The Strategy Manual

A step-by-step guide to the
transformational change of anything

Mike Baxter

Goal Atlas Ltd

My strategy …

… was to marry Cathy. My biggest success.

Acknowledgements

This book was a family effort. Cathy, much needed editor, with the patience of a saint. Keeva and Seaton, chief copy-editors; Jane, support copy-editor; Tom and Miles, advisors and mentors. Tate, for time-outs. Sarah (extended family), organiser, planner and publicist. And the many people, who are known affectionately as 'friends and family', who gave feedback (especially Peter), encouragement (especially my lovely 'brothers'), wise counsel (especially Joachim) and help in the run up to the book's launch, especially Ciaran, Jeremy, Mark, Peter (again) and Michael.

To you all, the most heartfelt thanks – this book wouldn't have happened without you.

About the author

Mike Baxter has been awarded a PhD in Science, a personal Professorship and Chartered Designer status. He has enjoyed a variety of careers: trawlerman, animal welfare scientist, product designer, higher education college dean, web entrepreneur, author, keynote speaker, business thought-leader and company director. He has been a business consultant since 2001 for some of the world's biggest brands (e.g. Cisco, Google, HSBC, Lilly, Skype, Sony PlayStation) and a long-term advisor to some of London's fastest growing tech start-ups.

Mike is, therefore, in a great position to resolve the challenges surrounding strategy success. As a scientist, he thinks from first principles and builds theories and models to turn principles into practicalities. As a designer, he can visualise and illustrate strategic models, making sense of them in terms of their component parts and how they interconnect. As a psychologist, he understands cognitive biases, knows how to manage their influence and recognises that engagement and commitment from front-line teams are essential for strategic success. And finally, as an expert consultant, business advisor and company director, he is a hands-on strategist, able to turn principles into practice, ensuring the effectiveness and success of strategy in a wide range of circumstances.

Mike lives with his family in a houseboat on the River Thames in West London.

About Goal Atlas

Mike's company, Goal Atlas Ltd, was established in 2014 to work with leaders and teams to facilitate the systematic, hands-on management of effective strategies. Goal Atlas delivers practical tools, training, expert guidance and unbiased advice to organisations in all sectors based on the latest strategy theories, models and frameworks described in this book, and utilising Goal Atlas's bespoke strategy mapping software.

We believe strategy is for everyone. To help you DO strategy rather than just think about it, all of our models, frameworks and templates in The Strategy Manual will be released under Creative Commons License. This means they are free for you to use in your presentations and strategy documentation.

Sign up at goalatlas.com/models

CONTENTS

Introduction

The origins of 'The Strategy Manual'

Throughout the early years of my consultancy, I felt a lingering sense of frustration that strategy shouldn't be this difficult. Because it usually was difficult. Really difficult! It felt like I had to reinvent how to do strategy to deal with each new client and the slightly different challenges they presented. It's not that the world is short of books and articles on strategy. I've read hundreds of them and my thinking has been profoundly changed by dozens of them. But I came to realise most of these were 'perspectives' on strategy. They say you must analyse your competitors and you must innovate but have little to say about actually writing your strategy or what, specifically, to do with it after it was written.

So began the tough but exhilarating journey to try to devise my own manual for not just 'doing' strategy, but for doing it well. The scientist in me sought the underlying first principles of strategy that would apply to the transformational change of anything. The consultant in me demanded these first principles were translated into readily-applied practicalities. Fortunately, my 10,000+ billable hours of consultancy across retail, technology, pharmaceuticals, financial services, travel, gaming and education sectors gave me plenty of opportunity to test, refine and consolidate these ideas. I am now, many years into this journey, at the point of having confidence they are robust and repeatable enough to be released into the world in the form of this book.

Mike Baxter, September 2020.

About this book

The Strategy Manual is a step-by-step guide on how to do strategy well for anyone with an interest in strategy:

- Those with responsibility for the governance of strategy, e.g. directors, trustees, governors…
- Those responsible for creating, delivering, assessing, planning, managing or measuring strategy, e.g. senior leadership, strategists, functional managers, team leaders, analysts…
- Those teaching or learning about strategy, e.g. lecturers, trainers, students, aspiring strategists and managers…
- Those who need to work with or work alongside strategy, e.g. suppliers, consultants, employees, agencies…

Strategy is about transformational change. This is a practical handbook to help make those transformations more manageable, more fit-for-purpose and result in more successful outcomes. To do this, you will find models, frameworks, templates and case studies throughout the book. Here's how they differ (Fig. 1):

- A **model** is a representation (usually graphical) of a concept, system or process that identifies its component parts and the relationship between them.
- A **framework** is a model combined with a process for applying it.
- A **template** is a document to print off and fill in, guiding you through the process and capturing how you apply this model to your situation.
- A **case study** provides a worked example of the model, framework and template.

Some models are broad and expansive. Chapter 8, for example, features a triple-loop model illustrating the entire strategy development process. Other models are narrower and more specific. The Hallmarks of Good Strategy model, for example (also in Chapter 8) identifies the five criteria for what makes a good strategy. All of the models and frameworks devised by Goal Atlas are listed in the glossary at the back of the book.

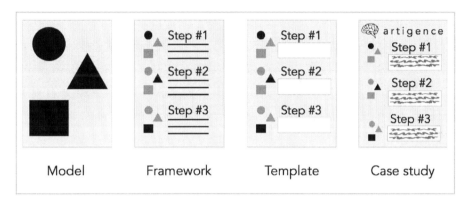

Figure 1 Models, frameworks, templates and case studies

There are a lot of images in this book. Often the images amplify or contextualise what is written in the text, and help you grasp a concept or clarify a complex issue. Sometimes they simply present the written concepts in a graphical way. Hopefully, they accommodate the needs of readers with either visual or verbal learning styles. The use of icons and models is useful for visual-first thinkers in support of the explanations in the text.

We believe strategy is for everyone. To help you DO strategy rather than just think about it, all of Goal Atlas's models, frameworks and templates in *The Strategy Manual* will be released under Creative Commons License.[1] This means they are free for you to use in your presentations and strategy documentation (see goalatlas.com/models).

A practical manual from 'first principles'

In 1994, Charlie Munger, Vice Chairman of Berkshire Hathaway (the largest financial services company in the world)[2] gave a famous commencement speech at the University of California, Business School.[3] He began by asking what worldly wisdom was.

> *"Well, the first rule is that you can't really know anything if you just remember isolated facts and try and bang 'em back. If the facts don't hang together on a latticework of theory, you don't have them in a usable form.*
>
> *You've got to have models in your head. And you've got to array your experience—both vicarious and direct—on this latticework of models. You may have noticed students who just try to remember and pound back what is remembered. Well, they fail in school and in life. You've got to hang experience on a latticework of models in your head."*

A latticework of mental models is a lovely way to describe what this book sets out to provide.

The overriding aim of this book is to be practical: to help you to produce strategy, have that strategy adopted by your organisation and then adapt that strategy as necessary, throughout its lifespan.

To be practical it needs to be deep; deep thinking goes beyond beliefs, preconceptions and opinions to investigate, analyse and reflect in depth about an issue. As Kurt Lewin, the 'founder of social psychology', said, "Nothing is as practical as a good theory."[4] Stephen Kosslyn, a psychologist and expert on the science of learning, explains, "Good theories allow one to explain novel phenomena and anticipate how events will unfold in unfamiliar contexts. Good theories are useful."[5]

Good theories come from 'first principles thinking',[6] which breaks down complicated problems into basic elements and then reassembles them from the ground up. In the 4th century BCE, Aristotle proposed first principles thinking as a core method of physics. He suggested that scientific knowledge reaches a point of understanding "when we have identified the primary causes and the first principles."[7] Aristotle's teacher, Plato, described a method of enquiry called Socratic Questioning (Plato was, himself, a student of Socrates), which has become recognised as a classic method for first principles thinking:[8]

1. What is the topic I am thinking about and where do my ideas on this topic come from? (Why do I think this? What exactly do I think?);

2. What assumptions shape my understanding of this topic? (How do I know this is true? What if I thought the opposite?);

3. What evidence do I have that my understanding of the topic is good? (How can I back this up? What are the sources?);

4. How could I think about this topic differently? (What might others think? Are there different assumptions I could make?);

5. What are the implications of me understanding this topic in this way? (What if I am wrong? What difference will it make if I am right or wrong?);

6. Did these five questions that I've just asked give me confidence I have come to a robust conclusion? (Was this a good reasoning process? What did I miss? What could I have asked differently?).

One of the best-known first-principles thinkers of current times is Elon Musk. Here is what he said, in an interview in 2012.[9]

> "... look at the fundamentals and construct your reasoning from that, and then you see if you have a conclusion that works or doesn't work, and it may or

may not be different from what people have done in the past."

He goes on to give this example:

"… on batteries, people would say, 'historically, it costs $600 per kilowatt-hour. And so it's not going to be much better than that in the future.' So, the first principles would be, what are the material constituents of the batteries? What is the spot market value of the material constituents? It's got cobalt, nickel, aluminium, carbon, and some polymers for separation, and a steel can. So, break that down on a material basis; if we bought that on a London Metal Exchange, what would each of these things cost? Oh, jeez, it's … $80 per kilowatt-hour. So, clearly, you just need to think of clever ways to take those materials and combine them into the shape of a battery cell, and you can have batteries that are much, much cheaper than anyone realizes."

So, this book will take you back to first principles and strive to build robust models and frameworks about, for example, what strategy is, how Key Performance Indicators (KPIs) work and how strategies need to be agile. It will then guide you in the hands-on work that defines, and then achieves, strategic success. By building from first principles, strategy can be used for the transformational change of anything.

The scope of this book

This book comes from over 20 years of independent consultancy undertaken on the strategies of some of the world's biggest organisations (find out more in 'About the author'). Strategies for organisations in retail, technology, pharmaceuticals, financial services, travel, gaming and education sectors have shaped the thinking behind this book and provided the testing-ground for its models and frameworks. It is, therefore, designed to be sector-agnostic. Regardless of which sector your organisation operates in, this book will help you achieve strategic success. It is also the result of intense focus over the past two years on strategy in one sector: higher education. Universities in the UK have the sector-wide custom and practice of publishing their strategies openly, for anyone to read, or for a strategy researcher to analyse. In April 2019, Goal Atlas published an analysis of 52 university strategies, including insights from strategy discussions held with over 25 different university leaders and strategists. Once published, the findings were presented at university events (e.g. Universities UK Annual Conference, Russell Group Directors of Strategy and in presentations to senior leadership / boards of the university sector). The author also undertook several in-depth consultancy projects on strategy with individual universities. This enabled further testing and validation of several of the key models and frameworks in this book, demonstrating their relevance and application across a range of sectors.

The thinking behind this book has also been helped enormously by the development of Goal Atlas's own strategy mapping software.[10] Turning this kind of thinking and decision-making process into software is a remarkably effective way to ensure your approach is structured, formalised, tested and refined!

Throughout the book strategy is discussed as it applies to organisations. This is not to say that individuals seeking transformation cannot have strategy. It is just that applying strategy to an organisation is strategy at its most complex, and hence the bigger challenge. The principles of strategy, however, as the sub-title to the book suggests, apply to the transformational change of anything. Strategy is also referred to as singular, as if there was only ever one strategy. This clearly isn't always the case. There will often be an overarching corporate or institutional strategy, but underneath may be financial, marketing, sales, operations, estates and digital strategies. Under the digital strategy may be a cloud storage strategy, an apps strategy, a digital on-boarding strategy and a bring-your-own-device strategy. And so on. The intention in writing the book was to make the models and frameworks as applicable to organisation-wide strategies as they are to the functional strategies that sit underneath. Many of the models and frameworks have been tested and refined on functional as well as organisation-wide strategies.

Finally, this book has been designed for anyone with an interest in strategy success and transformational change. The contents of the book apply equally to individuals and business start-ups as to public-, private- and third-sector enterprise-scale organisations.

How to use this book

This is not intended to be a book you take on holiday or read in the bathroom (sorry, if you are already at the airport with your family or sitting on the loo!). It is a manual for 'doing' strategy. Its place is by your side in the office, suggesting what to do next and how, guiding you with frameworks and templates and prompting you with completed examples, as you sweat the details of your own strategy. It is designed to enable you to 'do' – to take the action needed to deliver strategic success. Before you 'do' you will need to 'decide', and before you 'decide' you will need to 'understand'. Hence the first-principles approach described above. This, however, is not a book aimed at understanding for the sake of understanding. The understanding is only needed to inform and guide your work on strategy on a day-to-day basis. So, use it as a manual to inform, enable and hopefully even inspire strategic success. If you also share it with your colleagues, you will all be thinking and working on strategy in the same way, using similar frameworks, models and tools. That's a great first step on the road to strategic success!

You also don't need to read this book cover to cover. Dip into whatever section helps you get your strategy work done. In the writing and editing process, each chapter has been made as free-standing as possible, with cross-references to other parts of the book you might want to read first, to get the job done.

To bring the issues raised in each chapter to life within your organisation, at the end of each chapter you will find some suggestions on how to prompt a deeper level of conversation about that chapter's content.

With something as complex as strategy, it is vital that you have a collection of key words and phrases that you use in the same way to mean the same thing when you discuss strategy. You will find a comprehensive glossary of the terms used throughout The Strategy Manual at the back of this book. The glossary is also the place to find a list of all the models devised by Goal Atlas in this book.

The first six chapters of the book are about aspects of strategy that apply across the entire strategy lifecycle. These include the fundamentals of strategy (Chapter 1), frameworks for representing, analysing or making sense of strategy (Chapter 2, 3 and 4 on the strategy lifecycle, core models of strategy and strategy mapping) and then key ways that strategy needs to be managed (Chapters 5 and 6 are on strategy governance and strategy measurement).

The next five chapters guide you, step by step, through the strategy lifecycle, showing you how to:

- produce your strategy, by first scoping it (Chapter 7) and then developing it (Chapter 8);

- ensure that your strategy is adopted across your organisation (Chapter 9);

- adapt your strategy to changing circumstances (Chapter 10);

- review your now-finished strategy in preparation for the next one (Chapter 11).

The case study

To try to maximise the coherence of the chapters that follow, a single case study will be referred to repeatedly. This will help you track how the choices considered and the decisions made at one step in the process follow through to subsequent steps.

The company chosen for this case study is a new-ish, fast-growing business in the software-as-a-service (SaaS) sector, reflecting the author's experience as an advisor to some of London's fastest growing SaaS start-ups and consultant on SaaS projects for enterprise clients. It is, however, entirely hypothetical: it is a made-up organisation, with made-up people leading and operating it. The case study reflects real-world issues, however, to safeguard commercial confidentiality and to enable lessons from multiple companies to be combined, the content is for illustrative purposes only and does not represent an actual client or an actual client's experience. Although the case study features a rapidly scaling start-up, this could equally be a new business unit in an established enterprise.

You don't need to know about SaaS businesses to understand this case study, although a few of the basics will help you gain a richer understanding of the strategic decisions made by our case study company. In the early days of the software industry, you bought software as a product. You paid the price, downloaded the software (or received it wrapped in a box containing CDs or DVDs) and installed the product on your computer. By contrast software-as-a-service enables you to pay for *access* to the software. It is like a rental or a subscription. As a result, SaaS companies have a very distinctive business model. When they get a new customer they expect this new customer will pay them an on-going monthly or annual fee, typically for several years. Annual revenue, therefore, doesn't have the same meaning as it does for most companies, where payments happen in single transactions. SaaS companies, instead, talk about *Annual Recurring Revenue* (ARR)

– how much money they expect to make cumulatively from the customers who signed up this year plus those they retained that signed up in previous years. Our SaaS case study will use ARR rather than annual revenue as a measure of performance.

Another key measure of the financial health of a SaaS business is how much they make from each customer per year. This is measured as *Average Revenue Per Account* (ARPA). This is important because a SaaS company could slash its subscription prices, sign up huge numbers of new customers and still increase their Annual Recurring Revenue. They couldn't, however, keep doing this. A healthy SaaS company will have a growing Annual Recurring Revenue, with a stable or growing Annual Revenue Per Account.

The hypothetical company, Artigence Ltd., was founded in London five years ago by Katerina, a former Chief Information Officer at a global technology business, and Daniel, a software engineer and start-up veteran, who had created and sold three technology businesses in the previous ten years. The Artigence software platform uses a variety of artificial intelligence technologies to analyse large data sets to identify insights and summarise the data behind those insights for inclusion into dashboards, reports and presentations. The platform is marketed as the 'analyst that never sleeps' and examples of its use include price and discount optimisation for retailers and cash reserve optimisation for finance teams in small and medium sized businesses.

Artigence have been on a steady growth curve from year two. They took on their twentieth employee in year four and will soon take on their fortieth around the same time as they reach £10M Annual Recurring Revenue. Their two major investors are both pleased with the business's progress so far but have different views on how best to move forward. Sensing potential difficulties ahead, Katerina and Daniel have decided they need a robust 5-year strategy that they, their investors and their growing team can commit to. Over the remainder of this book, you will be a fly-on-the-wall observer across the lifecycle of this strategy as it is produced, adopted, adapted and finally, 5 years hence, reviewed in preparation for its successor.

Katerina   Daniel

Co-founders

Notes on Introduction

(all web content accessed between April and September 2020)

[1] Creative Commons. *Share your work*. https://creativecommons.org/share-your-work/

[2] Wikipedia. *Berkshire Hathaway*.
https://en.wikipedia.org/wiki/Berkshire_Hathaway

[3] Farnam Street Blog. *A Lesson on Elementary Worldly Wisdom As It Relates To Investment Management & Business* (transcript of Charlie Munger's commencement speech in 1994). https://fs.blog/great-talks/a-lesson-on-worldly-wisdom/

[4] Lewin K, 1943. *Psychology and the process of group living.* Journal of Social Psychology, 17: 113– 131. Reprinted in *The complete social scientist: A Kurt Lewin reader,* (Martin Gold, Ed) (1999) (pp. 333–345). For anyone wanting a more in-depth perspective on Lewin's Maxim, as it has become known, Katherine McCain has identified three different wordings of the maxim used by Lewin in a variety of his publications and went on to analyse how it has subsequently been cited: McCain KW 2016. *"Nothing as practical as a good theory" Does Lewin's Maxim still have salience in the applied social sciences?* Proceedings of the Association for Information Science and Technology. https://asistdl.onlinelibrary.wiley.com/doi/full/10.1002/pra2.2015.1450520 10077

[5] Kosslyn SM, 2017. *Practical Knowledge.* Chapter 2 of Kosslyn SM and Nelson B (Editors) *Building the Intentional University: Minerva and the Future of Higher Education.* MIT Press.

[6] Farnam Street Blog, 2018. *First Principles: The Building Blocks of True Knowledge.* https://fs.blog/2018/04/first-principles/

[7] Mouzala MG, 2012. *Aristotle's Method of Understanding the First Principles of Natural Things in the Physics* I.1 PEITHO / Examina Antiqua 1 (3). https://philarchive.org/archive/MOUAMO-3v1

[8] Adapted from Farnam Street Blog, 2018. *First Principles: The Building Blocks of True Knowledge.* https://fs.blog/2018/04/first-principles/

[9] Rose K, 2012. *Foundation 20 // Elon Musk.* https://www.youtube.com/watch?v=L-s_3b5fRd8 The relevant section of the Kevin Rose's interview with Elon Musk starts at 22.36.

[10] See https://goalatlas.com/strategy-mapping

Chapter 1

The fundamentals of strategy

Strategy is how you move from where you are now to where you want to be by defining the future state you seek to bring about.

Strategy is a slippery concept.[1] It is understood unclearly, inexactly or imperfectly by many people. It is defined or interpreted differently by different individuals or groups. It can be specific or general, depending on the context. It is often overused and applied to so many different situations that it can mean everything or nothing. It often reflects common misconceptions about the meaning of the word.

The aim of this chapter is to introduce some of the content of the forthcoming chapters and to develop a common understanding of this thing called 'strategy'. To do so, here are four fundamental questions you will work through:

1. What exactly is strategy?
2. What is strategy for?
3. How does strategy work?
4. What are the benefits of strategy – do I really need one?

1.1   What is strategy?

1.1.1   Six elements of strategy

You're going to start by exploring six different things strategy can be claimed to be: analysis, choice, positioning, design, storytelling and commitment. You will then pull these elements together to synthesise a more coherent view of what strategy is.

1. **Strategy as analysis.** Strategy is all about where you are now and where you could potentially get to, as a result of strategic success. Defining where you are now takes analysis. Some of this may be straightforward and come from your working knowledge of your organisation and its marketplace. You may, however, need to take it to a deeper level to make it useful for strategic purposes. What, for example, are the core differentiating features between you and your competitors? This is not an analysis of your product's feature-set versus the feature-set of your competitor's product. This is a much deeper question. What are the differences in your organisation's DNA? What is it you do significantly, consistently and meaningfully better than your competitors? That's the stuff strategy is made from.

2. **Strategy as choice.** "The essence of strategy is choosing what not to do", according to Harvard Business School Professor Michael Porter.[2] No organisation, no matter how rich and powerful, can do everything! Certainly, you cannot do everything well. The possibilities need to be prioritised and then everyone needs to focus effort on those priorities (Fig. 2). You must decide, out of all the things you could potentially do, which ones are going to be the most beneficial, the most lucrative, the most competitively advantageous. The inescapable logic that underpins every strategy is, therefore, that strategy is about choice. It defines what you, as an organisation, are going to do and what you are going to ignore or

deliberately avoid. It explains why just having a strategy can be an advantage over an organisation that doesn't – you are more focused than they are, have a higher probability of getting work completed without overworking staff, and more likely to do it well. This, on its own, can justify the investment of time and effort producing strategy. AG Lafley, former CEO of Procter and Gamble says "In my now forty-plus years in business, I have found that most leaders do not like to make choices. They'd rather keep their options open. Choices force their hands, pin them down, and generate an uncomfortable degree of personal risk ... in effect, by thinking about options instead of choices and failing to define winning robustly, these leaders choose to play but not to win."[3]

Figure 2 The logic underpinning strategy

3. **Strategy as positioning.** Of all the strategic choices you will make there will be some that 'position' you strategically. Strategic positioning defines where your strategy proposes to locate you on one or more significant dimensions. Here are two examples (Fig. 3):

a. **Price-value positioning.** Where would you like your products to be positioned on a price-value map, relative to your competitors? This reveals whether you aspire to high-value, high-price positioning or competitive value for a low price or a niche position (e.g. best value at a particular price point, for a particular type of customer).

b. **Shareholder positioning.** There are three key factors to balance out to ensure your strategy has the right positioning for shareholders:

    i. how much investment is demanded by your strategy;

    ii. how much shareholder value will be returned in increased share price;

    iii. how much shareholder value will be returned in increased dividends.

This positioning clearly needs to be sensitive to the preferences of your particular profile of shareholders for increased capital value or increased dividend payments.

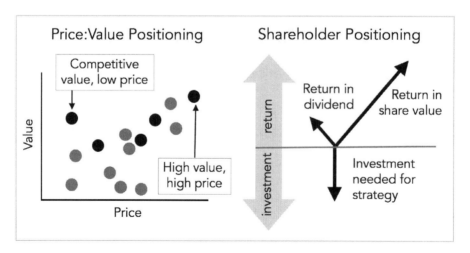

Figure 3 Strategy as positioning

4. **Strategy as design.** Nobel prize-winning economist and psychologist, Herbert Simon, suggests that the "natural sciences are concerned with how things are", whereas the sciences of the artificial are "concerned with how things ought to be, with devising artefacts to attain goals."[4]   Design, he suggests, is about devising "courses of action aimed at changing existing situations into preferred ones. Design, so construed, is the core of all professional training; it is the principal mark that distinguishes the professions from the sciences. Schools of engineering, as well as schools of architecture, business, education, law, and medicine, are all centrally concerned with the process of design."[5]   This is good news for a theory of strategy. A great deal of what Simon suggests as being common to all sciences of the artificial could actually have been written specifically about strategy. Strategy is all about how things ought to be, about how to attain goals and about changing existing situations into preferred ones.

5. **Strategy as storytelling.** If it is going to succeed in securing the engagement and commitment of the change-makers in your organisation, your strategy probably ought to be more than a spreadsheet. It needs to tell a story. A compelling, absorbing story that makes the change-makers excited about the future they are striving to bring about. It needs to captivate their interest. It needs to be credible and plausible. Ideally it should be identifiable in some way – it should make people feel they can help to make it happen.

6. **Strategy as commitment.** So far, most of your exploration of 'what strategy is' has been about ways of thinking about strategy. Whilst it is true that a lot of the hard work involved in strategy success involves deep thinking, it must never end there. Strategy without action changes nothing. Strategy is about engaging the change-makers and securing their ongoing commitment to the point that strategic goals have been achieved.

Figure 4 Six elements of strategy

Using these six elements of strategy, you can now synthesise a notion of 'what strategy is':

- Strategy requires *choices* to be made. Which, of the many strategic possibilities, are you going to include in your strategy, and which are you going to exclude?

- These choices need to be informed by *analysis* and they need to add up to a clarification of your strategic *positioning*.

- Strategy is about a lot more than choosing between the options in front of you. Strategy is also about inventing possibilities that don't exist right now. Strategy *designs* a future that you then strive to bring about.

- Strategy is more than just thinking. It needs to turn thought into action and align a multitude of individual actions to bring about transformation. This needs the *commitment* of change-makers and that commitment will be more readily secured if your strategy tells a *story* they can engage with, get behind and make happen.

This shows that strategy is multifaceted. It can be seen as being different things by different people in different situations but does, in fact, comprise all of these different elements (Fig. 4).

1.1.2 The risk and complexity of strategy

Strategy is both risky and complex. Just how risky is revealed by examining what's involved in strategy.

1. **Strategy is multi-dimensional.** It is to do with customers and competitors, products and services, prices and costs, risks and rewards.

2. **Strategy has multiple stakeholders.** The senior leadership who create it, the board and shareholders who ratify it, the employees and suppliers who need to make it work and the customers who need to love the outcome.

3. **Strategic success or failure will have multiple causes.** Throughout its lifecycle, strategy will be buffeted by a multitude of forces. New laws or regulations may appear. The economy may flourish or contract. Technology will evolve. Customer demographics will shift, tastes will change, and cultural norms will adjust. Market research, competitor analysis, scenario planning, trend extrapolation; strategy is informed by many signals and obscured by lots of noise.

4. **Strategy has multiple symptoms.** Symptoms are the circumstances, good or bad, that arise on account of the strategy. Strategy can impact performance, organisation design and culture, all of which themselves can become causes of strategic success or failure.

5. **Strategy has multiple solutions.** Popular strategy books suggest different ways of achieving strategic success, such as build core competencies,[6] find sustainable competitive advantage,[7] exploit transient advantages,[8] find your Blue Ocean,[9] decide where to play and how to win,[10] design a winning value proposition.[11]

6. **The key determinants of strategy success are constantly evolving.** When it was written, your strategy could have been masterful in its analysis and insights, inspired in its creativity and prescient in its projections. Yet by the time you came to look back on its performance, its insights turned out to be misinformed, its creativity misguided, and its projections flawed.

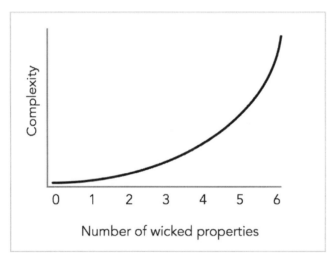

Figure 5 Complexity increases the more the properties of wicked problems combine

This list, some of you may have realised, is a description of strategy using the properties of wicked problems.[12] In their book *Wicked and Wise: How to Solve the World's Toughest Problems,*[13] physician and neuroscientist Alan Watkins and philosopher Ken Wilbur propose that complexity increases exponentially the more the six key properties of wicked problems combine. Figure 5 shows the graph they use to portray this relationship.

So, the more multi-dimensional, multi-stakeholder, multi-cause, multi-symptom, multi-solution and constantly evolving an issue is, the more complex it is. By this logic, and the analysis of strategy you have just read, strategy is amongst the most complex things humans ever attempt to do. Wow! No wonder you need a Strategy Manual! So, let's move on now to the second fundamental question about strategy: what is strategy for?

1.2   What is strategy for?

You are going to explore four key purposes that strategy serves:

1. Strategy provides one of several *identity marks* that define and distinguish an organisation;

2. Strategy provides a single, constant, long-term *navigational beacon* that can be used to align or re-align action and inform decision-making;

3. Strategy is an *investment in organisational transformation*;

4. The purpose of this investment is to *replenish the value that has been eroded* by the changing dynamics of customers and competitors.

1.2.1 Strategy as an identity mark

Organisations have a variety of 'identity marks' they use to signal what type of organisation they are, what they stand for and what they aspire to (Fig. 6). These include vision, mission, values and strategy.

When the time comes to write a new strategy, a decision needs to be made on whether this strategy needs to fit within the current vision, mission and values or whether new vision, mission and values need to be devised alongside the new strategy. This is typically a decision that would be taken by the board, following consultation with shareholders and senior leadership (see Chapter 5 on strategy governance).

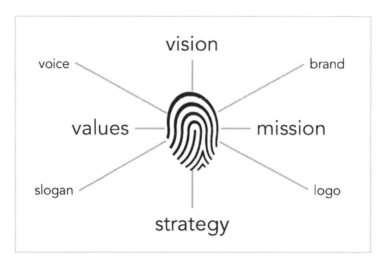

Figure 6 The identity marks of organisations

Figure 7 The House of Strategy Model

The House of Strategy Model (Fig. 7) provides a way to audit your current identity marks and to devise new ones, if required. You will learn about the House of Strategy Model, and its frameworks and templates, in Chapter 3 on core models.

1.2.2   Strategy as a navigational beacon

Freek Vermeulen, Professor of Strategy at London Business School, tells the story of how Frank Martin, CEO of Hornby, turned the company's fortunes around with his new strategy.[14] Hornby started making toy trains in 1920, but by the mid 1990's it was struggling financially. In 2000, Frank Martin was appointed as their new CEO and his new strategy aimed to:

1.   make perfect scale models (rather than toys);

2.   sell to adult collectors (rather than children);

3.   appeal to a sense of nostalgia (reminding adults of their childhoods).

This immediately gave people across the organisation meaningful guidance that helped them make decisions in the own work. It could inform decisions on distribution channels, advertising messages, point-of-sale displays and new product development. It provided a *navigational beacon* for front-line teams, guiding them on which of their many possible directions of travel to choose.

The value of strategy as a navigational beacon depends on how it endures changing circumstances. This is something that might appear to conflict with many organisations' ambitions to be 'agile'. Even the most agile working practices, however, still need some sense of where all this agility is intended to get you. As management consultants, McKinsey, have emphasised, agility depends on underlying stability.[15] This applies in sport as well as business; to be agile needs a firm footing and good grip. You will learn more on strategic agility in Chapter 10.

1.2.3 Strategy is an investment in transformation

Strategy is about the future; it is about transformational change and so doesn't have a great deal of value for managing business-as-usual. A fundamental responsibility of your 'board' (e.g. Board of Directors, Board of Trustees, Council) is to decide the nature and extent of the transformation sought by strategy and the proportion of the organisation's resources that will be invested in strategic change. There is no right and wrong answer here; what is important, however, is that the board has a view on how much of which resources your organisation invests in strategy. This is the essence of the Boundary Model of Strategy (Fig. 8).

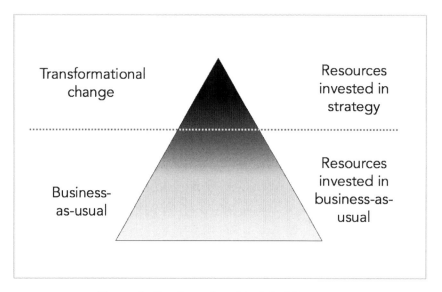

Figure 8 The Boundary Model of Strategy

The other key boardroom decision on 'strategy as investment' is who are the intended beneficiaries of strategy. Clarifying the purpose of your organisation is part of the foundation upon which any strategy is built. The Value Model of Strategy (Fig. 9) helps you define what value you deliver and for whom; what good do you seek to do in the world and what does it mean to work well to achieve that good? (see Chapter 3).

Value will be defined differently for different stakeholders, whether they are shareholders, customers, employees, suppliers, communities or, indeed, humankind or planet Earth. Strategy as investment is explored further in Chapter 5 on strategy governance.

Figure 9 The Value Model of Strategy

1.2.4 Strategy replenishes eroded value

Let's begin this section with a commercial answer to the question 'what is strategy for?' The market economy is a mechanism that matches the supply of goods and services to the demand for their consumption by means of price adjustment.[16] Imagine you are a successful business with a significant competitive advantage within your market. The reason you gained that competitive advantage was because you were the first to see that customer needs were changing, and you innovated to meet these new needs. Customer needs, of course, haven't stopped changing and hence the advantage you first enjoyed will diminish as customers acquire new needs and your innovation meets these less well. In the meantime, your competitors will have been busy. Your success may have hurt some of them badly, for example if you 'stole' their market share. Propelled into action by that pain, some may simply have copied your innovation. Others may have found more honourable ways to provide equivalent functionality without copying. Inspired by your success, a few may have set out to leapfrog over you into market leadership. Whatever path they chose, all these competitors will have put further dents in your competitive advantage. The combined effect of continuously changing customer needs and the actions of your competitors progressively erodes your competitive advantage.[17]

Clearly, every sensible business will try to minimise the rate at which this erosion takes place. Effective marketing, improved sales techniques and incremental improvements in your product or service will all help but they won't recover your original competitive advantage. Yet it's important to try to get it back. Market leaders enjoy many advantages. Your products and services will be considered-for-purchase by most buyers and preferred by many. As a result, you will enjoy greater brand loyalty and will probably be able to charge premium prices. Economies of scale are likely to reduce your costs, making you more profitable and hence able to invest in maintaining your market leadership.

So, what to do? The answer is strategy: a concerted effort by many people across the organisation to replenish eroded value and deliver a big improvement in your position in the market (Fig. 10). It's what some of your competitors did to you, when they leapfrogged over you into market leadership.

But here's the rub. The more this strategy becomes a 'big deal', the further into the future you push the outcome. This makes your destination harder to define and increases the risk of it going wrong. So, as you have seen, strategy, as a wicked problem, is risky and complex.

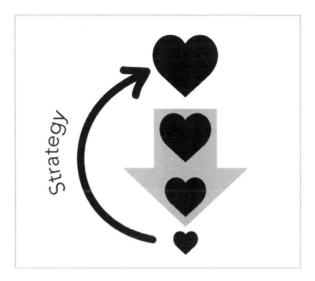

Figure 10 Strategy replenishes eroded value

1.2.5 Conclusion: What is strategy for?

You can now conclude that:

> *Strategy is a big investment, involving lots of people over a long period of time, to bring about a much bigger change than you could achieve by keeping on doing what you do currently. As a result, it is high risk and highly complex, but with the potential for high returns. Strategy is one of several identity marks that define and distinguish an organisation and, within the organisation, acts as a navigational beacon to align action and guide decisions.*

Described in this way, you now have an explanation of what strategy is for. This applies equally to non-commercial organisations (e.g. a charity, a university), as it does to business; strategy is a vehicle for large scale change that seeks to enhance the value delivered.

1.3   How does strategy work?

You have just learned that strategy is a concerted effort by many people across the organisation to replenish eroded value and deliver a big improvement in your position in the market. The first issue to resolve is how you can make strategy work as an organisation-wide endeavour.

Strategy needs to be made to work all the way from the boardroom to front-line operations. Figure 11 shows how authority typically flows through an organisation in relation to strategy. Clearly not all organisations will have a structure as delineated as this, and in smaller organisations several roles may be held by a single individual. However, the decisions relating to investment and identity, and the governance of strategy, will certainly be 'owned' by someone.

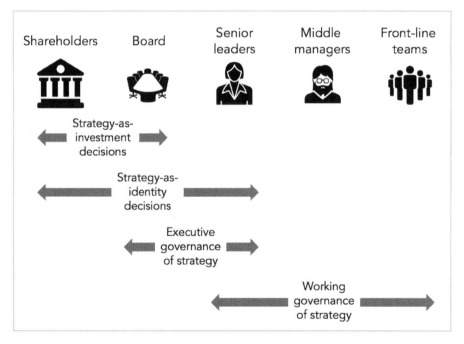

Figure 11 How authority flows through an organisation in relation to strategy

Working through this authority-flow, the shareholders and board need to agree what proportion of resources are to be invested in strategy, using the Boundary Model of Strategy (see Figure 8 and related discussion above). Issues related to strategy as an identity mark will typically be decided by shareholders, the board and senior leadership. How strategy is used as an identity mark is resolved using the House of Strategy Model (see Figure 7 and related discussion above).

1.3.1 Governance

Making strategy work as an organisation–wide endeavour requires strategy governance. The defining characteristics of strategy governance are that it:

1. structures and delineates authority, and thereby defines roles for both strategy governance and strategy management;

2. sets strategic goals and the rules by which these goals can be pursued (e.g. policies, compliance);

3. establishes reporting and control mechanisms related to strategy.

Figure 12 Strategy governance comprises executive governance and working governance

Strategy governance, as explained fully in Chapter 5, comprises two components, executive governance of strategy and working governance of strategy (Fig. 12).

Executive governance of strategy ensures the board and senior leadership are working effectively together towards strategy success.

Working governance of strategy ensures that strategy is effectively adopted across the organisation. This requires senior leadership to ensure that people and teams across the entire organisation know about the strategy, are committed to it and empowered to contribute to its success. Working governance encompasses the formalisation of authority and engagement and commitment.

1.3.2 Strategy Lifecycle

Having looked at the governance of strategy, the next step in resolving how strategy actually works is to consider the strategy process itself. The subtitle of this book promised a step-by-step guide on transformational change; at the heart of this step-by-step process is the notion of strategy lifecycle. Strategy progresses through distinct lifecycle stages within which very different types of strategic activities take place (Fig. 13).

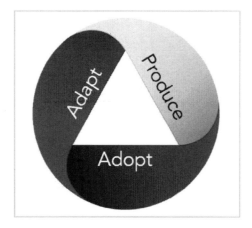

Figure 13 The Lifecycle Model of Strategy

Chapter 2 of this book looks in detail at the strategy lifecycle, and subsequent chapters explore the practical methods you can employ at each of these three stages: produce, adopt and adapt.

1. Stage #1: Produce

Strategy production, where the strategy is invented, designed, crafted and brought to life, happens in the 'produce' stage of the strategy lifecycle. As you will discover in Chapters 7 and 8, strategy production can be explained using two triple-loop processes, Strategy Scoping and Strategy Development (Fig. 14).

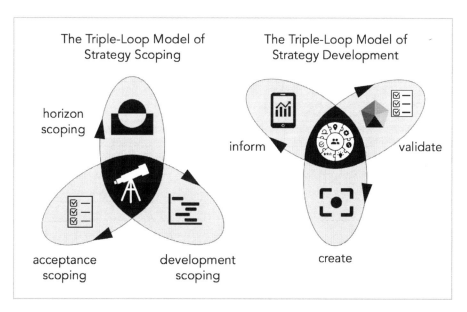

Figure 14 Strategy Scoping and Strategy Development

The strategy production stage of the lifecycle culminates in a completed strategy that defines your desired future state, identifies the benefits of achieving it and proposes the core methods needed to get there. You can visualise this as an interconnected cascade of goals (Fig. 15). Chapter 4 describes the process of strategy mapping which allows you to map out the interconnected cascade of goals required to bring about strategic success. Strategy mapping results in a validated, prioritised logic diagram (a 'strategy map') that can be used to manage and track the performance of strategy, assess strategic risks and ensure systematic strategy adoption, whilst helping to identify missing goals and opportunities for innovation.

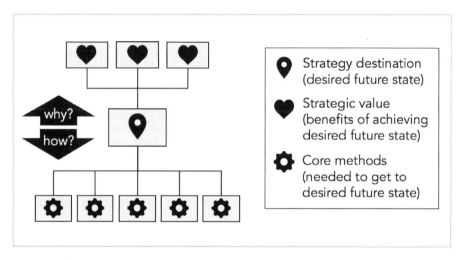

Figure 15 Strategy as an interconnected cascade of goals

One model used to devise strategic goals is The Value Model of Strategy (see Figure 9), one of your core strategy models, described in detail in Chapter 3, that can be used across the strategy lifecycle. The Value Model of Strategy takes, as its starting point, the fact that strategy is about action and must, therefore, encompass the three key defining features of any action:

1. Why are you doing it? What is its *value?* What value do you seek to deliver; what value do you get back in return?

2. What is it you need to do? This is your *effectiveness:* how, and how well, you deliver this value.

3. What, beyond effectiveness, does it mean to do it well? How do you make good use of resources? When does it need to be done by? This is your *efficiency.*

These are the fundamentals of performance as applied to any action or set of actions. Value, effectiveness and efficiency are therefore fundamental to strategy. What good do you seek to do in the world and what does it mean to work well to achieve that good?

2. Stage #2: Adopt

The 'Adopt' stage of the strategy lifecycle is covered in Chapter 9. Strategy adoption is where strategy moves from being owned by those who produced it, e.g. senior leadership, to being owned by those who need to align behind it and drive the changes necessary for strategy success, i.e. most people in the entire organisation (Fig. 16).

Figure 16 The 'H' Model of Strategy Adoption

Strategy adoption requires the active engagement and willing commitment of people across the organisation in order to produce a strategic plan that clarifies goal ownership, goal priorities and goal targets.

A key consideration here is strategy measurement; ensuring that metrics are in place to provide evidence of progress towards strategic goals and to inform the strategy adaptation stage of the lifecycle of the changes required to adjust and optimise the path to strategic success. A good strategic Key Performance Indicator (KPI) is actionable, measurable and purposeful, as shown in the AMP Model (Fig. 17) and described in Chapter 6 on strategy measurement.

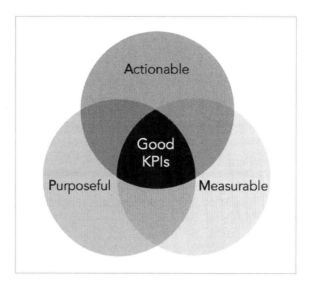

Figure 17 The AMP Model of Good KPIs

3. Stage #3: Adapt

The final stage of the strategy lifecycle is the 'adapt' stage, which is a combination of strategic resilience and strategic agility. Strategy never operates in unchanging circumstances and hence strategy is never static. It needs to adapt. It needs to respond to ongoing insights from strategic KPIs. Strategy adaptation, which you will learn about in Chapter 10, is summarised in the Pyramid Model of Strategy Adaptation (Fig. 18).

- Strategy adaptation operates by working through a repeated cycle of ongoing adaptive activities: sense-making, decision-making and change-making.

- Strategy adaptation is underpinned by robust capabilities, built over time. These are surveillance capabilities, commitment capabilities and responsiveness capabilities.

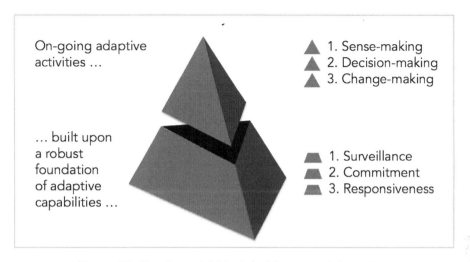

Figure 18 The Pyramid Model of Strategy Adaptation

1.3.3 Strategy Review

When your strategy has reached the end of its lifecycle, either by design or circumstance, the final task is to perform a strategy review, described in Chapter 11. The strategy review looks both backwards and forwards. Looking back, you evaluate the extent to which your strategic goals were met and what lessons can be learned to feed into the next strategy lifecycle. Applying these lessons looking forward blends the strategy review with the strategy scoping for your new strategy (Fig. 19).

Figure 19 The look ahead component of Strategy Review Model will blend into strategy scoping

1.4   The benefits of strategy - do you actually need a strategy?

This is not a rhetorical question. A great many organisations get along just fine without a strategy. Many more get by with a strategy-in-name-only. They have a document with 'Strategy' on the cover, but it is rarely, if ever, read. It plays no part in shaping the prioritisation, the resourcing, the measurement of success or the reward and recognition within the organisation. And it certainly never drives business transformation.

Okay, so, why is strategy needed? Here, in response, is the strategy manifesto arising from this chapter:

1. The more your organisation operates in a dynamic marketplace, the more you need a strategy. Not having one exposes you to the risk that your competitors do have one, and that makes them more focused, more productive and more likely to transform in ways that leave you behind.

2. A critical part of your board's responsibility for maximising shareholder value comes from having a minority of high-risk, high-potential-return activities blended with the safe-and-profitable majority of activities. Strategy is what defines these high-risk, high-potential-return activities.

3. No organisation can do everything. If senior leadership are to prevent your organisation from descending into stress, over-work and inefficiency, they need to clarify what you, as an organisation do and don't do. Some of that comes from policies, processes and standard ways of working. The rest comes from strategy.

4. To avoid the crisis of engagement afflicting the majority of organisations' front-line teams, they need to feel engaged, need

to feel their work matters and that they are able to make tangible progress towards meaningful goals. This is hard without a strategy.

So, if your organisation needs to stay alert to make sure your competitors don't get too far ahead of you, if your board and senior leadership want to do their jobs fully and well, and if you want to save your front-line teams from apathy and disinterest … you definitely need a strategy!

1.5   Time to get started!

So, now you know you need a strategy. You know what strategy means. You know what purposes strategy serves and, at a high level, the process you need to work through to manage a strategy throughout its lifecycle. All that is left is to actually do it!

Figure 20 visualises key steps in your forthcoming journey and some of the highlights you will see along the way. You have just covered the defining aspects of strategy in this chapter on strategy fundamentals. The Strategy Lifecycle Model is the centrepiece of Chapter 2. The House of Strategy Model and the Value Model of Strategy are core models, described in Chapter 3, and applicable at several different points across the strategy lifecycle. Strategy mapping (Chapter 4) enables any strategy to be transformed into a logic diagram, making its development systematic and its content readily validated. The Hourglass Model of Strategy Governance explains, in Chapter 5, how strategy shapes organisational culture. The AMP Model, in Chapter 6, proposes that KPIs should be Actionable, Measurable and Purposeful. Chapters 7 to 11 walk you through the practicalities of managing strategy across its lifecycle, using Triple-Loop Models of Scoping and Development, the 'H' Model of Strategy Adoption, the Pyramid Model of Strategy Adaptation and the Strategy Review Model.

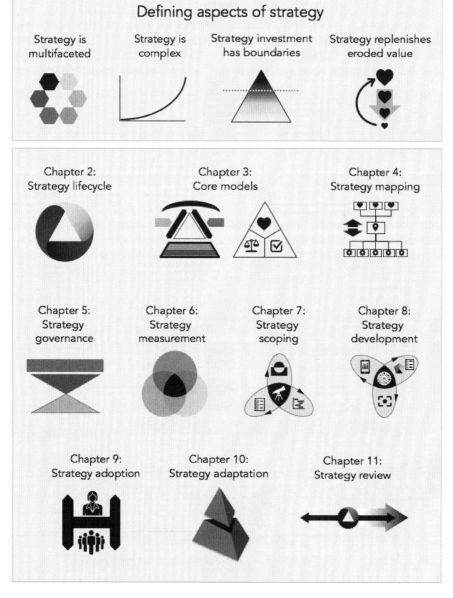

Figure 20 The Fundamentals of Strategy

1.6   Summary and key takeaways from Chapter 1

1. **What is strategy: Defining aspects of strategy**

    a. **Strategy is multifaceted** – it is a synthesis of analysis, choice, positioning, design, storytelling and commitment.

    b. **Strategy is a wicked problem** – it is both risky and complex, but with the potential for high returns.

2. **What strategy is for:**

    a. **Strategy is one of several identity marks** that define and distinguish an organisation.

    b. **Strategy acts as a navigational beacon** to align action and guide decisions.

    c. **Strategy is an investment in transformation.** It commits the entire organisation to bring about a much bigger change than could have been achieved by continuing with business-as-usual. Strategy investment has boundaries and beneficiaries.

    d. **Strategy replenishes eroded value** – strategy is a vehicle for large scale change that seeks to enhance the value you deliver in order to replenish the value eroded due to the changing dynamics of customers and competitors.

3. **How strategy works:**

    a. **Strategy is an organisation-wide endeavour** – it extends from top to bottom of organisations: from shareholders to board to senior leadership to middle managers to front-line teams. This is achieved by means of executive governance and working governance.

b. **Strategy passes through distinct lifecycle stages**, produce, adopt and adapt, during which different types of strategic activities are undertaken.

c. **Strategy production** involves two processes: strategy scoping and strategy development. A completed strategy defines your desired future state, identifies the benefits of achieving it and proposes the core methods needed to get there.

d. **Strategy is an interconnected cascade of goals.** Strategy mapping can be used to present strategic goals in a prioritised, validated logic diagram (strategy map) that can be used to manage and track the performance of strategy, assess strategic risks and ensure systematic strategy adoption.

e. **Strategy adoption** requires the active engagement and willing commitment of people across the organisation in order to produce a strategic plan that clarifies goal ownership, goal priorities and goal targets.

f. **Strategy measurement** requires strategic Key Performance Indicators (KPIs) that are actionable, measurable and purposeful.

g. **Strategy adaptation** equips the organisation to cope with changing circumstances by means of both strategic resilience and strategic agility.

h. **Strategy review.** The strategy review looks both backwards and forwards, applying lessons learned to the scoping of your new strategy.

4. **The benefits of strategy.** Strategy enables your organisation to stay alert to make sure your competitors don't get too far ahead of you,

your board and senior leadership to do their jobs fully and well and saves your front-line teams from apathy and disinterest.

1.7   Let's talk about… the fundamentals of strategy

Use these questions to prompt deeper conversations on the fundamentals of strategy across your organisation:

1. *Who, within your organisation really needs to understand the fundamentals of strategy? And do they?*

2. *How will you convey a working understanding of these fundamentals to the rest of your organisation? What do they need to understand? How can this be conveyed simply and concisely?*

3. *Do you agree that strategy is a complex challenge for your organisation? In what way is your strategy complex?*

4. *Do you agree that strategy is only about change? Does it mean that a company that doesn't seek change doesn't need a strategy?*

Notes on Chapter 1

(all web content accessed between April and September 2020)

[1] This definition of slippery concepts comes from Teaching with Themes article on *Concept Development: Clarifying the Meaning of Slippery Words & Concepts.* https://teachingwiththemes.com/index.php/projects/concept-development-slippery-concepts/

[2] Porter ME, 1979. *What is Strategy?* Harvard Business Review 74(6): 61–78. p70.

[3] Lafley AG, 2013. *Strategy as Winning.* In Lafley AG and Martin RL, 2013 *Playing to Win: How Strategy Really Works.* Harvard Business Review Press, Boston. p48.

[4] Simon HA, 1996. *The Sciences of the Artificial.* 3rd Edition. MIT Press, Cambridge, Massachusetts. p114.

[5] Simon HA, 1996. *The Sciences of the Artificial.* 3rd Edition. MIT Press, Cambridge, Massachusetts. p111.

[6] Hamel G and Prahalad CK, 1996. *Competing for the Future.* Harvard Business School Press, Boston.

[7] Porter ME, 1985. *Competitive Advantage: Creating and Sustaining Superior Performance.* Free Press, New York.

[8] McGrath RG, 2013. *The End of Competitive Advantage. How to keep your strategy moving as fast as your business.* Harvard Business Review Press, Boston.

[9] Kim WC and Mauborgne R, 2004. *Blue Ocean Strategy: How to Create Uncontested Market Space and Make the Competition Irrelevant.* Harvard Business School Press, Boston.

[10] Lafley AG and Martin RL, 2013. *Playing to Win: How Strategy Really Works.* Harvard Business Review Press, Boston.

[11] Osterwalder A, Pigneur Y, Bernarda G and Smith A, 2014. *Value Proposition Design: How to Create Products and Services Customers Want.* John Wiley and Sons Inc, New Jersey.

[12] Wicked problems are difficult or impossible to solve because of incomplete, contradictory, and changing requirements that are often difficult to recognise. They have better or worse solutions, not right or wrong ones – wicked problems are said to be tamed rather than solved. Summarised from Wikipedia. *Wicked Problem.* https://en.wikipedia.org/wiki/Wicked_problem

[13] Watkins A and Wilbur K, 2015. *Wicked and Wise: How to Solve the World's Toughest Problems.* Urbane Publications Ltd, Chatham, Kent, UK.

[14] Vermeulen F, 2017. *Many Strategies Fail Because They're Not Actually Strategies.* Harvard Business Review, 8 November 2017.

[15] Aghina W, De Smet A, and Weerda K, 2015. *Agility: It rhymes with stability.* McKinsey Quarterly, 1 December 2015.

https://www.mckinsey.com/business-functions/organization/our-insights/agility-it-rhymes-with-stability

[16] Wikipedia. *Market Economy.*
https://en.wikipedia.org/wiki/Market_economy

[17] Winston A, 2012. *Your Competitive Position Is Always Eroding.* Harvard Business Review. 20 March 2012.

Chapter 2

Strategy lifecycle

Strategy progresses through stages.

The stages are sequential.

The stages are functionally different.

This chapter discusses and explores the 'lifecycle stages' of strategy. Many authors have, in the past, suggested that strategy can be usefully understood as comprising a number of different parts (Fig. 21). Mintzberg and co-authors[1] say strategy "typically involves two major processes: formulation and implementation". Professor Fred David, in his classic strategy textbook, *Strategic Management: Concepts and Cases,*[2] insists the strategic-management process consists of three stages; Dave Ketchen and Jeremy Short's open source strategy textbook, *Mastering Strategic Management,*[3] now used worldwide, says the strategy management process has four elements; the International Project Management Association (IPMA) proposes *'Seven steps to a strategy for your organisation'*[4] and the Balanced Scorecard Institute identifies nine steps for strategic planning and management.[5]

You will notice that the authors above label the component parts of their models in different ways: two *processes*, three *stages*, four *elements*, seven or nine *steps*. With this many different opinions, it might be tempting to think that the stages involved in strategy are arbitrary. We, however, don't believe they are, and to explain why, let's tighten up on what we mean by 'lifecycle'.

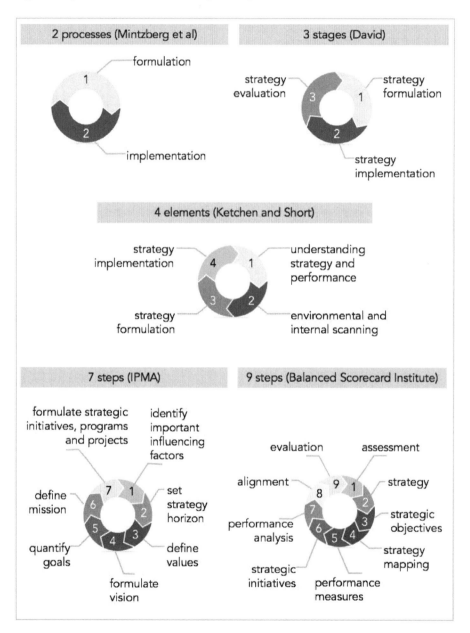

Figure 21 'Stages' of strategy lifecycle

2.1   The lifecycle stages of strategy

The concepts of lifecycle and lifecycle stages usually apply to animals (e.g. egg, caterpillar, chrysalis, butterfly) and plants (e.g. seed, seedling, plant, flower, fruit).[6] They have value because organisms look different and work in different ways at the different lifecycle stages. Caterpillars have bodies with thirteen segments and eat leaves.[7] Butterflies have bodies with three 'tagmata' (head, thorax and abdomen) and eat nectar.[8]

When it comes to strategy, it is important to distinguish between stages and processes. Lifecycles go through stages and these are discrete and sequential. There are no 'caterflies' or 'butterpillars'. First you are a caterpillar and, when you are done with that, you move on to becoming a butterfly (with a pause to be a chrysalis if you want to stay true to the biology). It is the same with strategy. The strategy needs to be written before you can start rolling it out across the organisation.

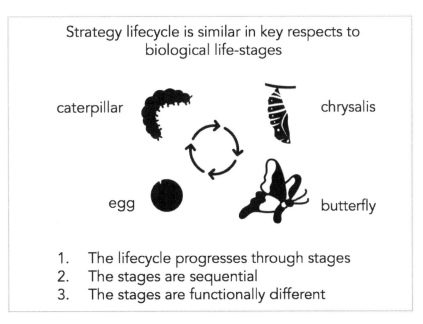

Figure 22 The lifecycle-stages of strategy

So, in the terminology you will see in this book, the strategy lifecycle divides into stages. Each stage is distinct from the other stages in two ways. Firstly, the stages are sequential. Stage 1 must end before stage 2 begins. Secondly, different stages involve doing different things, just as the biology of caterpillars is different from the biology of butterflies (Fig. 22).

Just to be clear on what this says about strategy:

1. Strategy progresses through discrete stages across its lifecycle;

2. These stages happen in a particular sequence;

3. The activities that happen within these stages are functionally different.

2.2   The Strategy Lifecycle Model

Henry Mintzberg, Professor of Management at McGill University, wrote a paper called the *Fall and Rise of Strategic Planning* in 1994,[9] making the strategy lifecycle a defining issue for strategy in general.

Mintzberg distinguished between:

a. *Strategic ways of thinking,* which are intuitive, creative and designed to produce synthesis; an integrated perspective on the organisation, a vision of the future you seek to bring about.

b. *Planning ways of thinking,* which are analytic and designed to break a goal down into steps, formalise them for implementation and anticipate their outcomes so progress can be measured.

He concluded that:

> "*Strategic planning isn't strategic thinking. One is analysis, and the other is synthesis.*"

The essence of Mintzberg's argument was that planners should not create strategies. Instead, they should supply data, facilitate strategic thinking by strategists and, once the strategy is decided, planners need to program and monitor the activities needed to achieve strategic success. His intention was not primarily to constrain the work of planners but rather to leave a clear space for strategists to be strategic: to be creative in synthesising a coherent, integrated vision of their organisation's future. Strategy, he claimed, was not primarily a matter of calculation and deduction but rather a matter of imagination and commitment.

In terms of strategy lifecycle, Mintzberg couldn't be much clearer. Strategy creation and strategic planning are in different stages. They involve different types of activities and the boundary between them is clearly demarcated by the production of a finished strategy.

The Separation Model of Strategy provides a clear structure for this idea (Fig. 23).

Figure 23 The Separation Model of Strategy

The essence of the Separation Model of Strategy is that strategy and strategic planning need to be forced apart so they can serve their different purposes within the organisation. Whilst strategy provides a compelling vision of the future, strategic planning devises the transformational change programme to get there. Whilst strategy is all about destination and path, strategic planning is all about people, priorities, resources and deadlines. Perhaps most critically for the practicalities of managing strategy, strategy doesn't change, but strategic plans can, and usually do, change.

The strategy lifecycle model you will use throughout this book has three stages: produce, adopt and adapt. Each stage marks its completion with a specific output (Fig. 24)

Figure 24 The Strategy Lifecycle Model

The three stages are defined as follows:

1. **Produce:** This stage is strategy production, where the strategy is invented, designed, crafted and brought to life. At the end of strategy production is … (no surprise here!) … the strategy.

2. **Adopt:** This second stage could have simply been called 'strategic planning'. We, however, opted to call this stage 'strategy adoption'; it is where strategy moves from being owned by those who produced it, e.g. senior leadership, to being adopted by those who need to align behind it and drive the changes necessary for strategy success, e.g. most people in the organisation. It involves not just planning but engagement and commitment across the entire organisation. The strategy adoption stage results in a strategic plan.

3. **Adapt:** This stage is strategy adaptation, involving both strategic resilience and agility. The strategic plan you have at the end of strategy adoption, sadly, won't last long in its original form. The world will move on. Circumstances will change. And the plan will need to be adapted. If the plan changes so much it can no longer meaningfully derive from the strategy, it is time for a new strategy – remember strategic plans change but strategy doesn't. And if you are going to produce a new strategy, what better place to start than with a review of the current strategy? Strategy adaptation, therefore, ends with a strategy review.

To grasp the notion of the three stages of the lifecycle and their outputs, it may be helpful to think of the analogy of 'going on holiday'. In the strategy production stage, you scope out the possibilities, consider all the options and decide on the destination, timeframe and who will go along. This is your holiday 'strategy'. The strategy adoption stage turns your strategy into a viable plan. This involves not just planning (booking travel and accommodation, acquiring currency and all the things you will need for your trip, learning about your destination, checking you have your passport etc.) but also the commitment and engagement of all those involved, from the travellers themselves, to those enabling your journey in other ways (colleagues covering you at work, the hosts at your destination, the dog-sitter at home etc.). This leads to the 'strategic plan' for your holiday – it's all about the people, priorities, resources and deadlines. The final stage is the holiday itself –

you're off! You will, however, find that this is a stage of adaptation, where you respond, with no small measure of agility and resilience, to the changing circumstances that will affect the plans you have made (the travel updates, the weather, the people you meet… all the opportunities and challenges that arise along the way). You may want to extend your stay, or even cut it short, but at the end of your, hopefully successful, holiday, you will look back at what worked and what didn't work so you can start to think about the next one, based on the lessons learned and the experiences you have had. This is your holiday 'review' (Fig. 25).

Figure 25 The lifecycle of 'going on holiday'

Having discovered the stages of the strategy lifecycle and their outputs, you can now delve down inside the three stages.

2.3   Processes within lifecycle stages

Figure 26 is a representation of the processes required within each stage of the strategy lifecycle. Unlike the lifecycle stages themselves, which occur in a fixed order, the processes within each stage don't. The looping connections between them show that they don't necessarily occur in any fixed sequence. You find yourself looping through these processes iteratively or even nesting one process inside another.

Figure 26 Strategy lifecycle stages and the processes inside them

2.3.1 Lifecycle stage #1: Produce

The strategy production stage is complete when the strategy is produced and launched. Strategy production has two core processes:

1. **Scoping –** Strategy scoping is how you prepare to develop the strategy. A key purpose is to reduce the complexity involved in strategy development by defining the following:

a. What you can say, right now, about where this new strategy is likely to take you and why. This defines what you can see 'on the horizon' for your forthcoming new strategy – is there anything that needs to be included in the strategy? Or anything that must be excluded?

b. How the strategy will be developed. What are the key decisions that you are likely to have to make, and what data, evidence and insights are you likely to need in order to make those decisions? What jobs need to be done to develop the strategy? Who is going to do what and by when?

c. The acceptance criteria for the decisions and jobs scoped out for strategy development. How will you tell if the strategy you have written is good enough to be launched and made official?

Strategy scoping sets out to make strategy development a lot more focused, more effective and more efficient than it would otherwise have been. It can also serve a vital communication role across the organisation, by explaining simply and clearly what is going to be done in order to produce this strategy. The key output from strategy scoping is the announcement of the strategy: "here is the sort of strategy we are about to start developing; here is how we plan to go about developing it; here is how you can contribute." Chapter 7 is all about strategy scoping.

2. **Development** - Strategy development is how you analyse, synthesise, imagine and commit to a new strategy, and how you write it and prepare it for dissemination throughout the organisation, following its launch. It includes processes of strategy validation, where you 'set the brief' for your strategy and then check against it to ensure that the strategy you develop makes sense, has internal consistency and is conducive to adoption and adaptation. Development involves the creative imagination of strategic ideas, informed by research and analysis. Chapter 8 looks at the detail of

strategy development and the processes you can use to ensure the right strategy is launched at the end of the development process.

2.3.2   Lifecycle stage #2: Adopt

At the end of the strategy production stage, the intended strategy has been communicated to the organisation via its launch. The strategy adoption stage of the strategy lifecycle then takes this completed written strategy and creates a delegated, scheduled, prioritised, measured and resourced plan necessary for its strategic success. This stage moves strategy from the domain of those who created it into the hands of those who will make it happen – it is the process of adoption of the strategy across the organisation. Calling it strategy *adoption* reveals the active participation and willing commitment by front line teams needed to make the strategy a success. It also hints at the process by which adoption is undertaken. Strategy needs to be interpreted and applied to local circumstances. High-level strategic goals need to be elaborated, to translate them into local, team-specific goals that can then be delegated. The individuals and teams to whom goals are delegated need to be trained and coached to ensure they can attain the goals they've been given. Local targets need to be set and then checked that they aggregate back up to strategic success.

> Strategy adoption is a process that turns the aspiration of a strategy into the action of front-line teams to bring about strategic success.

Strategy adoption requires:

1. **Planning** – translating high-level, organisation-wide strategic goals into the actionable goals that front-line individuals and teams can

achieve, and identifying priorities, timescales and targets for strategic success.

2. **Engagement and Commitment** – securing active interest and a willingness to get involved in the strategy. This is brought about by high levels of consultation, influence and autonomy being afforded to individuals and teams across your organisation.

2.3.3 Lifecycle stage #3: Adapt

Strategy adaptation is the cycle of sense-making, decision-making and change-making that keeps the organisation responsive to significant change.

The strategy adaptation stage of the strategy lifecycle begins with a completed strategic plan and manages the adaptation of that strategic plan to cope with changes in circumstances and the discovery of new ways to achieve strategic success. This stage usually takes up most of the strategy lifecycle. At some point it will be in the best interests of the organisation (or individual) to develop a new strategy rather than continuing to adapt the existing strategy. In these circumstances, this stage of the strategy lifecycle should end with a review of the strategy throughout its lifecycle, as a starting point for the production of a new strategy.

Strategy adaptation requires:

1. **Resilience** – the process of making the strategy resilient to changes both inside the organisation and outside in its operating environment.

2. **Agility** – the process by which the organisation becomes innovation-ready and capable of responding at pace to either the need or opportunity to change.

Adaptiveness includes the activities needed to 'be' resilient and agile as well as the longer-term capability-building to make the organisation more change-ready (more on this in Chapter 10).

To make sure you are clear about the lifecycle stages and the processes within them, here is how they would roll out in a strategy timeline (Fig. 27).

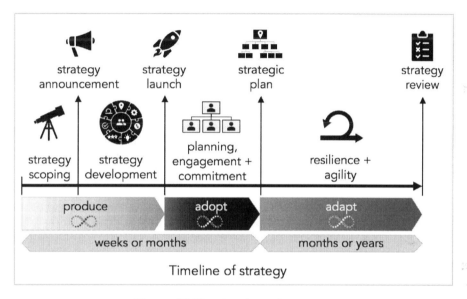

Figure 27 The timeline of strategy

2.4   Summary and key takeaways from Chapter 2

1. **Strategy progresses through discrete stages across its lifecycle.** These stages happen in a particular sequence. The activities that happen within these stages are functionally different.

2. **Strategy creation and strategic planning are in different stages.** They involve different types of activities and the boundary between them is clearly demarcated by the production of a finished strategy.

Strategy and strategic planning need to be forced apart so they can serve their different purposes within the organisation.

3. There are three stages in the strategy lifecycle:

    a. **Strategy production**. The strategy production stage is complete when the strategy is produced and launched. Strategy production involves:

        i. Strategy scoping;

        ii. Strategy development.

    b. **Strategy adoption**. This is a process that turns the aspiration of a strategy into the action of front-line teams to bring about strategic success. Strategy adoption results in a delegated, scheduled, prioritised, measured and resourced plan and involves:

        i. Planning;

        ii. Engagement and commitment.

    c. **Strategy adaptation**. This is the cycle of sense-making, decision-making and change-making that keeps the organisation responsive to significant change. It requires:

        i. Resilience;

        ii. Agility.

2.5   Let's talk about… strategy lifecycle

Use these questions to prompt deeper conversations on strategy lifecycle across your organisation:

1. *How does your organisation manage strategy differently, at different stages of its lifecycle?*

2. *In what ways are strategy and strategic planning separate processes throughout your organisation?*

3. *Given that most of the strategy lifecycle is spent adapting to new and emerging circumstances, how do people at all levels in your organisation stay current in their understanding of how to achieve their strategic goals?*

4. *Given where you are now in the strategy lifecycle, can you justify the work done on strategy so far? Is it robust enough for the future success of your strategy?*

Notes on Chapter 2

(all web content accessed between April and September 2020)

[1] Mintzberg H, Lampel JB, Quinn JB and Ghoshal S, 2002. *The Strategy Process: Concepts, Contexts, Cases.* Pearson, NY.

[2] David FR, 2011. *Strategic Management: Concepts and Cases* (13th Edition). Prentice Hall, New Jersey. p6.

[3] Ketchen D and Short J, 2018. *Mastering Strategic Management, v 2.0.* Flat World Knowledge, Creative Commons License. Available, for example, in Canada (https://opentextbc.ca/strategicmanagement/) and Hong Kong (http://www.opentextbooks.org.hk/tertiary-institutions/17986).

[4] International Project Management Association. *Seven steps to a strategy for your organisation* https://www.ipma.world/seven-steps-to-a-strategy-for-your-organisation

[5] Balanced Scorecard Institute. *How to Create a Balanced Scorecard: Nine Steps to Success.* https://balancedscorecard.org/about/nine-steps/

[6] Wikipedia. *Biological life cycle.* https://en.wikipedia.org/wiki/Biological_life_cycle

[7] Wikipedia. *External Morphology of Lepidoptera: Caterpillar.* https://en.wikipedia.org/wiki/External_morphology_of_Lepidoptera#Caterpillar

[8] Wikipedia. *External Morphology of Lepidoptera: general body plan.* https://en.wikipedia.org/wiki/External_morphology_of_Lepidoptera#General_body_plan

[9] Mintzberg H, 1994. *The Fall and Rise of Strategic Planning.* Harvard Business Review, January-February 1994.

Chapter 3

Core models

---

*Models that apply across the
entire strategy lifecycle have
something fundamental to
say about your strategy.*

Throughout this book you will discover a great many models and frameworks to enable strategy to work well in your organisation. Most of these will be specific to one stage of the strategy lifecycle. In strategy production, for example, you will use Triple-Loop Models of both Strategy Scoping and Strategy Development. You will use the 'H' Model of Strategy Adoption and the Pyramid Model of Strategy Adaptation.

There are, however, two models that apply across the entire strategy lifecycle and, perhaps because of this, have something fundamental to say about your strategy. They are the House of Strategy Model and the Value Model of Strategy.

3.1   The House of Strategy Model

You learned in Chapter 1 that organisations have 'identity marks' signalling what type of organisation they are, what they stand for and what they aspire to. Figure 28 shows that, of the many identity marks, such as brand and logo, the four most relevant to you here are vision, mission, values and strategy.

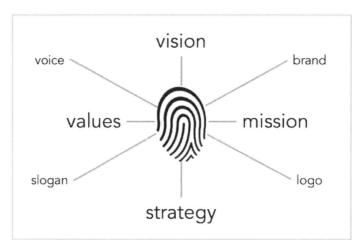

Figure 28 Identity marks for organisations

The House of Strategy Model shows graphically how vision, mission, values and strategy come together for an organisation (Fig. 29).

Figure 29 The House of Strategy Model

Let's work through the model:

Your 'current organisation' is the baseline for any strategy. For all but the freshest of start-ups, your organisation's current state will be derived from its heritage; how the organisation originated and what capabilities it has since acquired. Current state ought to be characterised, to a large extent, by 'mission'.

An organisation's mission is a statement of core purpose and focus, that normally remains unchanged over time.[1] It answers the question, "Why does our business exist?".[2] A mission statement communicates the organisation's purpose to its employees, customers, suppliers and other stakeholders and creates a sense of identity for its employees.[3] It is about NOW! Why do you exist, right now?

An organisation's 'vision' is almost a counterpoint to its current state. It defines not where you are currently, but where you want to be. An organisation's vision is a picture of its potential,[4] an audacious dream of its future.[5] It should inform, inspire and energise everyone in the organisation.[6] Since vision typically stretches into the future, it can also be what gives continuity from one strategy to the next.

It is important to distinguish clearly between mission and vision. It is not your mission to become the market leader in your business sector because that is an aspiration for the future. Your mission is your reason-for-being now. It could be to offer market-leading value for money or to delight customers with your services. If your organisation remains on-mission, you may then be able, in the future, to realise your vision. And that vision could be an aspiration for market leadership.

Values are what ought to both drive and constrain your organisation. The word 'values' literally means principles or standards of behaviour; one's judgement of what is important in life;[7] the moral principles and beliefs or accepted standards of a person or social group.[8] Values are the ethical ideals of the organisation.[9] They are the important and lasting beliefs or ideals shared by the members of a culture about what is good or bad, and desirable or undesirable.[10]

Your organisation is continually surrounded by 'opportunities and obstacles' presented by your operating environment. These can include changing customer needs, emerging technologies and new laws or regulations.

In the House of Strategy Model, strategy is what is needed to fill the hole left by mission, vision and values. Strategy joins up where you are now with where you want to get to. It defines a desired future state, explains its benefits and proposes a handful of core methods by which you will get there.

3.1.1 Using the House of Strategy Model

There are two main ways to use the House of Strategy Model:

1. To *audit* existing vision, mission, values and strategy;
2. To *create* new vision, mission, values and strategy.

Where the model is particularly useful is in ensuring these identity marks are aligned, compatible and mutually supportive. It checks the validity of each in relation to the others. Here is a practical, real world example. On several of its global websites Samsung have what they call their Vision 2020[11] (Fig. 30). It is not clear when these were produced.

Samsung's vision is to 'Inspire the World, Create the Future'. This is a great vision, although it could belong to the latest AI tech start-up, an upstart fashion retailer or possibly even the White House. It, therefore, needs a lot of substantiation and support from Samsung's other identity marks.

Figure 30 Samsung's published Vision 2020

Their mission is 'To inspire the world with innovative technologies, products and designs that enrich People's lives and contribute to a socially responsible and sustainable future'. This sounds a lot like an expansion of their vision, rather than a statement of core purpose and focus; a declaration of why they exist now. Powerful ideas feature within their Vision 2020 statement that could be developed into a mission statement, such as innovating to enrich lives, being creative and creating new markets and focusing on Infotainment and Lifecare. Right now, however, their mission doesn't explain how their purpose equips them to 'Inspire the World, Create the Future'.

The biggest omission in Vision 2020 is strategy. They propose three 'Strategic Directions': Creativity, Partnerships and Great People, with no further explanation. They sound as if they might be values, along with the operational excellence and innovation prowess they allude to elsewhere in their Vision 2020. Strategy is meant to define a specific future state that you want to get to, explain the benefits of getting there and propose a handful of core methods by which you will get there. Samsung define several quite specific goals that get us closer to an understanding of their strategy. These include a specific sales target (USD 400B by 2020) and a specific brand ranking (Global top 5 by 2020) as well as several qualitative goals (e.g. innovative company, best workplace). This, however, still doesn't answer key questions about their strategy – why do they aspire to these defined goals (do they have an over-arching purpose, with a clear destination to aim for) and how do they plan to get there?

Using the House of Strategy Model to audit your current vision, mission, values and strategy in this way ensures that they are aligned, compatible and mutually supportive. The model translates into a template that you can fill in for your own organisation (Fig. 31).

Figure 32 shows this template completed for Samsung's Vision 2020.

| Strategy: | Prepared by: |
| | Date: |

House of Strategy

Vision = a picture of the potential of your organisation. An audacious dream of the future.

vision

*Vision is almost the counterpoint to mission – it is where you are **not** now but want to be. It is intended to inform, inspire and energise everyone to realise that shared vision.*

Strategy = the handful of core methods by which you join up where you are now with where you want to get to.

strategy

Strategy 'imagineers' a specific future state, explains its benefits and proposes a handful of core methods by which you will get there.

values

Values = important and lasting beliefs or ethical ideals shared by the members of your organisation.

opportunities *obstacles*

What are the key **opportunities** and **obstacles** faced by your organisation?

Values are used to guide what is acceptable and unacceptable, what is desirable and undesirable in your organisation.

Opportunities and obstacles arise both inside and outside the organisation. They create the key aspirations and drivers of strategy.

Mission provides a sense of identity for employees, customers, suppliers etc., and normally remains unchanged over time. It is about NOW! Why do you exist, right now?

Mission = the core purpose and focus of your organisation

mission *current situation*

Figure 31 House of Strategy Template

Figure 32 House of Strategy for Samsung's Vision 2020

These same templates can also be used to help in the *creation* of identity marks. Typically, you would start with your current organisation and heritage; these are the foundations upon which you will build your mission. Firstly, identify key features of your current organisation and your heritage. Think deeply about them. When distilled to its essence, what is distinctive, important, promising, exciting or compelling about your organisation? If you have a strong, stable set of values, write them down too. Be careful to make sure they are significant, impactful and distinctive (Figure 33).

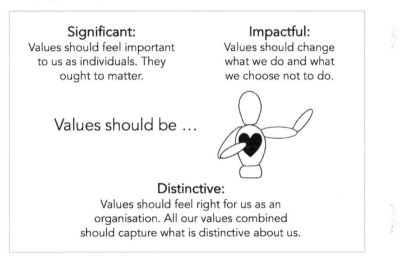

Figure 33 Attributes of good values for organisations

Now, what do the essence of your organisation and your values suggest about your mission? Why does your business exist? What is your core focus and purpose? Remember mission is about *now*. What is it you do and what are you for, right now?

Next, list the opportunities and obstacles facing your organisation. Make them current and keep them broad. You're not listing the annoyances that you need to resolve this afternoon. These are the big issues facing your whole organisation over a timescale of months or years, such as political, economic, social or technological (PEST) changes, or a new competitor entering your marketplace.

How well does your mission enable you to exploit the opportunities and overcome the obstacles you foresee? Is there a way to re-phrase your mission to make it better-suited to respond to these obstacles and opportunities? Or conversely, are there different obstacles and opportunities an organisation with your mission would be better placed to tackle? This might suggest you are currently operating in the wrong marketplace. You may need to redefine where you play, from a strategic point of view.[12]

This is as much as you can do with information about the present. The remainder of the House of Strategy requires you to venture into the future. A vision, you have seen, is a picture of your organisation's potential, an audacious dream of its future. Strategy is a desired future state. Both require a degree of analysis – how do you envisage the world is going to be in the future? They also require a degree of creative imagination – what is the world you would like to help create?

The House of Strategy template is not just about giving you a space to write these things down and prompts about what to write. Where it comes into its own is when you print ten copies of the template and re-write your ideas again and again to get vision, mission, values and strategy aligned, coherent and fit to respond to the opportunities and obstacles you anticipate you might face. You are devising your identity marks by successive approximation. This can also be done collaboratively, e.g. in a workshop.

The House of Strategy Model can also be applied at other stages of the strategy lifecycle to challenge and align your thinking, for example as a framework for strategy scoping. Here you will turn each element into a question about scoping; what do your current vision, mission and values say about the future of your organisation? You will see the House of Strategy template completed as part of strategy scoping for our Artigence case study in Chapter 7.

3.2 The Value Model of Strategy

The Value Model of Strategy (Fig. 34) takes, as its starting point, the fact that strategy is about action and must, therefore, encompass the three key defining features of any action:

1. **Value:** What is the purpose of the action? Why are you doing it? What value do you seek to deliver and what do you get back in return?

2. **Effectiveness:** What, specifically do you need to do? What would make the difference between doing this action in a satisfactory or unsatisfactory way? How, and how well, do you deliver value?

3. **Efficiency:** Was the action undertaken in the best possible way, or was time, energy or money wasted in the process? How do you make good use of resources? When does it need to be done by?

Value, effectiveness and efficiency can, therefore, be considered to be fundamental to strategy.

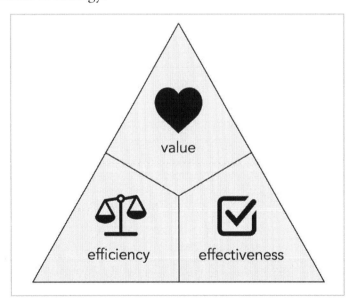

Figure 34 The Value Model of Strategy

Specifically, the word 'value' is used to refer to a *value exchange* between you and the world. What do you offer to the world and what do you get in exchange? If you are a business operating in a commercial marketplace your value exchange may be simple: you offer goods and services that meet an otherwise unmet customer need. In exchange, you get money: the price you charge for those goods and services. For businesses looking to "purpose beyond profits,"[13] as the Business Roundtable recommended, they seek to add other dimensions of value to the world, such as reducing waste and pollution, increasing recycling, becoming carbon-neutral, promoting diversity and inclusion amongst employees and committing a proportion of revenue or profit to charitable causes.

Strategies, of course, also need to work in non-commercial environments. Some operate in an ideas market[14] where the value you offer might be your contributions to the growing digital commons.[15] What you get in exchange is social credibility within the community. This credibility might, at some time, enable you to get other members of the community to support a project you initiate. Others operate in a virtue market,[16] where the value you offer might be saving lives or alleviating suffering. Recognition for this good work leads to donations, which in turn enable you to continue the good work.

Effectiveness and efficiency need to be thoroughly teased apart if you are to avoid being tripped up by their similarity. The most concise distinction, and one to keep in your head as a reminder, is that effectiveness is 'doing the right thing', whereas efficiency is 'doing the thing right' (Fig. 35).

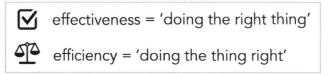

Figure 35 Defining effectiveness and efficiency

Digging a little deeper reveals two sides to both effectiveness and efficiency. One side is operational. Operational *effectiveness* involves doing lots of different 'right things'. You must know what you need to do, you must be able to do it all and you must do it in a way that achieves your purpose. Effectiveness is typically measured in terms of outputs or the benefits arising from those outputs. Operational *efficiency* tries to ensure you 'get more out than you put in' across a wide range of tasks. It is about cutting waste, reducing costs, compressing timelines or increasing return on investment. Efficiency is usually measured using rates, ratios or comparisons with benchmarks – costs per new customer, time to deploy new software, percentage of calls answered within 30 seconds of calling.

The other side of effectiveness and efficiency could be labelled 'ultimate'. Ultimate *effectiveness* is the sum total of all your operational effectiveness. It is the *impact* you are able to make. It is how much of the value, defined by your chosen value exchange, you are actually able to deliver. Ultimate *efficiency* is the sum total of all your operational efficiencies. In commercial organisations, the measure of ultimate efficiency is profit. You design and manufacture products which you offer to your customers for a price. When they purchase and pay the price, the value exchange is transacted. They get the value offered by the product they just bought; you get the money. Part of that money pays for the design and manufacture of the product just purchased. The remainder (value received minus the cost of value delivered) is profit; or, described generally enough to cover both commercial and non-commercial strategies, *residual value*.

As shown in Figure 36, 'impact' is what sits between effectiveness and value – it is how much value you are able to deliver, by means of the work you do. Similarly, 'residual value' sits between efficiency and value – by making good use of your resources, the cost of you delivering value to the world doesn't use up all the value you receive in exchange.

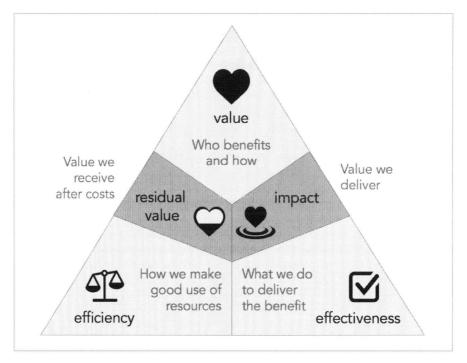

Figure 36 The Value Model of Strategy (full version)

3.2.1 The Value Model of Strategy and the Strategy Lifecycle Model

In Chapter 2 you were introduced to the Strategy Lifecycle Model. You can put the Value Model of Strategy, which represents your general theory of strategy, at the heart of the Strategy Lifecycle Model (Fig. 37). One of the key roles of strategy production is identifying how your organisation seeks to add value to the world and get value back in exchange. Once this is done, strategy production also needs to identify the high-level methods by which you will achieve this value exchange. So, as shown in Figure 37, it is fitting that strategy production sits alongside value and effectiveness in the Value Model of Strategy.

Strategy adoption seeks to drill down into the actions needed for effectiveness and to explore ways of making them efficient. Adoption is what blends effectiveness and efficiency together for the first time.

Strategy adaptation is where the strategic plan is adjusted to suit changing circumstances. The constant reference-point amidst all of this adaptation is the value exchange defined in the strategy. This is such a fundamental feature of any strategy that, if this needs to adapt, it is time for a new strategy. So, having strategy adaptation closing the loop back to value is also fitting.

Figure 37 Combining Value Model of Strategy with the Strategy Lifecycle Model

A fascinating provocation related to the Value Model of Strategy comes from Tim O'Reilly, founder of O'Reilly Media, one of the world's biggest specialist publishers of technology books and courses. His motto is 'create more value than you capture'. In a TEDx talk[17] he explains, "I was told by more than one internet billionaire that they started with an O'Reilly book. I thought, how wonderful is that. We sold someone a book for say $30 and they went on to build a billion-dollar company." He goes on to give the following examples: "Look at the enormous value that was created by Tim Berners Lee when he put the web into the public domain. Look at the enormous value that was created by Linus Torvalds when he made Linux available for free." So, his message is that you need to spend more effort considering the value you create – there is too much emphasis right now on the value captured, for example how much money you make by producing and selling something. To illustrate this, O'Reilly cites the 'Clothesline Paradox', which he attributes to Steve Baer, writing in Coevolution Quarterly in 1975. This paradox contrasts drying clothes in an electric dryer and on a clothesline outside. Drying clothes in a dryer is frequently cited as an environmental cost - it is a debit in our expenditure on fossil fuels. Yet drying clothes on a clothesline is rarely counted as a benefit from solar energy. So, when working with the Value Model of Strategy, think hard about the value you create and then maybe think even harder about how to create more value than you capture.

Figure 38 takes the full version of the Value Model of Strategy and translates it into a template to be filled in.

In order to show a completed version of this template, we have chosen Warby Parker, the innovative eyewear business in the USA. The reason they are of particular interest is, firstly, because they have disrupted the previously very traditional eyewear market and hence make an interesting strategy example. Secondly, and of particular relevance here, is that they have chosen to deliver value to a wide variety of beneficiaries, including offering free glasses to charities through their 'buy one, gift one' scheme (Fig. 39).

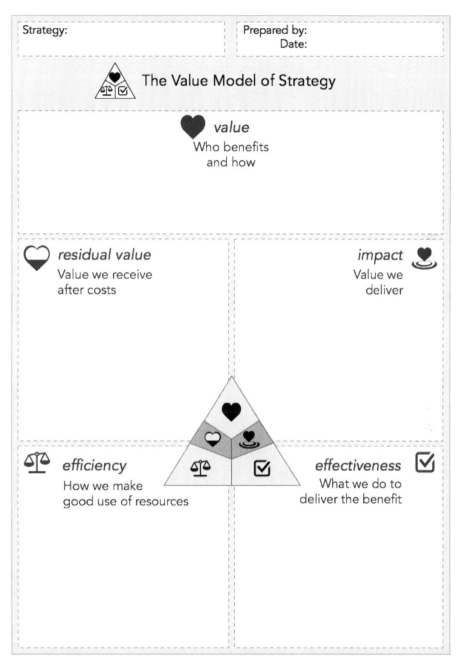

Figure 38 Template for the Value Model of Strategy

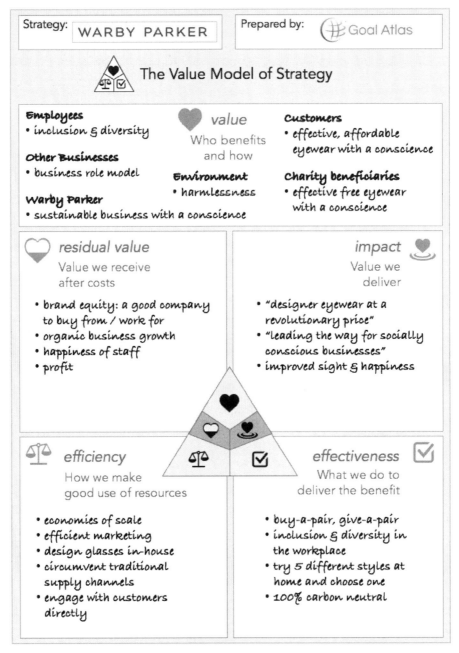

Strategy: WARBY PARKER **Prepared by:** Goal Atlas

The Value Model of Strategy

Employees
- inclusion & diversity

Other Businesses
- business role model

Warby Parker
- sustainable business with a conscience

value
Who benefits and how

Environment
- harmlessness

Customers
- effective, affordable eyewear with a conscience

Charity beneficiaries
- effective free eyewear with a conscience

residual value
Value we receive after costs

- brand equity: a good company to buy from / work for
- organic business growth
- happiness of staff
- profit

impact
Value we deliver

- "designer eyewear at a revolutionary price"
- "leading the way for socially conscious businesses"
- improved sight & happiness

efficiency
How we make good use of resources

- economies of scale
- efficient marketing
- design glasses in-house
- circumvent traditional supply channels
- engage with customers directly

effectiveness
What we do to deliver the benefit

- buy-a-pair, give-a-pair
- inclusion & diversity in the workplace
- try 5 different styles at home and choose one
- 100% carbon neutral

Figure 39 Value Model template completed for Warby Parker

3.3   Summary and key takeaways from Chapter 3

1. There are two models that apply across the entire strategy lifecycle; they are the **House of Strategy Model** and the **Value Model of Strategy**.

2. The House of Strategy Model shows graphically how **vision, mission, values and strategy** come together for an organisation.

3. There are two main ways to use the House of Strategy Model:

    a. To **audit** existing vision, mission, values and strategy,

    b. To **create** new vision, mission, values and strategy.

4. The Value Model of Strategy represents strategy in terms of the three key defining features of strategic action:

    a. **Value:** Who benefits and how. Value refers to a **value exchange** between you and the world.

    b. **Effectiveness:** Effectiveness is what you do to deliver value to your beneficiaries; how, and how well, you deliver value. It can be defined as 'doing the right thing'.

    c. **Efficiency:** Efficiency is how you make good use of resources. It can be defined as 'doing the thing right'.

5. **Impact** is how much value you are actually able to deliver, by means of the work you do.

6. **Residual value** is the value you receive, after costs, in exchange for the value you deliver.

3.4   Let's talk about… identity marks and value

Use these questions to prompt deeper conversations about identity marks and value across your organisation:

1. *How well aligned are your vision, mission, values and strategy currently?*

2. *How important is it that your identity marks are aligned? How well aligned do they need to be? What are the benefits of alignments and the costs of misalignment?*

3. *Are your values (beliefs and ideals) significant, impactful and distinctive?*

4. *Are you clear, as an organisation, what value you deliver and to whom? What value do you receive? How do you deliver value? How do you make good use of resources in delivering value?*

Notes on Chapter 3

(all web content accessed between April and September 2020)

---

[1] Business Dictionary. *Mission Statement.*
http://www.businessdictionary.com/definition/mission-statement.html

[2] The Balance, Small Business, 2020. *What Is a Mission Statement? Definition and Examples of a Mission Statement*
https://www.thebalancesmb.com/mission-statement-2947996

[3] Wikipedia. *Mission statement.*
https://en.wikipedia.org/wiki/Mission_statement

[4] Stoner JL. *What is Vision?* https://seapointcenter.com/what-is-vision/

[5] The Marketing Blender. *How to write mission and vision statements for B2B. And why it matters.* https://www.themarketingblender.com/vision-mission-statements/

[6] Change Factory. *The components of a good vision statement.* https://www.changefactory.com.au/our-thinking/articles/the-components-of-a-good-vision-statement/

[7] Oxford Dictionaries. *Value.* https://www.lexico.com/definition/value

[8] Collins Dictionary. *Values.* https://www.collinsdictionary.com/dictionary/english/values

[9] Ethics and Compliance Initiative. *Definitions of Ethical Values in Organizations.* https://www.ethics.org/resources/free-toolkit/definition-values/

[10] Business Dictionary. *Values.* http://www.businessdictionary.com/definition/values.html

[11] Samsung. *Vision 2020.* On the Samsung UK site at https://www.samsung.com/uk/aboutsamsung.html/aboutsamsung/ and on the Samsung Levant site at https://www.samsung.com/levant/aboutsamsung1/samsungelectronics/vision2020/

[12] Where to play, as a strategic decision comes from Lafley AG and Martin RL, 2013. *Playing to Win: How Strategy Really Works.* Harvard Business Review Press, Boston.

[13] Gartenberg C and Serafeim G, 2019. *181 Top CEOs Have Realized Companies Need a Purpose Beyond Profit.* Harvard Business Review, 20 August 2019.

[14] Coase R, 1974. *The Market for Goods and the Market for Ideas.* The American Economic Review, 64 (2): 384-391.

[15] Bowens M and Niaros V, 2016. *Value in the Commons Economy: Developments in Open and Contributory Value Accounting.* Heinrich Boll Foundation, Berlin. https://www.boell.de/en/2017/02/01/value-commons-economy-developments-open-and-contributory-value-accounting

[16] Maitland I, 1997. *Virtuous Markets: "The Market as School of the Virtues".* Business Ethics Quarterly, 7 (1): 17-31.

[17] O'Reilly T 2012. *Creating More Value Than You Capture.* TEDx Bradford. https://www.youtube.com/watch?v=5OEdy5HBGiI

Chapter 4

Strategy mapping

Strategy is a response to a complex challenge, defining the value, effectiveness and efficiency of that response, in terms of an interconnected cascade of goals.

Strategy mapping, as a process, is a remarkable strategic tool, and, as such, deserves a chapter all to itself. Strategy mapping provides a way to systematically validate every part of your strategy, and then put it into action by delegating, prioritising and measuring the progress of strategic goals in ways that ladder up to strategic success.

Just as the core models in Chapter 3 can be used across the strategy lifecycle, so too can strategy mapping. Based on an interconnected cascade of goals, strategy mapping is a simple, logical process that can be used to:

1. align the strategic actions across your organisation and hence make your overall strategy more purposeful;

2. make your strategy more innovative, by identifying alternative ways to reach your strategic goals;

3. validate your strategy to ensure its internal consistency by identifying missing goals (the things you should be doing) and surplus goals (the things you really don't need to be doing).

A strategy map can also inform and guide strategic planning by enabling:

1. effective delegation of goals (strategic actions), whilst giving everyone a genuine sense of ownership and involvement by linking their actions to the organisation's ultimate purpose;

2. prioritisation of goals to ensure maximum impact of strategic actions;

3. setting and tracking of targets that aggregate performance up to meaningful KPIs.

First though, you need to consider why a cascade of goals is an important way to think about strategy.

4.1   The importance of the strategy cascade

In their acclaimed book on strategy, *Playing to Win*, former CEO of Procter & Gamble, AG Lafley, and professor, author and leading management thinker[1], Roger Martin, suggest that the strategic choices made by any organisation "can be understood as a reinforcing cascade, with the choices at the top of the cascade …" (overall corporate strategy, business unit strategy etc) "…setting the context for the choices below …" (industry sector strategy, product category strategy and brand strategy) "… and choices at the bottom refining the choices above."[2]

They go on to explain how Procter and Gamble's strategy cascaded across four levels:

1. *Company strategy* (e.g. Procter and Gamble) covering multiple sectors;

2. *Sector strategy* (e.g. beauty or baby care), covering multiple categories;

3. *Category strategy* (e.g. skin care or diapers), covering multiple related brands;

4. *Brand strategy* (e.g. Olay or Pampers).

Chapter 1 characterised strategy as a concerted effort by lots of people over a prolonged period of time to bring about a much bigger change than you could achieve simply by keeping on doing what you do currently. This, in itself, is sufficient to produce a 'strategy adoption gap' (Fig. 40).

Figure 40 The Strategy Adoption Gap

Your starting point in understanding this gap is acknowledging that strategy is originally owned by senior leadership. There are two reasons for this. Firstly, strategy needs to represent the interests of the entire organisation and this is what senior leadership is charged with. Secondly, strategy needs to be ratified by the board and, once ratified, is then delegated to senior leadership to turn the intentions of strategy into the actions that will lead to strategic success. To do so will require the engagement and commitment of front-line teams across the organisation. Senior leadership's challenge in securing that engagement and commitment is how the strategy adoption gap is filled.

The solution, in principle, is simple. Two things need to happen:

1. The goals contained in the strategy need to be elaborated into sub-goals to a sufficient extent that they can be meaningfully delegated to the front-line teams who will deliver the necessary strategic change.

2. The actions of the front-line teams need to aggregate together harmoniously to ensure lots of individual changes add up to strategic success.

This defines more precisely what Lafley and Martin described as their strategy cascade: strategic 'choices at the top of the cascade set the context for the choices below, and choices at the bottom influence and refine the choices above'.[3]

What you need is a way of doing this elaboration and aggregation systematically and rigorously.

4.2   The logic of interconnected goals

Imagine you are wanting to run the London Marathon (something the author has experience of, having run it in 2013). As part of the marathon-running ritual, you will need to pester friends and family for sponsorship and raise some money for charity.

In running the London Marathon, you, therefore, will have two goals:

1. To *run a marathon* and

2. To *raise money for charity.*

One goal is clearly your 'purpose' – *raise money for charity* – and the other goal is your 'method' of achieving that purpose – *run a marathon*.

Figure 41 shows what these goals could look like in a diagram. Why will you *run a marathon*? In order to *raise money for charity*. How will you *raise money for charity*? You will *run a marathon*.

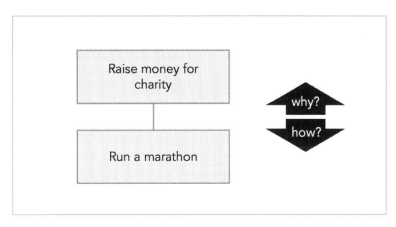

Figure 41 Connecting goals together for running a marathon

Taking this a step further, you realise that you are going to need to *train for six months* in order to be fit enough to *run a marathon*. Training becomes a further method under your goal of *run a marathon* (Fig. 42).

With the addition of this third goal, something magical has just happened. The goal *run a marathon* has been transformed into both a method AND a purpose. It is the method of *raise money for charity* and the purpose of *train for six months*. The magic that comes from this is that you can keep on connecting goals in this way, with each goal serving as the method of its 'parent' goal and the purpose of its 'child' goal.

You have just unlocked the secret of how to elaborate strategic goals from senior leadership to front-line teams, and then to aggregate them back up again to deliver strategic success.

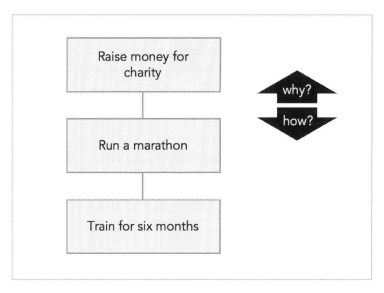

Figure 42 Expanding the goals for running a marathon

4.3   The origins of strategy mapping

In a presentation to the Society of American Value Engineers in 1965, Charles Bytheway christened this 'why-how logic' and explained that graphical mapping like this could be used to analyse any cause–effect relationship. In his book, *FAST Creativity and Innovation*, Bytheway gives the example of an incandescent light bulb.[4]

Light is produced by heating the filament, positioning the filament and preventing filament damage. The position of the filament is determined by the positioning of filament support wires, which in turn is achieved by fixing the filament support wires in the light-bulb base. The filament is heated by conducting current through it. This is achieved by providing connecting wires and providing an electricity supply. Filament damage is prevented by replacing oxygen with an inert gas. This is done by providing a glass bulb and sealing it with an air-tight seal against the light bulb base. All these interconnections are shown in a simplification of Bytheway's diagram in Figure 43.

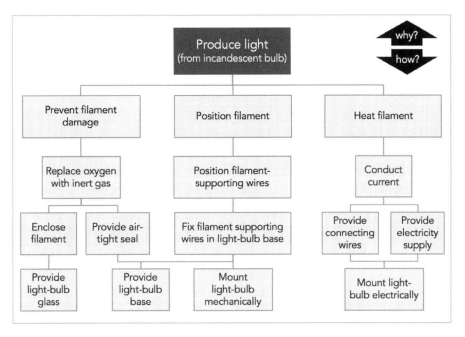

Figure 43 Simplified version of Bytheway's FAST diagram

Bytheway called this a 'FAST diagram', standing for Function Analysis System Technique, because it is a cascade of the functions performed by different light bulb components. Although Bytheway's diagram was new, function analysis was almost twenty years old. It was devised by Lawrence Miles of General Electric (GE) in New York in 1947.[5] Working as a procurement engineer in the post-war era, Miles faced day-to-day struggles to reconcile a manufacturing boom with materials shortages, still unresolved after the war. Function analysis was his way of asking suppliers to deliver the functionality GE needed, whilst leaving them to decide which products and parts to use. So rather than simply ordering nuts and bolts of a particular specification, for example, he would ask suppliers to propose a way of fixing steel sheets to a frame.

Engineering functionality is richly interconnected. Fixing steel sheets to a frame is a function that serves other functions: for example, preventing unintended access to manufacturing machinery behind the steel sheets. Preventing unintended access to machinery, in turn, serves other functions, such as preventing injuries (no hands or feet caught in moving machine parts) or preventing damage to the machinery (dropped tools are deflected before hitting the machinery). It was Bytheway's FAST diagram that enabled such functions to be interconnected systematically and with a logical rigour that Miles's function analysis hadn't previously had. Miles, and to a lesser extent Bytheway, built a whole new sub-discipline of engineering called Value Management on the back of function analysis. Over the intervening years, Value Management has grown to the point that it now has professional bodies worldwide.[6]

4.4   Introducing strategy mapping

The why-how logic that Miles and Bytheway used for value management turns out to be a great way to develop strategy and this is what we call 'strategy mapping'. Let's work through it from first principles.

A strategy map is made up entirely of goals. Many strategists like to distinguish between aims, objectives and goals, but in the absence of any standard way to differentiate between them, this probably confuses as much as it clarifies. So, within strategy mapping, everything is a goal.

A goal is an action, typically described by a verb-noun pair (e.g. *run a marathon*), often with qualifiers of different sorts (e.g. *raise* [verb] *money* [noun] *for charity* [qualifier]). To help stick to the language of goals, you may find it useful to write your goal by completing the sentence 'I want to ...' (Fig. 44). So, I want to *run a marathon*; I want to *raise money for charity*; I want to *train for six months.*

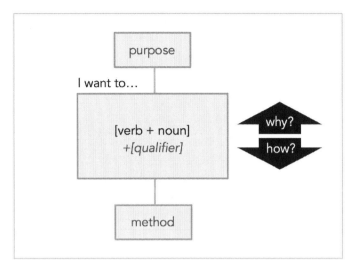

Figure 44 Goals are typically described using verb-noun pairs

There are also sentences you can complete to check that your goals connect together correctly (Fig. 45). So, for example,

> I want to …
>
> *run a marathon* [goal]
>
> … in order to …
>
> *raise money for charity* [purpose].

> In order to …
>
> *run a marathon* [goal]
>
> … I need to …
>
> *train for six months* [method].

Figure 45 also reinforces the idea that everything is a goal, typically described using a verb-noun pair. A purpose explains why you are doing the goal below it, but it is itself still a goal. A method explains how you are going to achieve the goal above it, but it too is a goal.

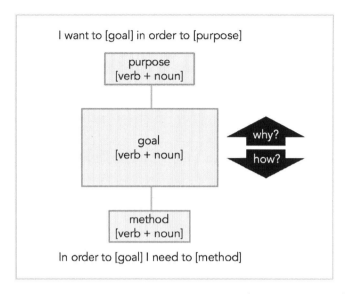

Figure 45 Sentence structures to ensure goals connect together

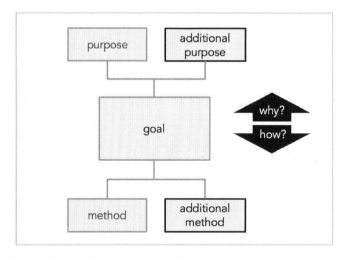

Figure 46 Adding purpose and methods to a strategy map

Figure 46 shows that you are now poised to elaborate the goals you started with by adding more methods and alternative purposes to each goal. If, for example, you want to *run a marathon* in order to *raise money for charity*, you need to do more than just *train for six months*. You also need to *secure a place in a marathon race*. This is an additional method for *run a marathon*. You may also realise that *run a marathon* will do more than *raise money for charity*. It will also help you *get fit*. This is an additional purpose of *train for six months*.

After a couple more rounds of elaboration, your goal of running a marathon has developed into a mini-strategy for your personal lifestyle (Fig. 47).

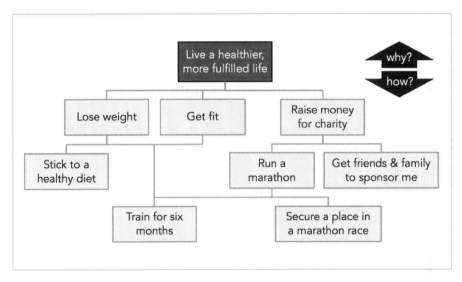

Figure 47 A personal lifestyle strategy

Just pause for a moment to reflect on how remarkably fortunate it is to have Miles and Bytheway providing the heritage for a tool to manage strategy:

- Firstly, their focus was on functions. Functions are descriptions on how to DO things. This heritage makes strategy mapping inherently action-focused;

- Secondly, the why-how logic that interconnects engineering functions can also interconnect elements of strategy. This crucially important feature is what enables strategy mapping to connect the aspirations of leaders with the actions of front-line teams.

To start exploring strategy mapping with real-world strategy examples, you are going to look at a strategy 'section'.

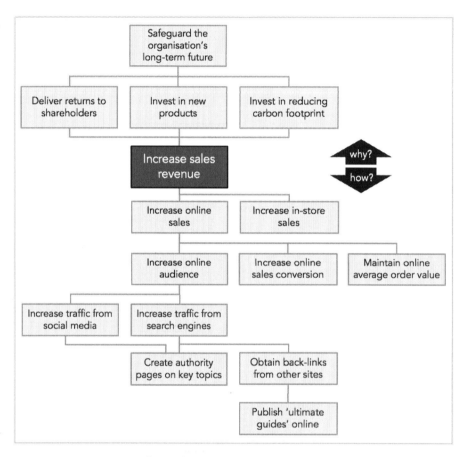

Figure 48 Section through a strategy map to increase sales revenue

You are borrowing the idea of a section from the world of microscopy. To examine a specimen under a light microscope, it needs to be sliced very finely so the light can pass through the specimen and into the optics of the microscope. This is usually done using a microtome and the slices it produces are called sections.[7] Figure 48 shows a strategy section that slices through an entire organisation, showing the methods (how?) and purposes (why?) of increasing sales revenue.

4.5   Five key features of strategy maps

You can now use this '*increase sales revenue*' example to explore the key features of strategy maps, as if it were your own organisation.

4.5.1 The wording of goals in a strategy map follows a common pattern

At the core of each goal is a verb–noun pair. What are you going to do? Verb. What are you doing it to? Noun. In the example above, you aim to increase audience, increase conversion and create pages. In all these examples, the verb–noun pair is qualified in some way. The audience you want to increase is your *online* audience. The conversion you want to increase is your *online sales* conversion. The pages you want to create are *authority* pages *on key topics*. Having verb–noun pairs at the heart of each goal, keeps the strategy map action-focused; something strategies often struggle with. To help you remain consistent in the way you write goals, try sticking to this sentence structure:

1. When moving 'down' the map to find 'how' to achieve your purpose, use the phrase "In order to [purpose], I need to [method]."

   a. In order to '*Invest in new products*', I need to '*Increase sales revenue*'.

   b. In order to '*Increase traffic from search engines*', I need to '*Create authority pages on key topics*'.

2. When moving 'up' the map to resolve 'why' you want to achieve your goal, use the phrase "I want to [method] in order to [purpose]."

a. I want to *'Increase traffic from search engines'* in order to *'Increase online audience'*.

b. I want to *'Invest in reducing carbon footprint'* in order to *'Safeguard the organisation's long-term future'*.

4.5.2 Strategy maps connect goals together recursively

Reading a strategy map involves moving up through the connected goals to find purpose (asking the question 'why?') and down through the connected goals to find methods (asking the question 'how?'). So, for example, the purpose of *Increasing online sales* is to *Increase sales revenue* and you want to do this in order to: a) *Deliver returns to shareholders*, b) *Invest in new products* and c) *Invest in reducing carbon footprint*. Your methods of *Increasing online sales* are to a) *Increase online audience*, b) *Increase online sales conversion* and c) *Maintain online average order value.* The key here, and this really is the secret sauce of strategy mapping, is that every goal is simultaneously the purpose of the goals below it and the methods of the goals above it. So, *Increasing online sales* is both why you want to increase online audience and how you will increase sales revenue. You have just introduced a 'recursive' method into the way you describe strategy. This isn't as complicated as it sounds but, since it makes strategy mapping one of the most powerful tools in your strategy toolkit, you need to take a moment to make sure you understand it fully.

Recursion is used in both mathematics and computer science and it means "the process of defining a function by the repeated application of an algorithm."[8] Here is a simple example from everyday life. John has just moved house and can't find his keys. As he searches through all of his belongings still packed in boxes, he uses a recursive search algorithm, illustrated in Figure 49.[9]

He opens the first packing case and goes through every item in that box. If any of these items is itself a box, he repeats the process – opens the box and goes through every item. If, inside this box, he finds another box he repeats the process again until he has searched inside every box to find his key, even if it is a box inside a box inside a box.

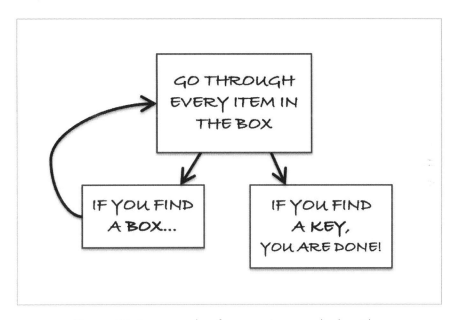

Figure 49 An example of a recursive search algorithm

Strategy mapping is recursive because the top goal is the purpose of the goal below it, just as the next goal down is the purpose of the goal below that, and so on until you reach the bottom of the strategy map. The bottom-most goal is the method of the goal above it, just as that second-to-bottom goal is the method of the next goal up. With a bigger, more complex strategy, this is astonishingly powerful, because it can connect together the goals of individuals from the top to the bottom of the organisation.

4.5.3 Strategy maps connect the goals of individuals across the entire organisation

The goal shown in dark grey in the strategy map in Figure 48, to *Increase sales revenue*, is 'owned' by your Director of Sales, who reports directly to the Chief Executive. The bottom goals, on the other hand, are owned by your front-line Content Team, which is part of the In-Bound Marketing Group within the Marketing Division. The Director of Sales doesn't need to know anything about authority pages or back-links. She just needs to know that 'stuff is being done' to increase traffic from search engines and that this will lead to increased online sales. Similarly, the Content Team doesn't need to know about in-store sales. They may not even want to know a great deal about *Increasing online sales.* They do, however, want to see how their work is *Safeguarding the organisation's long term future.*

Strategy mapping, therefore, connects the loftiest strategic objective with the most detailed and specific tactic in a strict logical step-chain. It enables the day-to-day goal of a member of a front-line team to be directly and explicitly connected to the five-year objectives of senior leadership.

4.5.4 Strategy maps don't care what you put in them, as long as you follow the logic

This isn't the first time the term 'strategy map' has been used. Over twenty years ago, US academics and consultants, Robert Kaplan and David Norton strategy mapping as part of their Balanced Scorecard system[10]. These strategy maps had four defined layers, corresponding to the four layers of the balanced scorecard system. Every element of strategy needed to be in either the financial layer, the customer layer, the internal business processes layer or the learning and growth layer. In addition, the layers were in a fixed order: financial, customer, internal business and learning and growth. Intuitively this makes sense. Learning and growth improves internal business processes, which enables you to serve customers better and this makes you more money. For organisations using the Balanced Scorecard system, this is perfect. Strategy is mapped in ways that conform to the specific way they have committed to transform their organisation. For the rest of us, however, there are some peculiarities. In a Balanced Scorecard strategy map, for example, the only way a new internal process can make more money is by causing customers to do something differently. Internal process improvements to streamline supply chains don't fit. Also, anything you learn (which lives in the learning and growth layer) can only have an impact on customers if it involves a change in an internal process. There isn't a place on their map for you to learn something and have it benefit customers by improving external processes (e.g. marketing agencies, delivery partners, franchisees).

Now, clearly a seasoned Balanced Scorecard professional would have workarounds for these issues. However, it's not the specific issues you are concerned with. It's the nature of the map you have produced. A map specialist would call it a *topological map* – a map that distorts spatial relationships to maintain a specific schematic representation of reality. London's Tube Map is probably the best-known topological map: it distorts the geography of London to ensure Underground Tube lines appear at 90- or 45-degree angles to each other. The Tube Map is the best way to navigate around London, if travelling by London Underground. If, however, you want to walk or drive around London, the Tube Map will get you hopelessly lost. Similarly, the Balanced Scorecard version of strategy mapping is an excellent tool if you run your business using the Balanced Scorecard system. Why-how strategy maps, on the other hand, offer less distortion, fewer constraints and a much more specific and tighter logic (why-how logic). Whenever strategy maps or strategy mapping are referred to in the rest of this book we mean those powered by why-how logic.

A strategy map can contain any type of goal and these goals can be arranged whichever way best suits your organisation, provided you stick to the why-how logic. Mapping in this way is so versatile it doesn't even need to be about strategy. You saw earlier how Bytheway mapped out the functioning of an incandescent light bulb. You can use the same why-how logic to document cookery recipes (in order to bake a cake I need to source ingredients, mix ingredients and cook ingredients) and to undertake risk analyses (in order for the engine to overheat, I need the cooling system to fail and the high-temperature warning to be missed).

4.5.5 Strategy maps branch up as well as down

When Charles Bytheway described his FAST diagrams, he called them FAST trees or function trees[11]. A single primary function is achieved by means of several methods and each of these, in turn, is achieved by several methods. The resulting diagram is, therefore, a tree branching out from a single start-point. Trees have unidirectional branching. Many branches sprout from a single trunk but none of these branches attach to a second, third or fourth trunk. If your strategy maps were actually strategy trees, as Bytheway suggests, this would mean that goals can only ever serve one purpose. You may already have noticed that the strategy map in Figure 48 has goals that serve more than one purpose. The goal *Increase sales revenue*, for example will enable:

1. *delivery of returns to shareholders;*

2. *investment in new products;*

3. *investment in reducing carbon footprint.*

A strategy map is indeed a map rather than a tree. It can branch up as well as down, because it can have goals serving multiple purposes.

With a tree diagram it is obvious where the main goal is – it is the trunk of the tree, from which all other goals branch. In a map with branches going up as well as down, it is less obvious where the primary goal is. Which is why, in our strategy maps, we always have one goal rendered darker to show the 'primary goal'.

4.6   Validating strategy to ensure its internal consistency

Validation is not a word often associated with strategy. To validate something means to prove it correct.[12] How can that happen with a strategy when its success lies some distance away in an unpredictable future? The answer is to prove the strategy's internal validity. Do the clusters of goals in a strategy map make sense and show internal consistency?

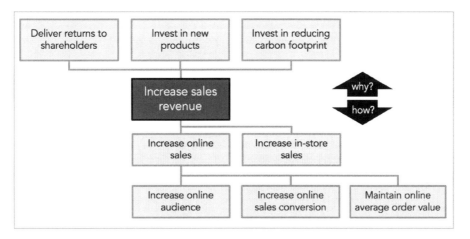

Figure 50 The middle part of the strategy map from Figure 48

The why-how logic of strategy mapping enables a degree of validation. If each goal is indeed the method of the goal above it and the purpose of the goals below it, and if this pattern repeats across the entire strategy map, you already have a considerable amount of validity in that map. This, of course, assumes the why-how logic has been applied rigorously. Part of the strategy map you explored previously in Figure 48 enables closer examination of this assumption (Fig. 50).

You start by asking the question 'how?' of your primary goal: how are you going to *Increase sales revenue*? The goal below should answer this: by *Increasing online sales*. Changes of wording like this should set off alarms in the strategy mapping process. Why do you have 'sales revenue' in one goal and 'online sales' in another? Does it matter? To answer this question, you need to pause and remind yourself what you are trying to do here. You are proposing a method by which a higher goal will be achieved. Does the logic hold true that if you *Increase online sales,* you will necessarily *Increase sales revenue*? No. Offering huge discounts online will increase sales volume, measured in numbers of orders, but might actually reduce online sales revenue. This is clearly a possibility you thought about because one of the methods of *Increasing online sales* is to *Maintain average order value.* Before deciding if this makes the strategy map okay, you need to re-examine the primary goal – *Increase sales revenue.* It serves three purposes: i) *Deliver returns to shareholders,* ii) *Invest in new products* and iii) *Invest in reducing carbon footprint.* Is *Increase sales revenue* the logical method of achieving these three goals? Not quite. These three goals depend on *profit*, not revenue and there are a variety of ways you could boost revenue at the expense of profit: increase spending on advertising, for example.

Ultimately this entire strategy map is about generating profits so they can be invested wisely. Currently the logic by which it does so isn't very rigorous. So, you try again, and come up with the map in Figure 51. Increased revenue from sales has been turned into *Increased profit from sales,* because profit is what enables returns to shareholders, investment in new products and investing in reducing carbon footprint. The methods of *Increasing profit from sales* have also been changed so they too refer to profit. One of the methods of *Increasing profit from online sales* has also been changed to maintain the profit-focus: *Maintain average profit margin per order.*

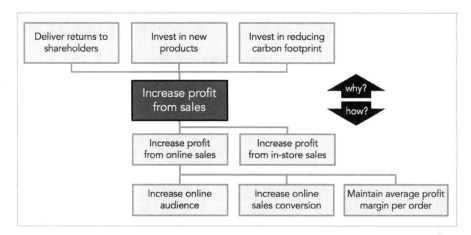

Figure 51 Strategy map refined after validation, with emphasis now on 'profit' rather than 'sales'

Your original strategy map wasn't that bad. It looked fine until you examined it in more detail, then the logic started to fall apart. This is strategy validation. It takes a strategy that looks okay, examines it in much more forensic detail, and can discover where its underlying logic lacks rigour.

4.6.1 The SaNity Check Model

Okay, so you've checked the why-how logic from top to bottom of the strategy map and it all looks fine. There's one more tool to deploy before you're done with validation. It's called the SaNity Check Model, so-called because it checks the **S**ufficiency **a**nd **N**ecess**ity** of the goals in the strategy map.

There is nothing quite so maddening as discovering that a strategy map, with rigorous why-how logic, still doesn't achieve the impact it was designed to deliver. The SaNity Check Model is designed to prevent this happening (Fig. 52).

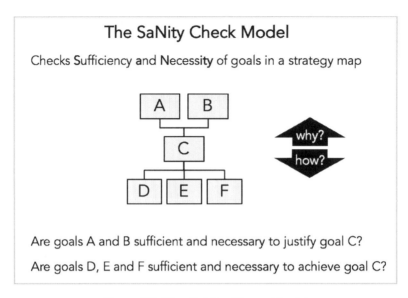

Figure 52 The SaNity Check Model

Look at the strategy map in Figure 51 again. Are the methods sufficient to achieve the goals they serve? If you want to *Increase profit from online sales,* is it sufficient to *Increase online audience, Increase online sales conversion* and *Maintain average profit margin per order?* Or is there something missing? Rigorous why-how logic can tell you if the goals you already have in the map are connected together correctly, but it can't say if anything is missing. For this you need to add the SaNity Check Model.

On reflection you think there may well be something missing. A few years ago, you thought new customers would be the answer to your financial woes. They weren't! They were expensive to acquire and most of them never returned for a second purchase. At the time, you promised never to underestimate the importance of your existing customers. Yet the way these goals are written makes you wonder if this strategy map is consistent with that promise. There are no goals focused on making the most of your existing customers. You decide to introduce clear customer acquisition and customer retention strands into your strategy (Fig. 53).

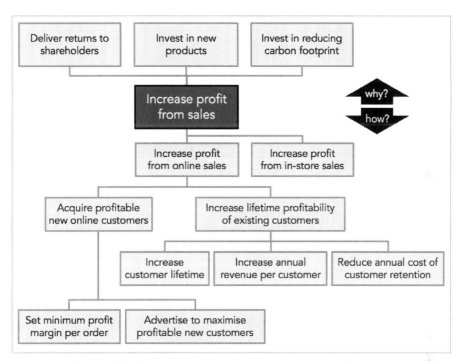

Figure 53 Strategy map refined after further validation

Now you have two methods of *Increasing profit from online sales*: i) *Acquire profitable new online customers* and ii) *Increase lifetime profitability of existing customers*. This, you feel resolves the insufficiency of the previous strategy map. It no longer underestimates the importance of your existing customers.

So far you have been SaNity Checking the methods in the strategy map. You can go through the same process with purposes. Of the three purposes you have for *Increasing profit from sales*, you could, for example, question the necessity of *Investing in reducing carbon footprint*. This isn't an issue of why-how logic. There is no doubt reducing your carbon footprint would come at a cost and that cost would need to come from profits earned through sales. The question of necessity is, therefore less of a yes / no kind of question and more of a requirement for assumptions to be explicit, the decision for its inclusion to be explained and its justification to be transparent. In this way, arguments for and against its necessity can be compared and evaluated.

4.7   Strategy mapping to make strategy more innovative

Strategy is about making choices, which is fine when you have a range of options readily available to choose between. Often this isn't the case and strategy mapping can be used to help you out here. This is one part of strategy mapping's why-how logic you haven't discovered yet and it is how to use strategy mapping to innovate – systematically!

Your strategy map in Figure 53, has two methods to *Increase profit from sales*: i) *Increase profit from online sales* and ii) *Increase profit from in-store sales*. If you wanted to make this part of your strategy more innovative, you could ask 'How else can we *increase profit from sales*?' Rather than increasing sales through your existing sales channels, maybe you could open up a new channel. Traditionally a customer support facility, your call centre has recently trialled tele-marketing campaigns, with some success. Which makes you decide to add a third method to *increase profit from sales*: *establish profit from call centre sales*, as shown in Figure 54. This is called *methods-focused innovation*.

This same approach can be applied to purposes, as well as methods. The goal *increase profit from sales* in Figure 53 already serves three purposes: *deliver returns to shareholders, invest in new products* and *invest in reducing carbon footprint. Purpose-focused innovation* asks, 'Why else could we do this?' So, why else do you want to increase profit from sales? Perhaps to make your business better prepared for an Independent Public Offering (IPO)[13] on the Stock Exchange. Or perhaps to commit a proportion of your profit to charitable causes (Fig. 55), by launching something like Warby Parker's buy-one, gift-one scheme, that you learned about in Chapter 3.

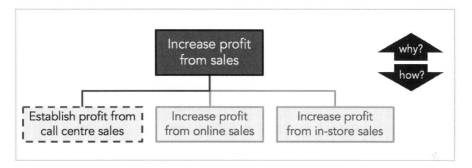

Figure 54 Strategy map with an innovative method added

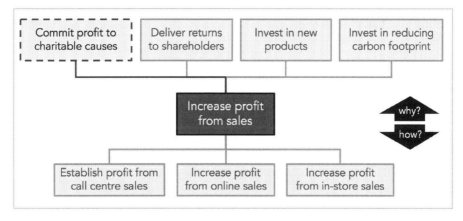

Figure 55 Strategy map with an innovative purpose added

4.8   The boundaries of strategy maps

Does a strategy map keep expanding until it covers every last detail of what an organisation does? It is all too easy for strategists to keep writing more and more strategy; you may have already encountered the idea that "if I don't write something about everyone, they won't feel strategically important". Strategy, however, is about *change*; if you are describing a change the organisation needs to undergo, include it in strategy; if not, leave it out. Of course, this just 'kicks the can down the road' and now you need to ask, 'what do we mean by change?'

Sergey Brin, cofounder of Google, was the first to apply the 70:20:10 rule to the management of innovation (you can read more on this in Chapter 5 on strategy investment as part of strategy governance).[14] As a general rule, he suggested, organisations should spend 70% of their time managing their current core business. This will include optimising it, refining it and repairing it when necessary but not seeking to fundamentally change it. 20% of an organisation's time should be spent innovating incrementally from that core business. This could be new products and services for existing customer segments or propositions to expand into adjacent segments. 10% of the time is spent on 'things that are truly new', 'blue skies thinking', inventing what your core business might become in a few years' time. Strategy then is not about how your organisation spends 70% of its time managing its core business. The extent to which it focuses on Brin's 20% or his 10% depends on how incremental or radical your strategy is, but it is not about business-as-usual. Strategy, and hence strategy mapping, has no place for lists of jobs that need to be done to maintain or refine business-as-usual. Make sure it remains the manifesto for change it is meant to be.

4.9   Multiple strategies

Many organisations, especially the larger ones, have multiple strategies. You learned, at the start of this chapter, about Procter and Gamble's strategies at four levels: brand, category, sector and company. These, however, are all market-facing strategies. What about more operations-facing strategies: IT strategy, people strategy, finance strategy? Then what about other outward-facing strategies: Investor relations strategy, PR strategy, environmental strategy?

This proliferation of strategies is in marked contrast to the view of Michael Porter, the Harvard Business School academic and author, known as the 'Godfather of Strategy'.[15] He thinks this idea of multiple strategies within an organisation "doesn't make any sense". He suggests "there can only be one strategy for any particular business, because strategy is inherently integrative. It is how the various pieces, activities, functions actually fit together. The more you break strategy up into various strategies … the more likely you are to not have a strategy at all."[16]

So, who's right? The solution to this lies in what you mean by strategy. On the one hand, a strategy can be seen as a published document. It declares a set of aspirations and how these aspirations should be achieved. As far as strategy documents are concerned, there is no reason why this cannot be specific to part of the organisation. Indeed, there can be dozens of strategy documents. In a sense, the more the merrier. If you want to find out what your organisation seeks to change over the next few years with regard to recognition and reward, you know that the People Strategy is the place to look. If you want to know if you are stuck with this elderly laptop and out-of-date software forever, you may find an answer in the IT Strategy.

Strategy documents are, however, a very different thing from the strategic thinking that lies behind them. Strategic thinking needs to be *really* joined up. It needs to provide clarity about what the organisation seeks to achieve and what changes to, for example, IT provision are essential to get there. If renewing everyone's laptop and upgrading software is part of these changes, joined-up strategic thinking needs to explain why. This joined up strategic thinking is what strategy mapping provides. It's why-how logic is perfectly designed to connect together multiple disparate activities with increasingly aggregated levels of common purpose.

So, the solution to the multiple strategies issue is that multiple strategy documents are fine, provided joined-up strategic thinking underpins these documents to maintain strategic coherence.

4.10 Building the strategic plan

So far, you have been learning about strategy mapping as a logic diagram: how do goals logically connect leadership aspirations with front-line actions. Now you are going to discover *goal attributes* and find out how to make strategy mapping work a lot harder for your organisation in building your strategic plan. Figure 56 shows four commonly used goal attributes: goal owner, performance indicator, priority and resources.

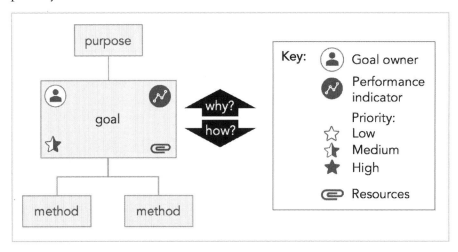

Figure 56 Attributes of a goal in a strategy map

1. **Goal owner** – this defines who this goal has been delegated to. They are responsible for taking the action specified by the goal and are

typically accountable to whoever owns this goal's purpose (the owner of the goal shown above this one in the strategy map).

2. **Performance indicator** – this shows how well this goal's objective is being achieved. This requires the goal to have a target set over a defined timescale and for progress towards that target to be reported.

3. **Priority** – this indicates the relative importance of this goal relative to other goals in the strategy map. The priority of an individual goal is usually defined using a simple priority scoring system (e.g. one, two or three-stars indicating low, medium or high priority). This priority can then be cascaded across the strategy map to give a far more subtle and nuanced prioritisation than you'd expect from a simple three-point prioritisation score. This will be explained and demonstrated in Chapter 9 on strategy adoption.

4. **Resources** – Part of the elegance of strategy mapping is the simplicity and conciseness of the goals (a verb-noun pair). This, however, cannot convey any of the context that a goal owner might need, as the goal is delegated to them. What evidence indicated the need for this goal? What models, processes or tools are available to be used in pursuit of this goal? Are there any policies or standards that need to be adhered to whilst achieving the goal? The resources attached to a goal include documents, spreadsheets, records and processes that give context to the goal and support its achievement.

Imagine your strategy is now complete. It has been developed. It has been drilled-down and delegated. It has been prioritised, timetabled and target-set. What does your strategy map end up looking like?

Figure 57 shows a section of a completed strategy map for a fictional company. It shows goal owners, performance indicators, priorities and resources. Figure 58 shows these attributes in detail, including a double-ring performance indicator. The outer ring shows how much of the time to the target deadline has elapsed – two-thirds of the time has elapsed leaving one-third remaining. The inner ring shows progress towards the performance target – less than two-thirds of the performance target has been attained so far. This shows, at a glance, that this goal is a little behind schedule.

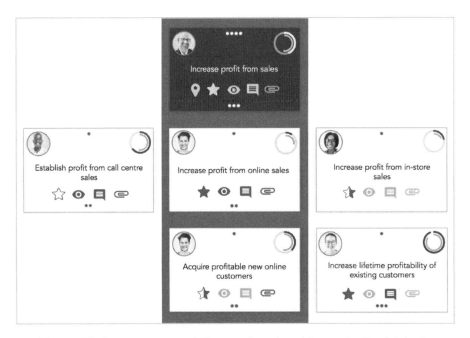

Figure 57 A strategy map fully populated and in use in Goal Atlas's strategy mapping software

Figure 58 also shows other attributes, such as whether comments have been made on this goal, and if it is being 'watched' by you, enabling you to track the progress of goals that are not your own. There is also an indication of the number of 'parent' and 'child' goals (i.e. purposes and methods) for each goal.

You are now clear on who owns which goals, how the goals connect together to aggregate up to strategic success and how you measure progress towards that strategic success. This is the hard part of strategic planning completed. The only task remaining is to divide the lifespan of your strategy into chunks of time and set targets that will indicate which goals are on track and which may be lagging behind and hence need adjustment to improve their performance. You will explore this in detail in Chapter 9 on strategy adoption.

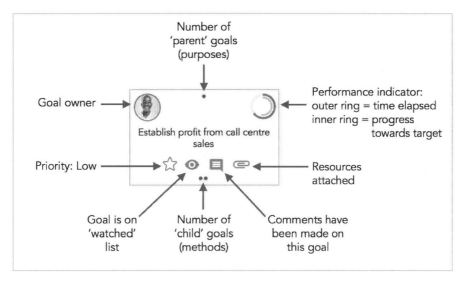

Figure 58 Goal attributes explained for Goal Atlas's strategy mapping software

4.11 Summary and key takeaways from Chapter 4

1. **Strategy mapping has a long and distinguished heritage,** having been devised as an engineering discipline over 70 years ago.

2. **Strategy mapping connects goals together using why-how logic in a strategy cascade.** By wording goals in a particular way (verb+noun pair) goals can, at the same time, be the **purpose** of the goal below and the **method** of the goal above in a strategy map. This enables a strategy map to systematically and logically connect the strategic aspirations of senior leadership to the tactical actions of front-line teams.

3. **Strategy maps ensure that the sum of all the small front-line changes add up to strategic success.** This gives everyone a clear sense of strategic purpose by seeing how their front-line achievements connect directly to overall strategic success.

4. **Strategy maps branch up as well as down** because goals can not only have multiple methods to achieve them but can also serve multiple purposes.

5. **Strategy maps facilitate innovation** in strategic thinking by enabling strategists to ask, 'How else can we achieve this purpose?' and 'Why else should we achieve this method?'.

6. **Strategy mapping provides joined-up strategic thinking** that underpins multiple strategy documents to maintain strategic coherence.

7. **Strategy maps facilitate strategy adoption** by clarifying goal ownership and the meaningful measurement of strategy.

8. **Strategy mapping supports strategic planning** through the delegation of goals and the measurement of progress toward timetable targets that lead to strategic success.

4.12 Let's talk about... strategy mapping

Use these questions to prompt deeper conversations on strategy mapping across your organisation:

1. *How well can you connect your strategic goals with the changes that will achieve them? Do front-line teams have clear line-of-sight between their actions and their strategic impact?*

2. *Is your strategy systematic and logical enough right now? How well would your key strategic goals connect using why-how*

logic? How else can you achieve each goal? Do your goals serve multiple purposes?

3. *How 'joined-up' are the strategies for different functional areas of your organisation? Do they lead to the organisation's overall strategic goals?*

4. *Do you have clear methods for delegating and measuring the progress of strategic goals?*

Notes on Chapter 4

(all web content accessed between April and September 2020)

[1] Thinkers 50, 2019. *Thinkers 50 Ranking and Awards.* https://thinkers50.com/awards/awards-2019/

[2] Lafley AG and Martin RL, 2013. *Playing to Win: How Strategy Really Works.* Harvard Business Review Press. p15.

[3] Lafley AG and Martin RL, 2013. *Playing to Win: How Strategy Really Works.* Harvard Business Review Press. p15.

[4] Bytheway CW, 2007. *FAST Creativity and Innovation: Rapidly improving processes, product development and solving complex problems.* J Ross Publishing, Fort Lauderdale, Florida. p111.

[5] General Electric, 1957. Value Analysis: Ten Years of Progress, 1947-1957. The Lawrence D. Miles Value Engineering Reference Center Collection, University of Wisconsin-Madison Libraries. https://minds.wisconsin.edu/bitstream/handle/1793/6374/418.pdf?sequenc e=1&isAllowed=y

[6] E.g. Association Française pour l'Analyse de la Valeur, https://www.afav.eu/, Society of American Value Engineers (SAVE), https://www.value-eng.org/default.aspx, Value Analysis Canada, http://www.valueanalysis.ca/, Hong Kong Institute for Value Management https://hkivm.org/introduction.htm/, Institute for Value Management,

Australia, http://www.ivma.org.au/, The Institute of Value Management, UK https://ivm.org.uk/.

[7] Wikipedia. *Microtome*. https://en.wikipedia.org/wiki/Microtome

[8] Dictionary.com. *Recursion*. https://www.dictionary.com/browse/recursion

[9] Carnes B, 2017. *How Recursion Works — explained with flowcharts and a video.* FreeCodeCamp. https://www.freecodecamp.org/news/how-recursion-works-explained-with-flowcharts-and-a-video-de61f40cb7f9/

[10] Kaplan RS and Norton DP, 2000. *Having Trouble with Your Strategy? Then Map It.* Harvard Business Review, 1 September 2000.

[11] Bytheway CW, 2007. *FAST Creativity and Innovation: Rapidly improving processes, product development and solving complex problems.* J Ross Publishing, Fort Lauderdale, Florida. p40.

[12] Cambridge English Dictionary. *Validation.* https://dictionary.cambridge.org/dictionary/english/validation

[13] Wikipedia. *Initial public offering.* https://en.wikipedia.org/wiki/Initial_public_offering

[14] Schmidt E, 2019. *Interview on The Tim Ferris Show*, 9th April 2019. https://tim.blog/2019/04/09/eric-schmidt/ (transcript – https://tim.blog/2019/04/11/the-tim-ferriss-show-transcripts-eric-schmidt-367/)

[15] Fisk P, 2016. *Is Michael Porter still relevant in today's fast and connected markets?* https://www.thegeniusworks.com/2016/10/michael-porter-still-relevant-todays-dynamic-digital-markets/

[16] Porter ME, 2016. *Strategy or Strategies?* https://www.youtube.com/watch?v=L9omLSOxYNQ

Chapter 5

Strategy governance

*Robust strategy governance
blows away the shifting sands of ill-defined
and ambiguous concepts of strategy to
provide a solid bedrock for the systematic
management of strategy.*

Strategy governance[1] is the means by which your organisation exercises authority to make a concentrated and coordinated effort to achieve strategic success. The mechanisms of strategy governance work in three ways:

1. They structure and delineate authority, and thereby define strategic roles;

2. They set goals (e.g. strategy) and the rules by which these goals can be pursued (e.g. policies, compliance);

3. They establish systems and processes for tracking and reporting progress of strategic change and enforcing the demands of strategy and commitments to strategy.

The benefits of strong strategy governance are:

1. Greater clarity on what strategy is, how it works and where responsibilities and accountabilities lie for its success;

2. Ensuring the right blend of executive ownership of the strategy and engagement and commitment to that strategy from across the organisation;

3. Laying the foundation for a strategic culture, in which the 'strategy matters', the 'strategy depends on all of us' and the 'strategy can be made to succeed'.

To illustrate the need for clarity around strategy, a recent analysis of the published strategies of 52 different UK universities revealed several different names being used for their main strategy documents without any underlying difference in what was in them (Fig. 59).[2]

With different labels meaning the same thing, and inconsistency in definitions, strategy has a shifting-sands-like quality to it. It means very different things to different people. Clearly, if you are ever going to manage strategy systematically inside your own organisation, you need to get rid of the shifting sands. You need to build a solid bedrock of shared understanding on what strategy is and how it works. This bedrock comes from strategy governance.

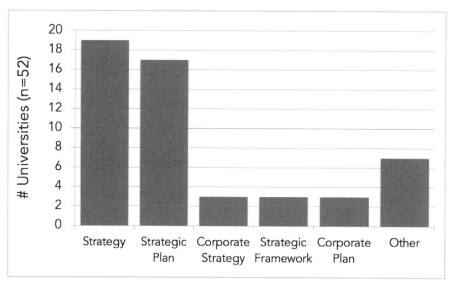

Figure 59 Naming of main strategy document for 52 UK universities

5.1 Making sense of governance

Since governance is the authority and control by which an organisation ensures effective, efficient, and safe operations, let's begin to make sense of the topic by exploring where authority comes from and what is done with it.

A typical for-profit, stock-issuing company is established by a registration process that identifies who owns what share of its stock.[3] Shareholders, by owning, controlling and receiving profits in proportion to their shareholding, are the ultimate authority within their company. A board of directors, comprising either these shareholders or their appointees, plus additional directors as specified in the constitution of the company, holds delegated decision-making power for the company, on behalf of the shareholders. The board manages this decision-making power in one of three ways.

Firstly, the board retains certain decision-making powers, such as approval of the annual report and accounts and the appointment and removal of all executive directors and the Company Secretary. Secondly, it delegates certain powers to committees of the board, such as an Audit Committee, Remuneration Committee or Nomination Committee. Thirdly, it will delegate certain powers to senior leadership, typically through the CEO. The most common instrument defining this is the job description of the CEO. This, however, only covers one side of the interaction between the board and the CEO and, as a result, can lead to problems. This is why organisations often have an explicit governance charter[4], defining how governance works and specifying how the roles and responsibilities of the board and senior leadership are intended to align.[5] You will come back to the concept of a governance charter in a moment, once your attention has narrowed from governance in general to strategy governance in particular.

5.2   Building a model of strategy governance

Governance covers several domains of responsibility, including financial reporting, risk management, legal / regulatory compliance and strategy. Whilst the above discussion was generic to all aspects of governance, you now need to focus attention on the main subject-matter of this chapter, strategy governance.

Strategy governance has two objectives. Firstly, it seeks to commit the organisation to a future destination. This is *executive governance of strategy* because it requires the board and senior leadership to work together to serve the best interests of the organisation. Secondly, it seeks to ensure that best endeavours are made to get there. This is *working governance of strategy* because it requires people and teams across the entire organisation to know about the strategy, to be committed to it and to be empowered to contribute to its success (Fig. 60).

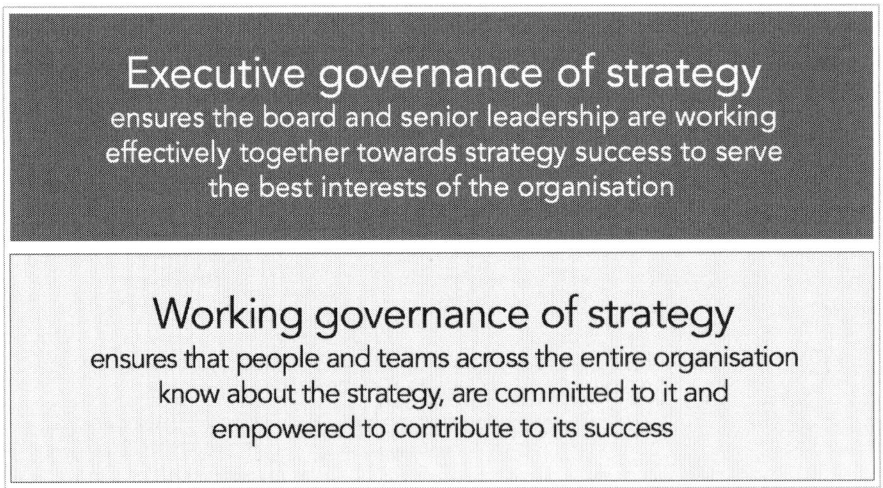

Executive governance of strategy
ensures the board and senior leadership are working effectively together towards strategy success to serve the best interests of the organisation

Working governance of strategy
ensures that people and teams across the entire organisation know about the strategy, are committed to it and empowered to contribute to its success

Figure 60 Executive and working governance of strategy

In the remainder of this chapter you will explore each of these, and their component parts, in greater depth.

5.3   Executive governance of strategy

Executive governance is the term for the working relationship between the board and senior leadership. Executives are people with the authority to make decisions and take action on behalf of entire organisations. Executive governance defines where this authority comes from and the terms under which it can be exercised.

Executive governance of *strategy*, therefore, is how the board and senior leadership work together to manage strategy to serve the best interests of the organisation.

This is how the UK Charities Commission describes[6] how the board and senior leadership work together on strategy:

1.   The board determines overall strategic direction;

2.   The Chief Executive prepares the strategy for consideration and approval by the board;

3.   The board considers and approves the strategy;

4.   The Chief Executive prepares corporate plans and annual budgets in line with the strategy;

5.   The board considers and approves the corporate plans and annual budgets.

Whilst this clarification of responsibilities and the back-and-forth interaction between the Charity Commission's board and senior leadership is useful, a lot more detail could be usefully added if these interactions were defined across the strategy lifecycle.

Figure 61 shows four goals critical to the executive governance of strategy within the strategy lifecycle, and Figure 62 shows how these key goals fit into the timeline of strategy.

Figure 61 Four goals critical to the executive governance of strategy

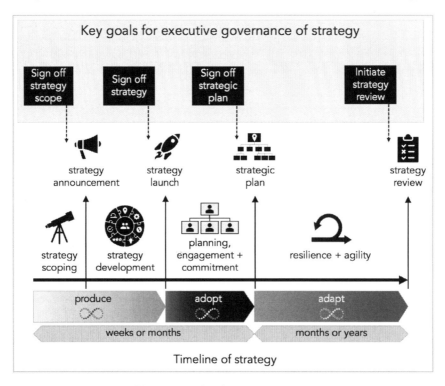

Figure 62 Timeline of key goals for the executive governance of strategy

1. **Sign off strategy scope.** Prior to the start of producing a new strategy, the board and senior leadership need to agree the scope of this new strategy. Is it a three-year strategy or a five-year strategy? Are vision, mission and values being revised at the same time or are they remaining as they were? What level of investment can the organisation commit to at this stage?

2. **Sign off strategy.** Once most of the hard work has been completed and the new strategy has taken shape, the board and senior leadership need to move to a point where the new strategy can be signed-off for official launch. Any changes to scope decided during strategy development should be explained and justified. The strategy production process, its robustness and its conclusions need to be reviewed: what were the key strategic choices considered, the key evidence gathered, the key strategic decisions made? What strategy validation was undertaken and what were its conclusions? What is the proposed wording of the new strategy and what are seen as the main risks associated with it?

3. **Sign off strategic plan.** Once the strategy adoption process is nearing completion and the strategic plan is clear, the board and senior leadership need to agree how the remainder of the strategy lifecycle is to be governed. What will senior leadership report routinely to the board regarding strategy? Under what circumstances will discussions take place between senior leadership and the board outside of this routine reporting (e.g. when strategic risk changes significantly; when a substantial change to the strategic plan is proposed; when an aspect of strategic success starts to look unattainable)?

4. **Initiate strategy review.** The board and senior leadership need to agree when strategy review is initiated. This is the first step in bringing the current strategy to an end prior to the production of a new strategy. For a strategy of fixed duration, the timing of strategy

review may be obvious: it needs to happen in time to learn lessons from the old strategy, so that the new strategy can be ready for launch soon after the old strategy's end-date. Under certain circumstances, strategy may need to be reviewed earlier than originally planned. All strategic objectives may have been achieved earlier than planned. Or the strategy may be struggling to achieve any of its objectives.

There are two other aspects of the executive governance of strategy that run across the entire strategy lifecycle, the management of strategic risk and the tracking / reporting of strategic progress.

5.3.1 Managing strategic risk

Since the board represents the interests of the entire organisation, it must ensure risks are managed effectively[7], including strategic risks. A critical time for assessing these risks and ensuring the board and senior leadership are satisfied they can be managed effectively is as soon as the strategy is written. These risks, however, will change, once the strategic plan is finalised and change again throughout strategy adaptation. A better approach to the governance of strategic risk, therefore, is to consider this an ongoing issue throughout the strategy lifecycle and put in place governance provisions to monitor and review it.

5.3.2 Tracking and reporting strategic progress

Whilst it is vital that the board and senior leadership agree what the organisation's strategy is, their responsibilities don't stop there. They need to ensure satisfactory progress is being made towards strategy success and, if it isn't, they need to take corrective action. This requires progress on strategy to be tracked, reported and reviewed as a matter of executive governance of strategy. This is far from a straightforward task, as you will discover in Chapter 6 on strategy measurement: it is hard to define a simple set of metrics to represent progress on the entirety of a strategy. The executive governance of this is easier. What are the key roles and responsibilities for tracking and reporting strategic progress and what specific governance goals, if any, need to be put in place across the strategy lifecycle?

Figure 63 shows how these further goals for the executive governance of strategy extend across the timeline of strategy.

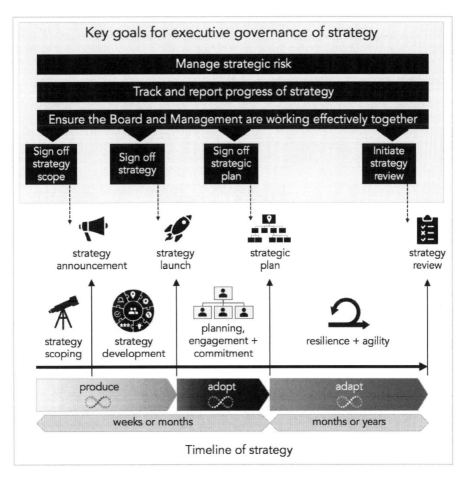

Figure 63 Key goals for executive governance of strategy across the strategy timeline

5.4   Key executive governance decisions

There are two key areas of decision-making that need to be made within executive governance – both of which were introduced briefly in Chapter 1: strategy as identity and strategy as investment.

5.4.1 Strategy as identity

You learned in Chapters 1 and 3 about the various identity marks organisations use to signal what type of organisation they are, what they stand for and what they aspire to. You also saw in Chapter 3 how vision, mission, values and strategy come together on the House of Strategy Model (Fig. 64).

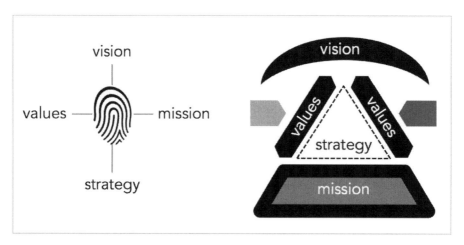

Figure 64 Vision, mission, values and strategy as identity marks and in the House of Strategy Model

The decision that needs to be made about strategy-as-identity, as part of the executive governance of strategy, is how strategy is intended to fit with other identity marks. The three possible decisions here are:

1. Strategy *needs to fit* with your current vision, mission and values;

2. Vision, mission and values *may be re-written* if they turn out to be incompatible with the new strategy you commit to;

3. Vision, mission and values *must be re-written* as part of strategy development because they are no longer considered to be fit-for-purpose.

The House of Strategy model, covered in detail in Chapter 3, can help deliver any of these decisions, using the templates described to help guide your thinking, as follows:

1. If strategy needs to fit with your current vision, mission and values, the House of Strategy model can be used to evaluate the current degree of fit and indicate how strategy may need to be refined to produce a better fit.

2. If vision, mission and values may be re-written if they turn out to be incompatible with the new strategy, the compatibility of the four identity marks can be assessed using the House of Strategy.

3. If vision, mission and values must be re-written as part of strategy development then House of Strategy can be used as part of the creative process to explore ideas for all four identity marks and evaluate how well they fit together.

5.4.2 Strategy as investment

One key responsibility of the board is to maximise shareholder value.[8] How, then, does the board achieve this through the investment of the resources at its disposal?

Figure 65 shows an investment pyramid and an innovation pyramid. The investment pyramid shows how good investment decisions set out to balance the different risk and return profiles of different types of investments. The pyramid shape reflects typical investment advice to keep the majority of your investment assets in low risk, low potential return investments, and a minority in high risk, high potential return investments.

The innovation pyramid shows a rule of thumb for innovation management that Sergey Brin, cofounder of Google devised. Here is Brin's initial explanation, as recalled by Eric Schmidt, former CEO and Chairman of Google, in an interview on The Tim Ferris Show. "70% [of resources go] on your core business, 20% on adjacent or nearby things, and 10% on wild bets…you need the 70% because you need the revenue, the revenue growth. You need the 20% because you need to extend your franchise, and you need the 10%, which is crucially important for the things that you will want to do five or 10 years from now."[9]

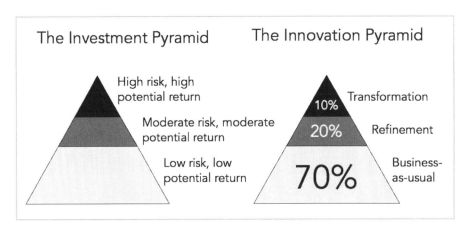

Figure 65 The investment pyramid and innovation pyramid

So, where does strategy sit in relation to these pyramids? Strategy doesn't have a great deal of value for managing business-as-usual. There are policies, processes, standard operating procedures and accepted ways of working for this. Effective business-as-usual needs competent management and efficient administration more than it needs strategy. Strategy is about the future. Strategy is about change. Strategy has much more to say about transformation. Presented like this, you get a hard-to-miss similarity between these two pyramids, which provides a fascinating theory of what strategy is for:

> *Strategic initiatives are what you spend a minority of your organisation's time and resources on, in order to provide the high-risk, high-return element of how your organisation invests for its long-term future.*

A fundamental responsibility of the board, therefore, is to decide the nature and extent of the transformation sought by strategy and the proportion of the organisation's resources that will be invested in strategic change. A Harvard Business Review article, by innovation consultants Bansi Nagji and Geoff Tuff, provides useful context to these decisions.[10] Firstly, they suggest that, whilst 70, 20, 10 are typical ratios for the innovation pyramid in 'high performing firms', these ratios can vary considerably for other types of firms (Fig. 66).

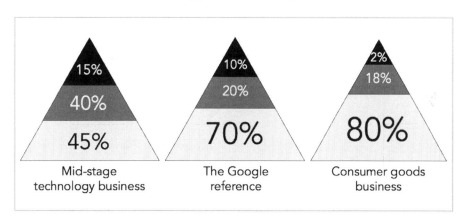

Figure 66 Different ratios for the innovation pyramid

Consumer goods businesses, for example, tend to focus almost entirely on small incremental innovations and hence only invest a tiny 2% on what Brin called wild bets (and even then, Google might not think of them as crazy-wild!). Mid-stage technology businesses are in much more continuous and rapid innovation and hence invest 15% on the wild bets, leaving only 45% to maintain business-as-usual.

Secondly, Nagji and Tuff's article inadvertently raises another key issue to be resolved. What is it that you are allocating, when you use 70, 20, 10 (or similar) ratios? They make it clear that they are talking about apportioning 'innovation investment'. So, of the resource allocated to innovation, 10% of it goes to transformational initiatives. This isn't what was originally meant by Google. In one of the first articles to discuss their 70, 20, 10 rule, Eric Schmidt says "everyone should spend 70% of their time on their core job, 20% as part of another team, and 10% on something blue sky".[11] So, Google is apportioning 10% of total resources, not just innovation-specific resources, to 'blue sky' initiatives. It's not important that you find a right answer here. What is essential, however, is that your board has a view on how much of which resources your organisation invests in strategy.

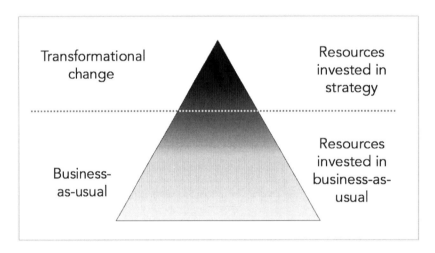

Figure 67 The Boundary Model of Strategy

Given the fact that maintaining and refining business-as-usual will take up the majority of available resources (budget and staff time), this leaves a minority of resources to be allocated to long-term, typically cross-functional activities aimed at business transformation. It is these transformational activities that strategy defines. So, deciding how much to invest in business transformation, as opposed to the maintenance of business-as-usual is to decide how much you are investing in strategy. This is the essence of the Boundary Model of Strategy (Fig. 67).

Whilst ultimately the proportion of resources invested in strategy will be a financial decision based on Return on Investment (ROI) projections, it will greatly assist in the development of strategy if this is managed more as a process of progressive refinement. By providing the strategy development team with a rough estimate of the likely resource available to be invested in strategy (a 'ball-park' figure), they can then use that figure to sense-check the various ideas they have about potential strategies (strategy 'candidates'). "Does this idea about strategy give us the right order of magnitude of transformation, given the resources we are likely to have, to bring this transformation about?" As the strategy firms up, so the ROI calculation can also firm up, using the performance indicator of overall success of the strategy (the Strategy Success Performance Indicator) to estimate the financial value returned from the investment.

The other key boardroom decision on 'strategy as investment' is who are the intended beneficiaries of strategy: you have seen that one of the board's responsibilities is to maximise shareholder value, but is it their *primary* responsibility? The Business Roundtable, an association of chief executive officers of America's leading companies, had, since 1997, argued forcefully that this was indeed the case: they said that corporations exist *principally* to serve their shareholders. Then, in 2019, they changed their mind. In a widely reported announcement they said:

"While each of our individual companies serves its own corporate purpose, we share a fundamental commitment to *all of our stakeholders.*[12] We commit to:

- Delivering value to our customers,

- Investing in our employees,

- Dealing fairly and ethically with our suppliers,

- Supporting the communities in which we work,

- Generating long-term value for shareholders."[13]

This commitment was signed by 181 CEOs of big US corporations, including Amazon, American Airlines, American Express, Apple, AT&T ... and that's just the ones beginning with 'A'.

So, clarifying the purpose of your organisation is part of the foundation upon which any strategy is built. Using the templates described in Chapter 3 for the Value Model of Strategy helps you define what value you deliver and for whom; what good do you seek to do in the world and what does it mean to work well to achieve that good? Value will be defined differently for different stakeholders, whether they are shareholders, customers, employees, suppliers, communities or, indeed, humankind or planet Earth.

5.5   The strategy governance charter

As discussed earlier in this chapter, organisations often adopt an explicit governance charter, defining how governance works and specifying how the roles and responsibilities of the board and senior leadership align.

Here are the key principles your strategy governance charter should seek to cover:

1. How does strategy review / the start of a new strategy happen? Are there any guidelines? Any constraints?

2. Strategy production – who is leading the production of the strategy? The board or senior leadership? It is typically senior leadership, but not always.

3. For each sign-off event (strategy scope sign-off, strategy sign-off and strategic plan sign-off), who does what:

a. How do you ensure there is initial alignment of strategic thinking?

b. What is actually going to be signed off? A single document, on its own? A single document for sign-off but with additional supporting documents?

4. How, in general terms, do you intend to manage strategic risk? How will the board be involved in this process?

5. How, in general terms, do you intend to monitor progress of the strategy? How will the board be involved in this process?

A strategy governance charter should always be simple and concise. If you find your charter reaches more than a handful of pages, you may need to review the working relationship between your board and senior leadership.

A template for producing a strategy governance charter is given in the practicalities section at the end of this chapter (Section 5.10).

5.6   Working governance of strategy

Working governance of strategy sets out to make sure that strategy is adopted effectively across the organisation, that everyone makes their best endeavours to have strategic impact and that these efforts, collectively lead to strategic success.

There are two ways of thinking about how strategy rolls out across organisations. Firstly, it can be thought of as rules and formalities that need to be imposed, complied with and enforced. This is the 'enforcement principle of governance' (Fig. 68). Secondly, it can be thought of as a set of goals, norms and conventions that individuals in the organisation co-create, engage with and commit to. This is the 'engagement principle of governance' (Fig. 69).

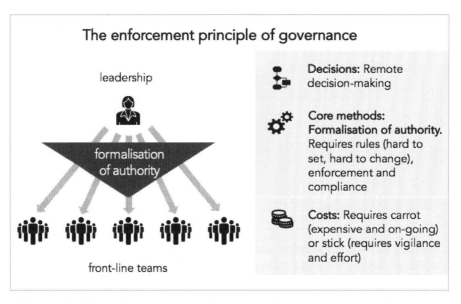

Figure 68 The enforcement principle of working governance of strategy

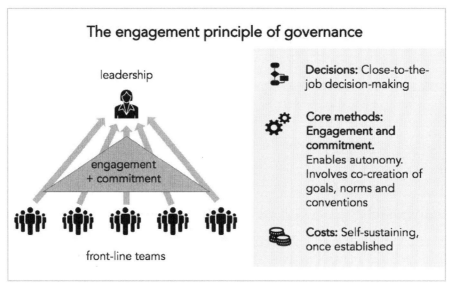

Figure 69 The engagement principle of working governance of strategy

There are good reasons why the engagement principle of governance should work better than the enforcement principle:

1. *Proximity of governance decisions.* The rules upon which an enforcement model is based are often made some distance away from where they apply. So, the rules you are required to comply with are likely to have been written by your manager, your manager's manager or possibly someone in corporate headquarters on a different continent. When, on the other hand, goals, norms and conventions are co-created by managers and their line reports, governance decisions are made closer to the work they are designed to govern.

2. *Easier to do well.* Governance requires rules to be complied with. Good rules, that apply to all foreseeable circumstances, are hard to set. In addition, once set, there is an often-unspoken assumption that if a rule is a rule, it must be right. The rules for enforcement-based governance are, therefore, hard to set and hard to change. Governance by engagement, on the other hand, accepts that whatever the best processes, frameworks and tools you have to hand are what you need to work with but, if improvements are found, they will be adopted as soon as possible. This enables much more front-line autonomy.

3. *Costs.* Enforcement of rules-based governance has costs attached. If the rules-compliance is incentivised, the payment of those incentives may have costs attached and if rule-breaking is punished, this will have the attendant cost of the vigilance and effort required to monitor and detect rule-breaking.

Among the well-documented advantages of the engagement principle of governance is the legendary case study of Toyota, a company that receives over 500,000 suggestions for improvement or innovation from their front-line employees per year[14] and implements an average of nine improvements per employee per year.[15] In his analysis of how Toyota 'pulls' improvement from the front line, Brad Power, a consultant and regular writer for Harvard Business Review, highlights two key ingredients for success:

1. *Context* – everyone has responsibility for continuous improvement and is actively encouraged to contribute. Toyota invests significantly in staff development. Supervisors, for example, ensure that production line teams have a deep understanding of their work and how it is designed to achieve its intended outcomes. Only with this understanding can useful suggestions for improvement emerge. Toyota also makes sure managers are receptive to suggested improvements from the front line – they don't see them as criticising or challenging managerial authority and they don't take the sceptical view that front-line suggestions are only ever intended to make workers' lives easier.

2. *Process* – suggestions follow a clear path through Toyota's organisation. Firstly, they are reviewed in peer-groups of front-line workers. The suggestions thought worthwhile by this group are then presented to managers and, if necessary, will work their way up through management to the required level needed to authorise the change. Senior managers strive to engage, face to face, with front-line teams during these processes. It is also the team, as opposed to any individual within a team, that is recognised and rewarded for their suggestions.

In a follow-up article, Power highlights how front-line improvement schemes often fail to maintain momentum and he lays a lot of the blame at the door of management.[16] Educated and trained to be the originators of innovative ideas, managers are not always good facilitators of other people's ideas. In addition, implementing change is often more time-consuming for managers than for the front-line teams that suggested them. Unless managers take ownership of change facilitation, make time for it and are recognised for achieving it, front-line improvement schemes may be unsustainable.

It is clear from the experience of Toyota that the working governance of strategy plays a key role in engendering the right culture for engagement and commitment and ensuring ongoing management support for that culture. You will learn more about the relationship between strategy adoption and organisational culture in Chapter 10.

Reaping the benefits of the engagement principle of governance doesn't mean you should, or can, avoid the enforcement principle of governance altogether. Are health and safety provisions optional? Are legal obligations such as financial reporting or data security engaged with and committed to as a matter of individual choice by each employee? Of course not. Rules are required to establish appropriate levels of responsibility, accountability, reporting and financial control, and to ensure compliance with legal and regulatory requirements. The enforcement principle of governance can also allow the standardisation and formalisation of routine procedures so that they don't need to be reinvented every time they are used.

Enforcement and engagement, therefore, both have a role to play in strategy governance, but engagement should be the default way of governing.

> Good strategy governance needs to combine elements of enforcement and engagement but should, wherever possible, default to engagement.

5.7   The Hourglass Model of Strategy Governance

The Hourglass Model of Strategy Governance combines all the governance principles you have discovered so far (Fig. 70). To make sense of this model and translate it into practicalities for strategy success, you need to understand the elements of the model and how they interact.

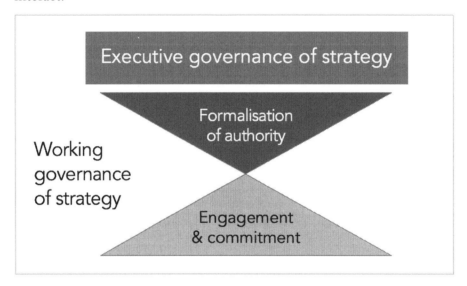

Figure 70 The Hourglass Model of Strategy Governance

The first and most obvious feature of the model is that executive governance and working governance of strategy are clearly separated. This, as you have already discovered in this chapter, is because executive governance of strategy ensures the board and senior leadership are working effectively together, whereas working governance of strategy ensures that strategy is effectively adopted across the organisation.

Secondly, working governance contains two components:

1.   Formalisation of authority;

2.   Engagement and commitment.

Formalisation of authority is how management enforces strategy upon the organisation, whereas engagement and commitment are how members of the organisation choose to adopt the strategy, of their own volition. The aim of the working governance of strategy is to make sure these enforcement and engagement components operate in harmony to achieve strategy success.

Now let's explore how formalisation of authority and engagement and commitment come about.

5.8   Working governance: formalisation of authority

There are typically five ways of formalising authority to enforce strategy (Fig. 71):

1.   organisation design;

2.   the use of RACIs;

3.   the deployment of policies and standards;

4.   the distribution of budget;

5.   the measurement of performance metrics against set targets.

5.8.1 Organisation design

The most obvious mechanism for formalising authority is by organisation design. Organisation design provides a reporting structure where everyone in the organisation has a line manager, and line managers report upwards: from front-line teams to their team leader; from the team leader to middle managers; from middle managers to senior managers and from senior managers to the CEO. Since all line managers have the delegated authority to define job descriptions, set performance targets and decide recognition, reward and promotion for their direct reports, this provides a powerful mechanism for rolling out strategic change initiatives across the organisation.

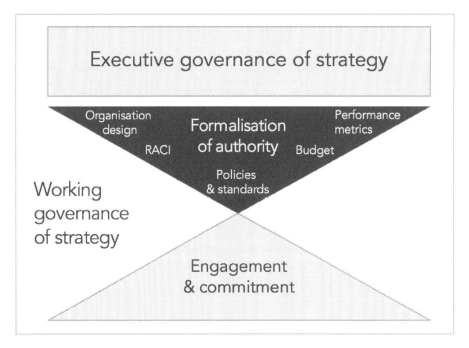

Figure 71 The formalisation of authority in pursuit of strategy

5.8.2 RACI

A RACI is another way to define working relationships. The acronym stands for:

1. *Responsible*: The person responsible for getting the work done or decision made.

2. *Accountable*: The person accountable for the work being done on time, with the right outcome and of the required quality. The person responsible typically reports to the person accountable.

3. *Consulted*: The people, often subject matter experts, who inform and advise on the work.

4. *Informed*: The people who need to know what is being done and what progress is being made but have no influence on the work's progress.

Different people often have different roles at different stages of the project, thereby producing a RACI matrix or table.[17] Figure 72 shows a generic, high-level RACI for strategy development.

	Chair	CEO	Director of Strategy
Produce strategy	Consulted	Accountable	Responsible
Sign-off strategy	Accountable	Responsible	Informed

Figure 72 Simple RACI matrix for strategy development

5.8.3 Policies and standards

Policies and standards are the organisation's way of saying 'this is how we do things around here'. A policy is a "a plan of what to do in particular situations that has been agreed to officially".[18] A standard is "a level of quality or achievement, especially a level that is thought to be acceptable".[19] Introducing new policies and standards can be a powerful way to drive strategic change. Failing to review and revise, or possibly even remove, old policies and standards is also an effective way to stop strategic change in its tracks.

5.8.4 Budget

The next way authority is formalised across an organisation is budget. Authorising or withholding budget can enforce strategic priorities. Since budgets are, in the first instance, approved by senior leadership, this is a common method of empowering those middle managers eager to make changes, or bringing reluctant middle managers into line on strategy.

5.8.5 Performance metrics

Following the adage that "what gets measured gets done"[20], the setting of performance metrics is another way to formalise authority across the organisation. This is a topic you will learn a lot more about in Chapter 6 on strategy measurement.

5.9   Working governance: engagement and commitment

As you will discover in subsequent chapters, strategy success comes from people, across the organisation, being actively engaged with, and willingly committed to, the strategy and their contribution to that strategy. Figure 73 shows how engagement and commitment are central to the strategy adoption stage of the lifecycle (find out more on strategy adoption in Chapter 9).

Figure 73 Engagement and commitment within strategy adoption

You will know you are getting engagement with the strategy when all the key people needed for you to achieve strategic success:

1. feel a sense of ownership of their own strategic goals;

2. understand the interdependencies between strategic goals connected to their own goals;

3. have clarity-of-purpose by seeing how their goals connect to organisation-wide strategic goals;

4. express confidence that they can make meaningful progress on their own goals.

These same people need to commit to their own goal-targets, their own goal timescales and their own goal performance metrics.

The role of strategy governance here is to ensure that authority is managed and delegated across the organisation in ways that promote strategy adoption. So, you could add a governance method to the strategy map in Figure 73 (Fig. 74).

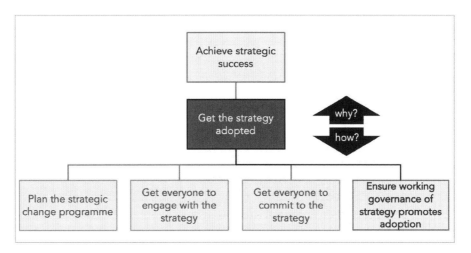

Figure 74 How working governance promotes strategy adoption

The worst-case scenario across the strategy lifecycle is when someone, whose contribution to strategy success is important, feels aggrieved:

1. Their opinions on strategy weren't sought;

2. When they tried to speak up, they weren't listened to;

3. The strategy ended up being weaker than it could have been if their input had been taken into account;

4. Even now, after the strategy has been finalised, their freedom to help the strategy succeed is curtailed by having to seek approval for every decision they should have been permitted to make on their own.

If the working governance of strategy is to avoid this, it needs three key elements of engagement and commitment (Fig. 75):

Figure 75 Working governance of strategy - engagement and commitment

1. **Consultation:** Strategy is consulted on widely enough to gather insights from across the organisation. If done well, this will also ensure everyone feels adequately consulted on strategy. Strategy consultation needs to be both meaningful (about the right things) and impactful (the insights gained need to drive change).

2. **Influence:** Everyone needs to feel that they have influence appropriate to their role, experience and their depth of understanding of the issues included in the strategy.

3. **Autonomy:** Strategy adoption gives people who are not senior leaders the authority to make their own individual contribution to strategic success. This requires appropriate levels of autonomy to take ownership of a goal, to try new methods of achieving this goal (particularly necessary for strategic goals) and to continually test and learn until their goal is achieved.

You now have a complete picture of the goals of both the executive governance of strategy and the working governance of strategy (Fig. 76).

Figure 76 Strategy governance goals

These can now be overlaid on the strategy timeline (Fig. 77).

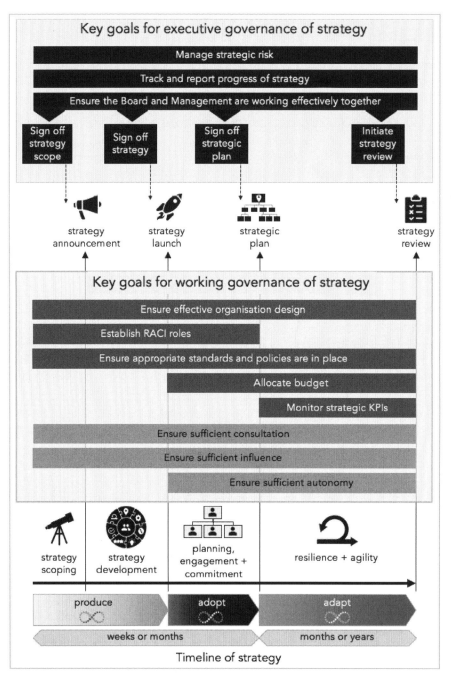

Figure 77 Strategy governance goals overlaid on the strategy timeline

5.10 The practicalities of strategy governance

Having worked through strategy governance from end to end, it is time to turn it into a practical process.

Task #1: Write your strategy governance charter

Figure 78 shows a template for writing a strategy governance charter, with space to define the key roles and responsibilities (senior leadership on the left and board on the right) across the strategy lifecycle under the following six headings:

1. **Strategy scoping:**

    a. Who is responsible for ensuring the views of the board and senior leadership are aligned on the new strategy before strategy production begins?

    b. Who will actually undertake the strategy scoping process? What are they expected to produce? What will they present for sign-off? Will this presentation need any supporting documentation?

    c. Who will sign-off strategy scoping?

2. **Strategy**

    a. Who is responsible for developing the strategy? What are they expected to produce? What will they present for sign-off? Will this presentation need any supporting documentation?

    b. How will the views of the board and senior leadership continue to be aligned throughout strategy development?

    c. Who will sign-off the strategy?

3. **Strategic plan**

    a. Who will lead strategy adoption and the development of the strategic plan?

b. What will be presented to the board and what is the board's role in reviewing this work?

4. **Strategy review**

a. What are the respective roles of the board and senior leadership in triggering a strategic review and initiating the production of a new strategy?

b. Are there any rules, processes or constraints on them doing so?

5. **Strategic risk management**

a. Who will be responsible for identifying, assessing and managing risks arising from strategy?

b. How will the board be informed of these risks and updated when they change?

c. How will the board ensure its effectiveness in strategic risk management?

6. **Strategy tracking and reporting**

a. Who will be responsible for deciding what is tracked and reported to the board to show strategic progress?

b. Who will be responsible for reporting strategic progress to the board?

c. How will the board ensure its effectiveness in tracking progress towards strategy success?

Figure 79 gives an example charter for our case study company Artigence. Note that this charter is limited to broad principles – no actions with names and dates! This is because it is always best to get principles agreed first before getting bogged down in the detail. The detail, however, is necessary and comes next.

Strategy: | Prepared by:
Date:

Strategy Governance Charter
Roles & responsibilities of senior leadership & board

Strategy scoping

Strategy

Strategic plan

Strategy review

Strategic risk management

Strategy tracking & reporting

Figure 78 Executive strategy governance charter

 **artigence** strategy

Prepared by: Katerina & Daniel
Date: 01 September

 # Strategy Governance Charter
Roles & responsibilities of senior leadership & board

Strategy scoping

Management leads strategy scoping, including aligning initial thinking, drafting strategy scope and then revising it following discussion.

The Board signs-off the strategy scope.

Strategy

Management leads a strategy away day with the Board, drafts the strategy and justifies the strategy development process.

 The Board provides input into strategy development and signs-off the strategy.

Strategic plan

Management leads strategy adoption drafts the strategic plan and justifies the strategy adoption process.

The Board signs-off the strategic plan.

Strategy review

Management may propose a strategy review to the Board at anytime (subject to any specific constraints agreed between the Board and Mgt).

The Board may propose a strategy review to Management at anytime (subject to any specific constraints agreed between the Board and Mgt).

Strategic risk management

Management leads strategy risk management and reviews it regularly with the Board

The Board's governance of strategic risk will be part of routine business and recorded in Board minutes.

Strategy tracking & reporting

Management leads tracking and reporting of progress of the strategy, including a handful of strategic KPIs and their timetabled progression.

The Board's governance of strategy tracking and reporting will be part of routine business and recorded in Board minutes.

Figure 79 Strategy Governance Charter for Artigence

Task #2: Build your strategy timeline

The aim of this task is to make sure the key governance goals work for you. Are there any other goals that are key for your strategy timeline? Examples might include appointing a new CEO or Board Chair, finalising a merger or completing a VC funding round. Then add your dates to the timeline. Figure 80 shows a model to guide your thinking and Figure 81 gives a completed version for Artigence.

Task #3: Define the key goals for the executive governance of strategy

Now is the time for you to identify the goals you need to commit to for the executive governance of strategy, with actions, names and dates. Figure 82 is a template for defining the specific goals, followed by a completed version for our case study, Artigence (Fig. 83).

Task #4: Review working governance of strategy

Ensuring that people and teams across the entire organisation know about strategy, are committed to it and empowered to contribute to its success is a big task and will be returned to on several occasions in the remainder of this book. In this section, you need to focus on governance only. The template in Figure 84 provides space to review all the different ways of achieving working governance of strategy. The key question is whether they are all conducive to strategic success.

Figure 85 shows this template filled in for Artigence, just after they have completed their strategy but before they start strategy adoption. At this stage, it is an internal review for circulation at a closed management meeting. The review will be repeated as part of senior leadership's quarterly review of strategy and actions will be delegated from it.

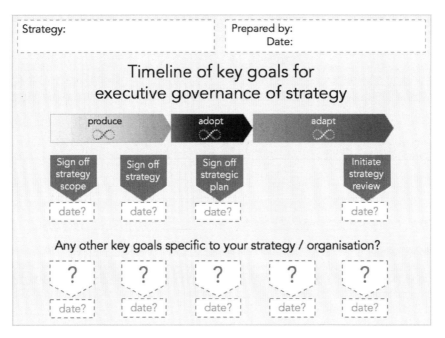

Figure 80 Make the strategy timeline your own

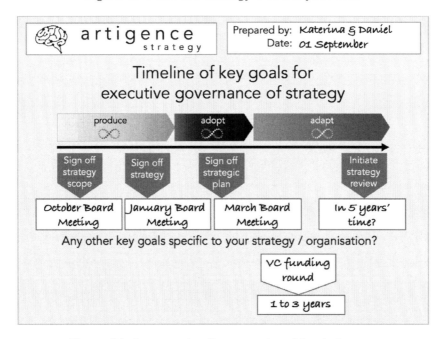

Figure 81 Strategy timeline completed for Artigence

Strategy:	Prepared by: Date:

Key goals for executive governance of strategy

	Owner	Date
⚠ Manage strategic risk		
〜 Track and report progress of strategy		
#1 Sign off strategy scope		
#2 Sign off strategy		
#3 Sign off strategic plan		
#4 Initiate strategy review		
#5 Goal description		

Figure 82 Key goals template for executive governance of strategy

artigence
strategy

Prepared by: Katerina & Daniel
Date: 01 September

Key goals for executive governance of strategy

	Owner	Date
⚠ **Manage strategic risk**	Exec	Ongoing
- Submit strategic risk audit for Board approval at the January Board meeting.	Kat	18 Dec
- Track and report strategic risks as appropriate to mitigate risks.	Mgt	Ongoing
📈 **Track and report progress of strategy**	Exec	Ongoing
- Submit initial strategic KPI proposals for Board approval (Jan)	Dan	18 Dec
- Submit final strategic KPI proposals for Board approval (March)	Dan	25 Feb
- Track and report progress on strategy at Board meetings.	Dan	10 Oct
#1 Sign off strategy scope	Board	24 Oct
- Arrange strategy away day (September) led by Management for Board & Management to discuss initial ideas for strategy scope.	Kat	07 Sept
- Finalise strategy scope document.	Mgt	05 Oct
- Submit scope document for Board approval at the Oct. Board Mtg.	Kat	10 Oct
#2 Sign off strategy	Board	18 Jan
- Arrange 2nd strategy away day (Dec) to review Management's strategy development docs, including draft strategy.	Kat	15 Sept
- Submit final strategy & launch plan for Board approval at the January meeting.	Mgt	18 Dec
#3 Sign off strategic plan	Board	20 Mar
- Circulate working governance of strategy proposals prior to 2nd strategy away day (December).	Dan	30 Nov
- Submit final strategic plan for Board approval at March Board meeting.	Dan	25 Feb
#4 Initiate strategy review	Board	5 yrs
- Approve 5-year strategy timespan.	Board	24 Oct
- Review annually.	Mgt	Oct
*See also Funding Round, below.		
#5 Proposed funding round	Exec	1-3 yrs
- Approve proposal that no strategy review will be initiated by either the Board or by Management before our funding round is completed and signed-off (expected to be complete within 3 years' time).	Mgt	Oct

Figure 83 Completed key goals for executive governance of strategy

Strategy:	Prepared by: Date:

Working Governance of Strategy Review

Formalisation of authority	Are all aspects of your organisation's formalisation of authority conducive to strategic success?
Organisation design	
RACI	
Policies & standards	
Budget	
Performance metrics	
Consultation	
Influence	
Autonomy	
Engagement & commitment	Are you supporting engagement and commitment in ways that are conducive to strategic success?

Figure 84 Template to review the working governance of strategy

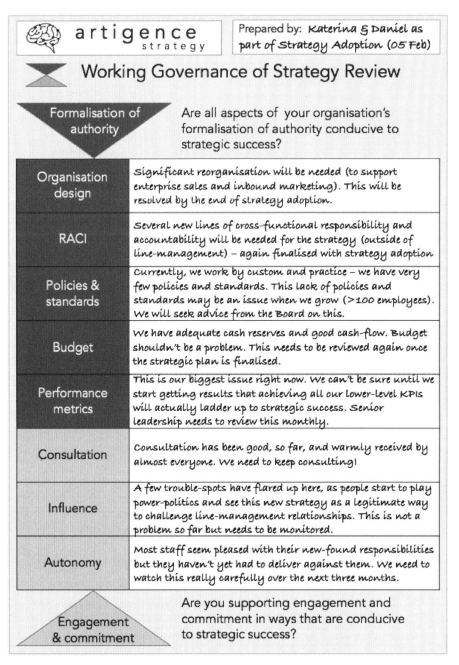

Figure 85 Completed template for working governance of strategy

5.11 Summary and key takeaways from Chapter 5

1. Core principles of governance:

   a. All organisations have an ultimate source of authority, defined by the documents establishing that organisation. For most businesses, this ultimate source of authority is the Board of Directors;

   b. This authority needs to be delegated to executives to provide them with the power to direct and manage the organisation;

   c. Executive power then needs to be held to account by control mechanisms retained by the ultimate source of authority;

   d. How authority is exerted and delegated in pursuit of strategy success can usefully be defined in a Strategy Governance Charter.

2. **Governance covers several domains of responsibility.** One of these is *strategy governance*, others include financial reporting and legal / regulatory compliance.

3. **Strategy governance** works in two ways: executive governance of strategy and working governance of strategy.

4. **Executive governance of strategy** ensures the board and senior leadership are working effectively together towards strategy success to serve the best interests of the organisation.

5. The executive governance of strategy can be defined by specifying the respective **roles and responsibilities** of the board and senior leadership at key strategy governance events across the strategy lifecycle, for example:

   a. Strategy scope sign-off;

   b. Strategy sign-off;

c. Strategic plan sign-off;

d. Strategy review initiation.

6. Executive governance of strategy must also ensure **the management of strategic risk** and the **tracking and reporting of strategic progress** across the strategy lifecycle.

7. There are two key areas of decision-making that need to be made within executive governance: **strategy as identity** and **strategy as investment.**

8. A **strategy governance charter** can be used to define how governance works and how the roles and responsibilities of the board and senior leadership align.

9. **Working governance of strategy** ensures that people and teams across the entire organisation know about the strategy, are committed to it and empowered to contribute to its success.

10. The working governance of strategy can operate according to two distinct principles. The **enforcement principle** imposes rules and formalities that need to be complied with and enforced. The **engagement principle** has goals, norms and conventions that individuals in the organisation co-create, engage with and commit to.

11. Governance-by-enforcement entails formalisation of authority through **organisation design**, the use of **RACIs**, the deployment of **policies and standards**, the distribution of **budget** and the measurement of **performance metrics** against set targets.

12. Governance-by-engagement is enabled by high levels of **consultation, influence and autonomy** being afforded to individuals and teams across the organisation.

13. Strategy governance should default to governance-by-engagement and only govern by enforcement when necessary.

14. Robust strategy governance blows away the shifting sands of ill-defined and ambiguous concepts of strategy to provide a solid bedrock for the systematic management of strategy.

5.12 Let's talk about… strategy governance

Use these questions to prompt deeper conversations on strategy governance across your organisation:

1. *To what extent is your senior leadership team in agreement about the relative benefits of governance-by-enforcement and governance-by-engagement?*

2. *How much of your strategy governance is by enforcement and how much by engagement?*

3. *How much time is set aside across the strategy lifecycle for strategy governance? Is that time well enough planned and managed to give strategy the best chance of success?*

4. *Is everyone across your organisation aware of their role in strategy governance?*

Notes on Chapter 5

(all web content accessed between April and September 2020)

---

[1] These definitions and concepts of governance are derived from Brown L, (Editor) 1993. *The Shorter Oxford English Dictionary*. Clarendon Press, Oxford. p1123 and Bevir M, 2012. *Governance: A very short introduction*. Oxford University Press, Oxford.

[2] Baxter M, 2019. *University Strategy 2020: Analysis and benchmarking of the strategies of UK universities.* Goal Atlas Ltd, London.

[3] This and the subsequent discussion of corporate governance is drawn from Renton T, 2001. *Standards for the Board (3rd edition).* Part of the Institute of Directors, Good Practice for Directors. Kogan Page London.

[4] A charter is a document granting authority or rights and defining the responsibilities of both the issuing authority and the recipient arising as a result of the charter. Summarised from Wikipedia. *Charter.* https://en.wikipedia.org/wiki/Charter

[5] A Governance Charter is a formal method of trying to resolve the 'principal – agent problem' in which the principal (the board) and their agent (Management) have different interests that may, at times conflict. See more at Wikipedia. Principal-Agent Problem. https://en.wikipedia.org/wiki/Principal%E2%80%93agent_problem

[6] Charity Commission for England and Wales 2018. *Governance Framework.* https://www.gov.uk/government/publications/charity-commission-governance-framework/governance-framework and Appendix 3 https://www.gov.uk/government/publications/charity-commission-governance-framework/appendix-3-levels-of-delegated-authority

[7] Board responsibilities for risk became prominent for UK businesses with the publication of the Turnbull Report in 1999. See ICAEW. Internal Control: Guidance for directors on the Combined Code. https://www.icaew.com/technical/corporate-governance/codes-and-reports/turnbull-report

[8] E.g. Business Roundtable, 2019. *Business Roundtable Redefines the Purpose of a Corporation to Promote 'An Economy That Serves All Americans'* https://www.businessroundtable.org/business-roundtable-redefines-the-purpose-of-a-corporation-to-promote-an-economy-that-serves-all-americans or Lipton M, Cain KL and Iannone KC, 2019. Stakeholder Governance and the Fiduciary Duties of Directors. Harvard Law School Forum on Corporate Governance. 12 August 2019. https://corpgov.law.harvard.edu/2019/08/24/stakeholder-governance-and-the-fiduciary-duties-of-directors/

[9] Schmidt E, 2019. *Interview on The Tim Ferris Show.* 9th April 2019. https://tim.blog/2019/04/09/eric-schmidt/ (transcript - https://tim.blog/2019/04/11/the-tim-ferriss-show-transcripts-eric-schmidt-367/)

[10] Nagji B and Tuff G, 2012. *Managing your innovation portfolio.* Harvard Business Review, May 2012.

[11] Hardy Q, 2011. *Google's Innovation –And Everyone's?* Forbes. https://www.forbes.com/sites/quentinhardy/2011/07/16/googles-innovation-and-everyones/#5d7ee9003066

[12] Emphasis added.

[13] Business Roundtable. 2019. *Statement on the Purpose of a Corporation.* https://opportunity.businessroundtable.org/ourcommitment/

[14] Hamel G and Breen B, 2007. *The Future of Management.* Harvard Business School Press, Boston. p23.

[15] Power B, 2011. *How Toyota pulls improvement from the front line.* Harvard Business Review, 24 June 2011.

[16] Power B, 2011. *How to sustain front line process improvement activities.* Harvard Business Review, 5 August 2011.

[17] Learn more about RACI at Haughey D. *RACI Matrix.* https://www.projectsmart.co.uk/raci-matrix.php

[18] Cambridge Dictionary. *Policy* https://dictionary.cambridge.org/dictionary/english/policy

[19] Collins Dictionary. *Standard.* https://www.collinsdictionary.com/dictionary/english/standard

[20] Often attributed to Peter Drucker (what gets measured get managed), it turns out the origin of this idea lies much further back in history. Software engineer and personal productivity hacker, Matthew Cornell, attributes its origin to astronomer and mathematician, Georg Joachim Rheticus (1514–1574). http://www.matthewcornell.org/blog/2007/7/30/whats-your-feed-reading-speed.html#1 See footnote 1.

Chapter 6

Strategy measurement

"… when you can measure what you are speaking about, and express it in numbers, you know something about it; but when you cannot express it in numbers, your knowledge is of a meagre and unsatisfactory kind …"
Lord Kelvin[1]

Strategy measurement seems, at first glance, to be one of the more straightforward aspects of strategy to understand. It's just a bunch of measurements – what could be hard about that? Yet, at the same time, if you ask people what the one thing was that they didn't get right about their last strategy, it is often strategy measurement that pops into their mind first. Strategy measurement is deceptively difficult.

Strategy measurement is dependent on Key Performance Indicators (KPIs). They are the workhorse of strategy measurement and, as such, will be the focus of this chapter. Here's what you need to know about them:

1. You need a *definition of a KPI* and its component parts – specifically you need to know what a *strategic* KPI is;

2. You need to know the *types of measurement* that are used for KPIs;

3. You need to understand the *criteria for good KPIs*.

4. You need to be familiar with different KPIs that serve *different purposes*:

    a. Leading vs lagging KPIs;

    b. 'Success-defining' KPIs vs 'Critical-to-success' KPIs.

6.1   What is a KPI?

As of 2020, the average company manages 800 terabytes of data,[2] enough storage for 761 miles of books on a shelf.[3] Making sense of that data is to 'drink from a very large firehose'. Every company, therefore, needs to identify the tiny subset of all the data at its disposal that is critical to its success – these are its Key Performance Indicators (KPIs). Figure 86 provides definitions for a KPI and also distinguishes between the concept of KPIs in general and strategic KPIs. Strategic KPIs are the subset of all the general KPIs used by an organisation to measure the performance of strategy.

✓ What is a Key Performance Indicator (KPI)?

Key	Performance	Indicator
Essential, critical, vital	Progress towards an intended outcome	A way of judging the presence or amount of something

A Key Performance Indicator (KPI) is a critical measure of progress towards an intended outcome.

A Strategic Key Performance Indicator is a critical measure of progress towards the change specified in a strategy.

Figure 86 What is a Key Performance Indicator?

Two things need to be clarified about these definitions. The first is why you need both KPIs and strategic KPIs. By describing them as *key* performance indicators, you are already designating them essential, critical or vital to the organisation. If they are 'key' then surely, they are also strategic, in which case, why do you need a separate label for 'strategic KPIs'? Is this not a bit like calling them *key* key performance indicators? The answer is that not all key performance indicators will be strategic. Remember, the Boundary Model of Strategy from Chapter 5 proposed that strategy is what the organisation spends a minority of its time and resources on to bring about impactful change across the organisation. The majority of time and resources, by contrast, are spent on 'business-as-usual'. This means that there will be KPIs for monitoring and improving business-as-usual, and KPIs for monitoring strategy.

The second clarification concerns the use of the word 'key'. It doesn't always need to be there. A 'performance indicator' is an entity in its own right. It is just a different thing to a '*key* performance indicator'. A performance indicator is an indicator of progress towards something, regardless of whether it is critical (or essential or vital). When you 'promote' a performance indicator to being a *key* performance indicator you are saying it is a critical measure of any aspect of performance that is important to your organisation's success, for example the profit you make across your entire organisation, your organic search ranking or how well your new website renders on mobile phones. Just calling it a key performance indicator doesn't indicate *what* it is a critical indicator of. Which is why you use the term strategic KPI – these are critical indicators of progress towards strategic success.

6.1.2 Component parts of KPIs

A KPI, whether strategic or not, comprises three parts (Fig. 87). It has a *target* – a threshold value that is deemed critical ('key') for the organisation, such as annual profit, organic search rank or page-load speed on mobile phones. Secondly, that target has a *date* – when should the target be reached by? Finally, it has a *measure of progress*, at a given moment in time, so performance at that time can be evaluated in relation to the target, for example projected quarterly profits or regular benchmarks against competitors.

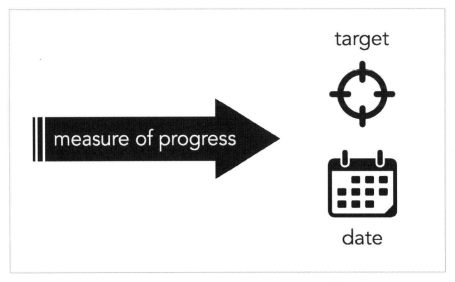

Figure 87 The three parts of a Key Performance Indicator

It follows from this that the difference between the current measure of progress and the target value is a measure of the *performance gap* to be filled by strategic activities between now and the target date. It also follows that KPIs can be measured at a series of dates to track the milestones reached along the way towards strategic success. This is sometimes known as the *KPI trajectory* and different trajectories will lead to different levels of performance at 'milestones' along the way towards the eventual target. Figure 88 shows three examples of KPI trajectories that lead to very different KPI targets as the strategy progresses.

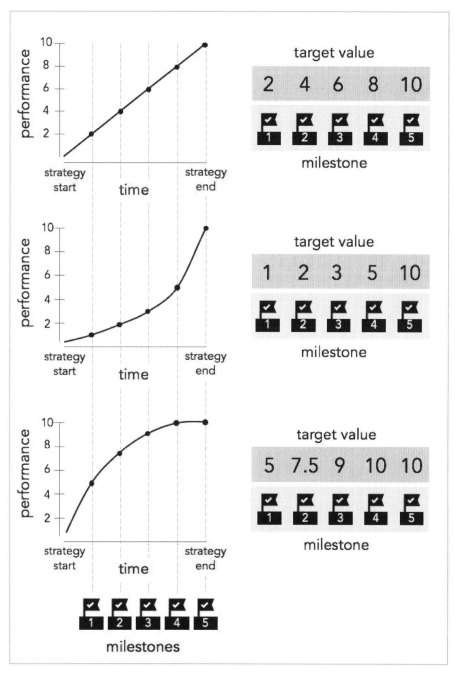

Figure 88 Different strategic KPIs may have different trajectories

6.2   Types of measurement used for KPIs

The science of measurement is a surprisingly confused and confusing place. There are at least three answers to the question 'How many different types of measurement are there?' Harvard psychologist, Stanley Stevens devised the first, and most widely used answer in 1946:[4] he proposed four levels of measurement: nominal, ordinal, interval and ratio. Statisticians, Frederick Mosteller and John Tukey disagreed.[5] According to them, there are seven levels of measurement: names, grades, ranks, counted fractions, counts, amounts and balances. Geographer Nick Chrisman goes further and proposes ten levels of measurement: [6] nominal, gradation of membership, ordinal, interval, log-interval, extensive ratio, cyclical ratio, derived ratio, counts and absolute. For present purposes, it is important to have a measurement system that is simple, intuitive and memorable. Hence the use of 'category', 'rank' and 'amount'.

6.2.1   Category

Progress towards strategy success can be measured categorically: for example, has the new Product Marketing Plan been written yet or not? Categories can be binary (yes or no) or have labels with no underlying order (such as country): which new markets have you launched your products and services in? Gartner's market research reports[7] categorise the products reviewed as 'Leaders', 'Challengers', 'Visionaries' or 'Niche Players' – being categorised as a 'Challenger' by Gartner could, therefore, be a strategy success KPI.

6.2.2   Rank

'Rank' is the next measurement system for KPIs: for example, where are you ranked in your ambition to be market leader in your sector? The key with ranks is that they are an ordered sequence but the difference between ranks is not necessarily consistent. So, imagine the star ratings given in product reviews. A one-star difference in reviews doesn't necessarily mean the same thing. Products given four- and five-star reviews might both be really liked, making their one-star difference in rating quite small. A three-star-rated product might still be quite liked, whereas a 2-star rated product is typically disliked, indicating a greater significance of the one-star difference.

6.2.3 Amount

Amounts are measures of magnitude, usually with reference to some absolute zero value. Amounts, by contrast to rank, have units that define quantity – how much of something you are aiming for. For example, annual sales revenue or profit in GBP (£), typically measured as EBITDA (Earnings Before Interest, Taxes, Depreciation and Amortisation), new customers measured as a number per month, or staff gender ratios measured as a percent (%).

Using categories, ranks and amounts are all great ways to measure progress towards strategy success (Fig. 89).

✓ Types of measurement used for KPIs		
Type of measurement	What is it?	Strategic KPI examples
Category	Naming, labelling or categorising (no underlying order) e.g. gender, nationality	• Produce Marketing Plan (Y/N) • New markets launched (FR, ES) • Gartner Quadrant (Challenger)
Rank	Ordered sequence (typically unknown magnitude of difference) e.g. happiness, IQ score	• Sector rankings (#1 in USA) • Net Promoter Score (NPS) • Brand preference (Pepsi>Coke) • Review rating (★ ★ ★ ★ ★)
Amount	Measure of magnitude (usually with reference to some absolute zero value) e.g. count, weight, money	• # new customers (number/month) • Profit (£) • Female:male managers (%)

Figure 89 Types of measurement used for KPIs

Another way of classifying different types of KPI is to check if they are intended to measure *impact* or *progress* – this brings you to the notion of leading and lagging indicators.

6.3　Leading and lagging indicators

Topic	Leading indicator	Lagging indicator
Diet	Calories consumed (kcal)	Weight loss (kg)
Marathon training	Training runs (miles/week)	Race finish time (hrs/mins)
Ecommerce	Online sessions (#) Bounce rate (%) Add-to-basket value (£)	Online revenue (£)
Sales	Calls completed (#) Sales pipeline (£)	Sales revenue (£)
Employee engagement	Absence rates (days/year) Participation rates (%) Customer complaints (#)	Staff retention (years) Net Promoter Score (NPS)

Figure 90　Examples of leading and lagging indicators

When measuring impact, you want to measure whether the intended outcome of your actions happened, even if you have to wait some time for the action to take effect and have its impact. Measuring impact, therefore, uses *lagging indicators*. These are measures of output or the consequences of actions.

If you are measuring progress, especially if you want to do so to 'fine-tune' your actions, you don't have the luxury of waiting for lagging indicators. By the time you get them, your actions will be long-since completed. So, to measure progress, you need *leading indicators* – measures either of your actions or their immediate consequences. These are what you expect to drive outcomes and hence you expect to be predictors of lagging indicators. Figure 90 gives a few examples to help you feel more comfortable with leading and lagging indicators.

6.4   The AMP Model of Good KPIs

Now you know what Key Performance Indicators are, what they are for and what types there are, it is time to learn what makes a good KPI.

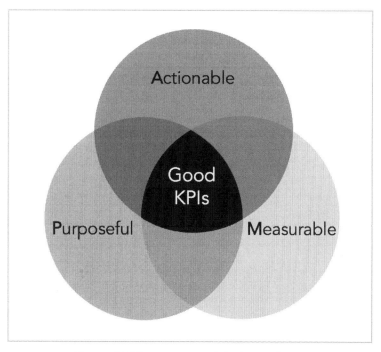

Figure 91 The AMP Model of Good KPIs

According to our AMP Model, a good KPI is Actionable, Measurable and Purposeful (Fig. 91). These are a distillation and simplification of the many published criteria for effective or useful KPIs.[8]

6.4.1 Actionable KPIs

To say that a KPI should be *actionable* begs the question, actionable by whom? As you discovered in Chapter 4 on strategy mapping, every strategic goal in a strategy map should have a goal owner. Indeed, good practice suggests any goal with a target ought to have a goal owner, otherwise who is held accountable for hitting this target? For Key Performance Indicators to be actionable, therefore, they need to be owned, they need to be visible to their owner and the owner must be able to influence their outcome. Goal owners must not simply be passive observers of the KPI moving towards or away from its target. They must be enabled to see a performance indicator drifting away from its target and take, what they hope will turn out to be, corrective action (Fig. 92).

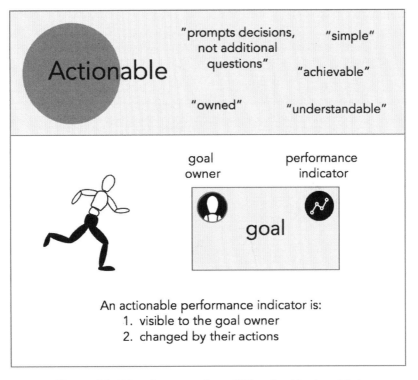

Figure 92 What it means for a KPI to be 'Actionable'

6.4.2 Measurable KPIs

For a KPI to be measurable, it must be a single, repeatable measure of sufficient accuracy and timeliness to serve its purpose:

1. *It needs to be precise and accurate* – it can be hard to remember exactly what these terms mean… unless you recall an image like Figure 93. This reminds you that 'accuracy' is how close your measurement is to the real world, whereas 'precision' is how repeatable your measurement is.

2. *The measurement should be timely.* It should present the measurement promptly after it was taken. Lag between measurement and reporting can impair the ability to respond and to adjust input parameters to improve performance.

3. *The measurement should be fit-for-purpose.* For a strategic KPI, it must measure something of strategic significance, and the measurement must, as you have seen, be actionable.

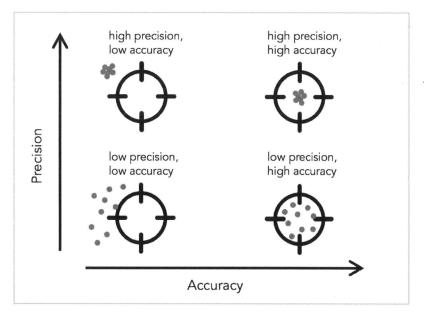

Figure 93 Making sense of accuracy and precision

Figure 94 shows what it means for a KPI to be measurable.

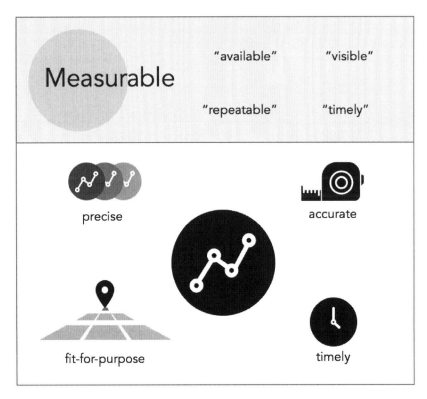

Figure 94 What it means for a KPI to be 'Measurable'

6.4.3 Purposeful KPIs

When you say a KPI needs to be purposeful, this means that its achievement needs to contribute to strategic success. It doesn't need to be a major contributor to strategic success. It could be a measure of a front-line action many line-managerial steps away from senior leadership. Yet it could be a critical cog in a much larger machine. The owner of this KPI needs to see the strategic importance of their actions. For this to happen requires a line-of-sight connection between their performance indicator and strategic success.

Figure 95 shows what it means for a KPI to be purposeful.

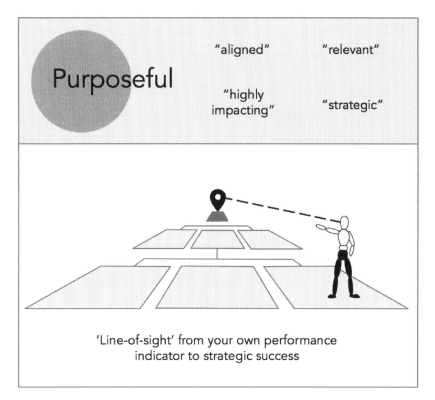

Figure 95 What does it mean for a KPI to be 'Purposeful'

6.5   Purposes of strategic KPIs

Having gained an understanding of strategic KPIs, you can now consider the interconnection between the purposes KPIs serve and the decisions they support. This requires you to take a step back from the detail of KPIs to think more broadly about what you are trying to achieve by measuring strategy, and how best to achieve it.

Figure 96 shows the Binary Star Model of KPIs. In astronomical terms, a binary star is a pair of stars locked in orbit around each other. 100,000 binary stars have now been catalogued by astronomers, many recognised by the distinctive wobble in their orbit as each exerts a gravitational influence on the other, proportional to their relative mass. The Binary Star Model demonstrates how strategic KPIs serve two distinct purposes, and how they exert a distinct 'gravitational influence' on each other.

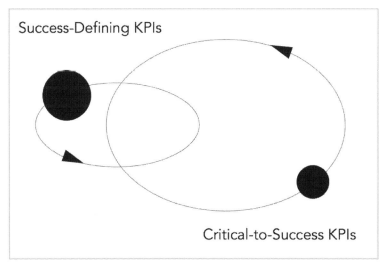

Figure 96 The Binary Star Model of Strategic KPIs

6.5.1 Success-defining KPIs

Every strategy needs an indicator of ultimate success – did the strategy achieve what it set out to achieve? A success–defining KPI sets the threshold at which your strategy will ultimately be judged to have succeeded or failed. There may, of course, be more than one success–defining KPI; strategy success may depend on several criteria being met, in which case you have multiple success–defining KPIs (for example sales revenue and number of new customers). Figure 97 shows that these success-defining KPIs can either be measures of the strategy destination or measures of the value realised from having reached that destination. Success–defining KPIs are identified during strategy development and are part of the documented strategy prepared for launch.

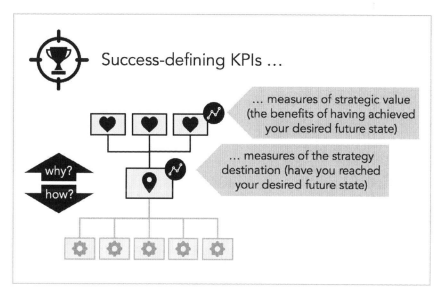

Figure 97 Success-defining KPIs

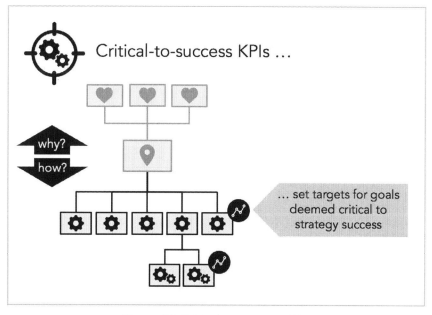

Figure 98 Critical-to-success KPIs

6.5.2 Critical-to-success KPIs

'Critical-to-success KPIs' are much more numerous than success-defining KPIs (Fig. 98). Each of your strategy's core methods may have a critical-to-success KPI. In addition, as you elaborate these goals to get the strategy adopted across the organisation, dozens, or in a big organisation, hundreds of other critical-to-success KPIs will be added. These KPIs need to be set and tracked as part of the strategic plan, as you will discover in Chapter 9 on strategy adoption. They also need to be adjusted and updated as part of strategy adaptation, as discussed in Chapter 10. Making sure these critical-to-success KPIs are *actually* critical to strategic success, and making sure they remain aligned and continue to aggregate up to strategic success, is a big and important task that ought to be reported directly to the senior leadership team. The senior leadership team should always seek to be reassured that if all the critical-to-success KPIs are achieved, the success-defining KPI will also be achieved. This is the basis of the Binary Star Model of KPIs.

6.5.3 Strategic decision-making

The different purposes that these KPIs serve relate to their role in supporting strategic decision-making. Success-defining KPIs, not surprisingly, enable decision-making on whether strategic success has yet been achieved. If not, they will help inform the decision on whether or not to persist in trying to achieve the success-defining KPI (Fig. 99). If, of course, you decide it is not worth persisting, this means the strategy is unattainable and a new strategy is needed, triggering a strategy review.

Critical-to-Success KPIs inform decisions about whether your strategic plan needs to be adjusted to improve its outcomes. This is a classic continuous improvement loop, using an iterative 'plan – do – check – adjust' cycle[9]. If, after checking (measuring) you discover you have run out of scope for adjustment, a decision needs to be made on whether to persist in trying to achieve the critical-to-success KPI (Fig. 100). If you decide not to persist, you would need to go back to strategy mapping to try to find a different way of achieving the critical-to-success outcome you need for the strategy to succeed. If this is not possible, it may signal the fact that strategy success is not attainable, and a new strategy is needed.

Figure 99 The decisions supported by success-defining KPIs

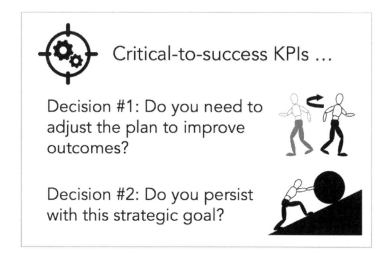

Figure 100 The decisions supported by critical-to-success KPIs

6.6   The practicalities of strategy measurement

As Lord Kelvin's quote at the start of this chapter illustrates, measurement of any kind is really important, and this is particularly so with strategy. Strategy measurement plays a key role in both strategy development and strategy adoption. To illustrate the practicalities of strategy measurement, the 'success-defining' and 'critical-to-success' KPIs of the case study, Artigence, will be explored in Chapter 8 on strategy development and Chapter 9 on strategy adoption.

6.7   Summary and key takeaways from Chapter 6

1. **A Key Performance Indicator (KPI)** is a critical measure of progress towards an intended outcome.

2. **A Strategic Key Performance Indicator** is a critical measure of progress towards the change specified in a strategy.

3. Key performance indicators comprise three parts: a **target**, a **date** and a **measure of progress** at a given point in time towards that target.

4. Three main types of measurement are used for key performance indicators: **categories, ranks** and **amounts.**

5. Key performance indicators are either **lagging indicators** (measures of impact, measures of output, measures of the consequences of actions) or **leading indicators** (measures of input, measures of action or their immediate consequences).

6. **The AMP Model of Good KPIs** proposes that good strategic key performance indicators are actionable, measurable and purposeful:

a. **Actionable** – visible to the goal owner to provide feedback on the performance of this goal and can be changed by the actions of the goal owner in pursuit of this goal;

b. **Measurable** – must be sufficiently precise, accurate and timely to be fit for purpose;

c. **Purposeful** – must contribute to strategic success.

7. **Strategic KPIs serve two distinct purposes:**

    a. **Success-defining KPIs** are ultimate indicators of strategy success. They enable you to decide if strategy success has been achieved and, if not, whether it is still wise to persist in pursuing it.

    b. **Critical-to-success KPIs** track the progress of goals upon which the success of the strategy depends. They enable you to decide whether plans need to be adjusted to improve outcomes, or whether a different way of achieving the same outcome needs to be found.

8. **The Binary Star Model of KPIs** demonstrates how success-defining KPIs and critical-to-success KPIs can exert a distinct 'gravitational influence' on each other. If all the critical-to-success KPIs are achieved, the success-defining KPI should also be achieved.

6.8   Let's talk about... strategy measurement

Use these questions to prompt deeper conversations on strategy measurement across your organisation:

1. *How fit for purpose has your measurement of strategy been in the past? What worked well? What worked badly?*

2. How important do you, as an organisation, think strategy measurement is, and as a result how much effort should go into doing it thoroughly?

3. Which aspects of strategy are you likely to struggle most to measure? What could you do to make these aspects of measurement more effective?

4. How does your organisational culture respond to targets? Are they a force for good? Are they set diligently? Once set, are they respected? Do they drive strategy forward in a positive way?

Notes on Chapter 6

(all web content accessed between April and September 2020)

---

[1] Kelvin 1883. *Electrical Units of Measurement.* A lecture delivered at the Institution of Civil Engineers, 3 May 1883.
https://archive.org/details/popularlecturesa01kelvuoft/page/72/mode/2up?q=meagre

[2] This number is extrapolated from the best data available. In 2016, IDG published the findings of their survey of 724 IT decision-makers and reported that the average company manages 162.9TB of data (average enterprise has 347.56TB of data, the average SMB has 47.81TB). IDG, 2016. *Data and Analytics Survey.*
https://cdn2.hubspot.net/hubfs/1624046/IDGE_Data_Analysis_2016_final.pdf In 2019 the Visual Capitalist published their *Data in a Day* infographic (https://www.visualcapitalist.com/how-much-data-is-generated-each-day/) that showed global data storage increased from 4.4ZB in 2013 to 44ZB projected for 2020, a ten-fold increase. Assuming (conservatively, because this growth is likely to be exponential) half of this increase occurred between 2016 and 2020, then the average company will manage five times the data in 2020 that they did in 2016 – hence 162.9x5=814.5TB, rounded to 800TB.

[3] Stegner B, 2020. *Memory Sizes Explained: Gigabytes, Terabytes, and Petabytes in Context.* https://www.makeuseof.com/tag/memory-sizes-gigabytes-terabytes-petabytes/ In this article 2GB of storage is stated to be enough to store 20 yards of books on a shelf. 800TB is therefore enough to store 819,200 yards of books on a shelf = 761 miles.

[4] Stevens SS, 1946. *On the Theory of Scales of Measurement.* Science. 103 (2684): 677–680.

[5] Mosteller F and Tukey J, 1977. *Data Analysis and Regression: A Second Course in Statistics.* Addison Wesley, Reading, MA.

[6] Chrisman NR, 1998. *Rethinking Levels of Measurement for Cartography.* Cartography and Geographic Information Science. 25 (4): 231–242.

[7] Gartner. *Positioning technology players within a specific market.* https://www.gartner.com/en/research/methodologies/magic-quadrants-research

[8] The sources used include 1. Optimize Smart *What makes a good KPI?* https://www.optimizesmart.com/understanding-key-performance-indicators-kpis-just-like-that/#a10 2. Phocas Software, 2020. *Business KPIs: 5 important characteristics to be effective.* https://www.phocassoftware.com/business-intelligence-blog/five-characteristics-of-an-effective-kpi

3. Liebowitz J (ed) 2014. *Business Analytics: An Introduction.* CRC Press, Boca Raton FL. p68.

[9] Wikipedia. *Plan, do, check, adjust (PCDA).* https://en.wikipedia.org/wiki/PDCA

Chapter 7

Strategy scoping

---

*Strategy scoping defines what
you can see of the new strategy from where
you are standing right now.*

Figure 101 shows the strategy lifecycle model that you learned about in Chapter 2.

Figure 101 The strategy lifecycle model, showing strategy scoping

In this chapter you are focusing on strategy scoping, the first part of the strategy production stage of the lifecycle. Strategy scoping comes immediately before strategy development and lays the groundwork for the strategy to be developed in a structured, systematic and unbiased way. Strategy scoping, which culminates in a strategy announcement, (Fig. 102) provides a clarity of thinking and a rigour of methodology that is hard to achieve otherwise in strategy development.

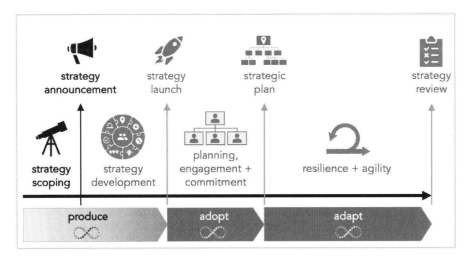

Figure 102 Strategy scoping on the timeline of strategy

7.1   Principles of strategy scoping

A story[1] to start with …

During a visit to one of the few remaining shipyards in the UK, a visitor from Asia, where shipbuilding was continuing to thrive, was asked if he noticed any differences between the approaches our different nations took to shipbuilding. He replied:

> *"At home, we take four years to design a ship and one*
> *year to build it. In your country you take only one year*

to design it and, as a result, it takes you four years to build it."

Strategy scoping is the design phase before you actually start to develop the strategy. It is the decision-making process right at the start of strategy production that sets out to inform the scope of the forthcoming strategy development process; what needs to be done, by whom and by when, for the strategy to be ready for launch.

Strategy scoping does not require in-depth research and analysis, rather it is an opportunity to think and reflect on what the new strategy will contain, and the requirements of effective strategy development. Strategy scoping should give readily-communicated focus to the forthcoming process of strategy development.

7.1.1   The iceberg principle of strategy scoping

Strategy scoping is not always an easy thing to sell within an organisation. It may seem to be yet another job to do in an already lengthy process. It might also appear to be a barrier preventing us getting started on strategy development.   Another concern is its feasibility.   How can you meaningfully scope a strategy you haven't even started to write yet?

Icebergs make a great metaphor for strategy scoping. A fundamental property of all icebergs is that there is more ice under the water than appears above the water: 7/8th of the mass of ice is below the water and 1/8th is above, according to people who should know![2] When you first start thinking about a new strategy, most of that strategy will lie tantalisingly out of sight, as will the work needed to write the strategy and the evidence needed for strategic decision-making. But that doesn't mean it is all out of sight. The visible part of an iceberg can be described perfectly meaningfully and, to a degree, characterised and defined without venturing under the sea. Similarly, strategy scoping describes what you can see, and decide about strategy, right now, without delving into strategy development (Fig. 103).

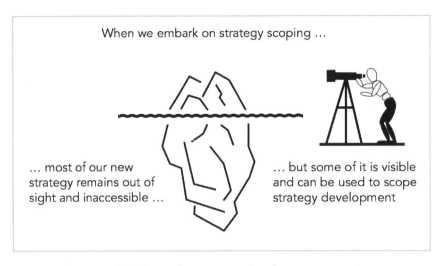

When we embark on strategy scoping ...

... most of our new strategy remains out of sight and inaccessible ...

... but some of it is visible and can be used to scope strategy development

Figure 103 The iceberg principle of strategy scoping

Strategy scoping aims to set 'good' boundaries for strategy, thereby reducing the range of strategic possibilities to be considered. Good boundaries define what you can 'see', from where you are 'standing' right now. From what you are able to see, you will be able to make some distinction between what needs to be included, and what's excluded, from the forthcoming strategy. 'Bad' boundaries, by contrast, set constraints on strategy development for no other reason than making the strategy-decision-maker feel less uncomfortable with the complexity they are facing. They are predicated on facts that cannot possibly be known at this stage.

If you focus on the parts of the forthcoming new strategy that are already 'above the water' and visible, they provide you with good boundaries by which you can start to reduce strategic uncertainty. Further uncertainty reduction can come from scoping the work needed to discover what remains 'under the water' right now. What research, what data analysis and what consultation looks as though it will be needed (from what you can see right now) to develop the new strategy to the point of strategy launch?

Strategy scoping presents, cleanly and simply, what could be in and out of scope for the prospective new strategy, and why. It is not the role of strategy scoping to evaluate and decide upon these strategic possibilities – this is done during strategy development. Rather, strategy scoping sets out what decisions need to be made, what data and insights will be needed within that evidence-base, and who will be responsible for which tasks and by when during the remainder of the strategy production stage.

7.2 The benefits of strategy scoping

Strategy scoping sets out to make strategy development more focused, more effective and more efficient than it would otherwise be. Any part of strategy you can scope in advance is a part you can plan, and consequently can make less complex to develop. It also serves a vital communication role across the organisation, by explaining, simply and clearly, what is going to be done in order to develop this strategy.

Expanding these benefits slightly, here are four reasons to persuade an unconvinced manager or board member that strategy scoping is a great investment of time and effort for any organisation:

1. **Simplicity** – Scoping makes strategy development simpler, more straightforward and more purposeful by identifying why the strategy is needed, which decisions need to be made and what evidence is needed to make them;

2. **Transparency** – Scoping makes strategy development more transparent and hence can lead to more, and better-quality, involvement across the organisation;

3. **Justifiability** – Scoping makes strategy development less prone to bias, more evidence based, more data-driven and hence a lot easier to explain and justify;

4. **Engagement** – Over the longer term, a simpler, more transparent and more justifiable strategy will be more readily engaged with, more willingly committed to and more eagerly adopted. It is more likely to achieve the strategic success it defines for itself.

These are benefits for:

1. the executives and the board who will ultimately own the strategy;

2. everyone involved in contributing to and developing the strategy;

3. anyone who will be affected by the new strategy, after it is launched.

7.3   Practicalities of strategy scoping

The practical process of strategy scoping can vary enormously. It could be completed in a one-day workshop or it could be a tightly coordinated, iterative process, involving dozens of individuals and lasting several months. The former is more typical in smaller businesses and start-ups; the latter in large multinational enterprises. Strategy scoping is usually led by senior leaders, such as the Chief Executive, although, in larger organisations, most of the work will be delegated to a Director of Strategy.

It is important, during strategy scoping, not to start trespassing into the territory of strategy development. This is *over-reach:* reaching further than you need to, for scoping purposes. If you need to analyse competitors, investigate customer needs or explore new technologies in order to write your new strategy, these are all jobs for strategy development. In strategy scoping you need, as far as possible, to define what these jobs are, roughly how long they might take and who might be best suited to undertaking them. Don't be tempted to start *doing* them within strategy scoping.

One key decision that can have a big impact on the duration of strategy scoping is who is doing the scoping? Scoping is what you can see of the new strategy from where you are standing right now. But who sees? And from standing where? In a small company, scoping is usually straightforward; the leaders responsible for strategy probably work closely together most of the time and simply need to set aside a day or two of discussions for scoping to be done. In a large enterprise, views on scoping may need to be gathered from across the organisation, potentially from around the world, then collated and reconciled before strategy scoping can even begin. Regardless of the scale and intensity of strategy scoping, however, it follows a similar process and has similar outputs.

7.3.1 The process of strategy scoping

Strategy scoping defines what you can see of the new strategy from where you are standing right now. The process of scoping a new strategy consists of three activities:

1. *Horizon scoping* – what direction is the strategy heading?

2. *Development scoping* – what work is needed to develop the strategy?

3. *Acceptance scoping* – how will you know when you've developed a good-enough strategy?

Each of these activities is a loop that can be re-visited several times in the course of strategy scoping. Together they form the Triple-Loop Model of Strategy Scoping (Fig. 104).

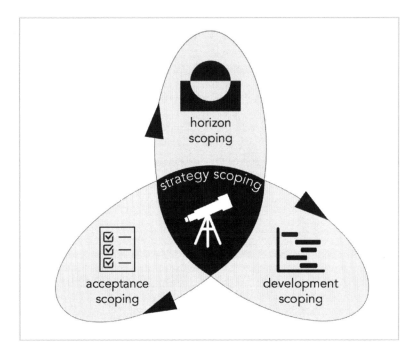

Figure 104 The Triple-Loop Model of Strategy Scoping

The scoping process is typically complete when the outputs of strategy scoping defined in all three loops are compatible and point towards a strategy that seems credible and plausible. At this point, the intended scope of the new strategy can be announced across the organisation.

Each of the activities in the strategy scoping process will now be reviewed in turn.

7.4 Strategy horizon scoping

A 'horizon' is the furthest place you can see from where you are standing[3]. Horizon scoping sets out to define what you can see 'on the horizon' for your forthcoming new strategy. What can you say, right now, about where this new strategy is likely to take you, with any degree of confidence, and why? There are a number of ways you can scope this strategy horizon (Fig. 105).

Figure 105 Scoping the strategy horizon

7.4.1 Situation analysis using the House of Strategy Model

Situation analysis is a review of the current situation for your organisation. The House of Strategy Model (Figure 106 and explained in detail in Chapter 3) is a visualisation of the relationship between the vision, mission, values, strategy and the obstacles and opportunities faced by an organisation.

To use the House of Strategy as a framework for strategy scoping, you need to turn each element into a question about scoping. What do your current vision, mission and values say about the future of your organisation? Do they provide a clear sense of direction? If so, write down what you think that direction is – it could be your new strategy horizon. If not, maybe your vision, mission and values need to be re-written alongside your new strategy?

How does your existing strategy (if you have one) impact on your new strategy? What lessons have you learned? What strengths of the current strategy would you want to re-use and what weaknesses would you want to avoid?

Figure 106 The House of Strategy for strategy scoping

Finally, are there any obvious opportunities or obstacles, external to your organisation, that are likely to shape your forthcoming strategy? If so, identify them in your strategy scope. They could be regulatory (e.g. new consumer protection law), a global trend or global shock (e.g. pandemic) or a new technology (e.g. artificial-intelligence-as-a-service). Consider the likely impact on your business: is there anything profound enough to demand a strategic response?

Figure 107 shows the full framework for strategy scoping and Figure 108 shows this framework completed for our case study, Artigence.

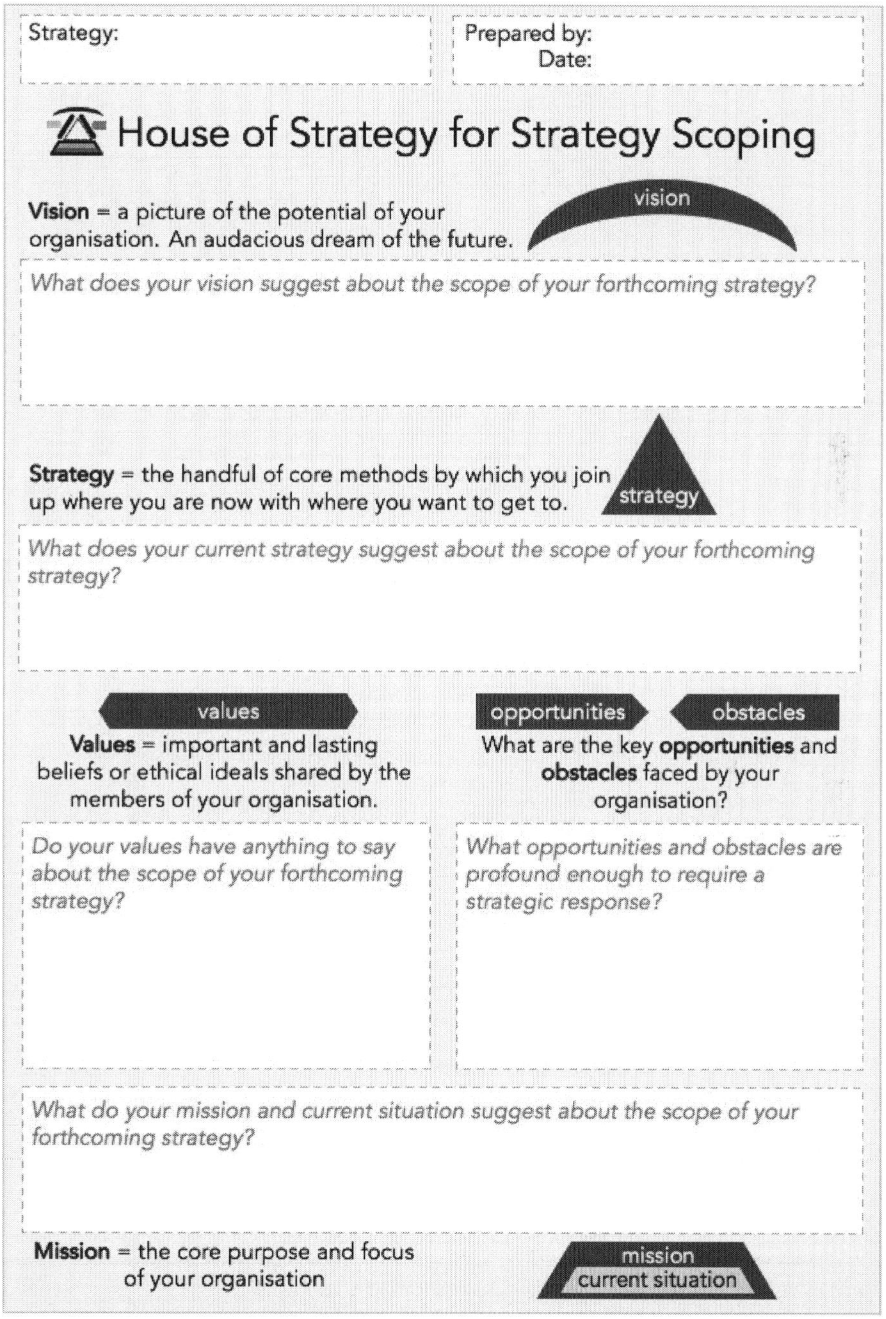

Strategy:

Prepared by:
Date:

△ House of Strategy for Strategy Scoping

Vision = a picture of the potential of your
organisation. An audacious dream of the future.

vision

What does your vision suggest about the scope of your forthcoming strategy?

Strategy = the handful of core methods by which you join
up where you are now with where you want to get to.

strategy

What does your current strategy suggest about the scope of your forthcoming strategy?

values

Values = important and lasting
beliefs or ethical ideals shared by the
members of your organisation.

*Do your values have anything to say
about the scope of your forthcoming
strategy?*

opportunities   obstacles

What are the key **opportunities** and
obstacles faced by your
organisation?

*What opportunities and obstacles are
profound enough to require a
strategic response?*

*What do your mission and current situation suggest about the scope of your
forthcoming strategy?*

Mission = the core purpose and focus
of your organisation

mission
current situation

Figure 107 House of Strategy Framework for Strategy Scoping

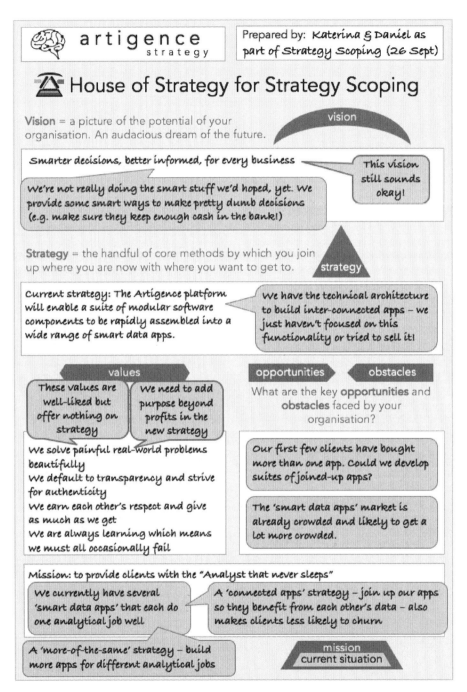

Figure 108 The House of Strategy Framework – case study

7.4.2 Strategy aspirations and drivers

Using the obstacles and opportunities identified in the House of Strategy situation analysis as a starting point, consider what the drivers or the aspirations of your new strategy might be (Fig. 109). Is, for example, the marketplace you sell into about to double or halve in size? Have competitors just announced they are about to launch new or cheaper technology that could challenge your current best-selling product? Or can you harness a new technology to competitive advantage? Are the materials your manufacturing depends upon just about to plunge into global scarcity? Or can you see an opportunity to contribute to global environmental preservation? Can you find new ways of working that would benefit both your customers and employees? By questioning what you can see 'on the horizon' for your forthcoming new strategy in terms of your strategy aspirations and strategy drivers, you contribute to the scoping of your new strategy.

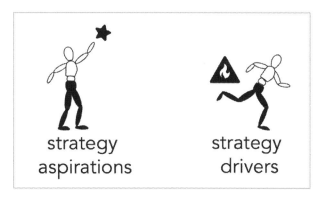

Figure 109 Strategy aspirations and strategy drivers

7.4.3 Strategy time-horizon

One final aspect of strategy horizon scoping you might want to consider is the lifespan for the new strategy – what period of time will elapse between its launch and its successful completion? This may, of course, be obvious. If the main driver of your new strategy is to achieve a particular target over a specific time period, then that's the lifespan of your strategy. More typically, lifespan needs to be decided and it is inevitably a somewhat arbitrary decision. For a large organisation in a mature market, five-year strategies are common. For smaller organisations in faster-changing markets, three years may be as long as you'd want to go. A growing number of strategists are beginning to think that limiting strategy to a fixed, predetermined lifespan is unnecessary. Dana O'Donovan and Noah Rimland Flower from Deloitte's Monitor Institute say, "In today's fast-changing world, why freeze your strategic thinking in a five-year plan?"[4] This is certainly consistent with more systematic strategy management techniques as advocated in this book. According to the Strategy Lifecycle Model (Chapter 2) strategy is adopted and adapted until it needs to be replaced – something perfectly consistent with strategies not having a fixed time horizon. Also, if strategy and strategic planning are to be kept separate, as advocated in the Separation Model of Strategy (refer to Figure 23 in Chapter 2), then strategy success can be measured throughout the strategy lifespan. You don't have to wait until the strategy has finished to discover if its targets were achieved.

7.5   Strategy development scoping

Scheduling strategy development is often a messy process. Here's how one company did it. The senior leadership team were scheduled to start work on strategy in a couple of weeks' time and started discussing it in their weekly Senior Management Meeting. "How long did it take to develop the last strategy?" someone asked. Everyone looked around for the answer but none of them were in-post five years ago. Help was sought from the CEO's Personal Assistant and five minutes later the answer came back – almost exactly 12 months from the day they started work on it to the day it launched. "Right, how about nine months for this one?" the Finance Director suggested. After lots of swiping through calendars, someone came up with a date in nine months and one week's time. It was a full board meeting. With no better ideas forthcoming, the date was fixed. The final strategy, ready for launch would be presented to the board for sign-off on that date.

Strategy development scoping is far from a precise science, but it provides a better way to schedule than pulling a strategy launch-date out of thin air. Figure 110 shows the activities in the development scoping loop.

strategy
development
decisions

strategy
development
evidence

strategy
development
jobs

Figure 110 Scoping strategy development

7.5.1 Strategy development decisions

You have already scoped out the horizons within which your new strategy will lie. Now you begin scoping strategy development by starting to think about the key decisions that will need to be made to produce that kind of strategy. Are your key decisions about customers? Or competitors? Or pricing and finance? Or technology and innovation? Are those decisions focused on growth of the organisation, or transformation and change-management or consolidation and efficiency?

7.5.2 Strategy development evidence

Once you have some understanding of the decisions needed to develop the new strategy, you can start to think about the evidence, analysis and insights that will be needed to inform those decisions. Are these decisions heavily evidence-based? If so, is the evidence readily available or do you need to acquire it? Once you have it, how easy will it be to analyse? How readily will it yield the insights needed for strategic decision-making? Or are the decisions better informed by expertise, in which case, where do you find reliable experts to support your decision-making? Or do the decisions depend on finding consensus-of-opinion (or diversity-of-opinion?) through a consultation process?

7.5.3 Strategy development jobs

Once you have some understanding of the evidence, analysis and insights needed, you can start to think about the jobs to be done, who will need to do them and how long they will take. Think through the work-flow needed for strategic decision-making. Research will be needed to gather the necessary evidence. Can you estimate how many discrete strands of research will be needed? Competitor analysis, for example, might split into three separate research strands: market research (which markets, what level of market penetration, what customer profile, which marketing channels?) product research (which products, what functionality, what after-sales support?) and financial research (pricing, costs and margins). How much of this is desk research and how much is field research? The analysis of this evidence is likely to uncover the need for further evidence. Can you estimate how many iterations of evidence-gathering and analysis are likely to be needed before sufficient insights are revealed for strategic decision-making?

When scoping the work to be undertaken during strategy development, it is important to think through all the different types of work that need to be done. In doing so, it is all too easy to assume everyone is simply going to do their usual day job but apply it to strategy. So, the Finance Director will do financial projections for strategy and the Sales Direction will run customer numbers against these financial projections. Whilst this is essential, it won't necessarily lead to any out-of-the-box thinking that might give rise to a breakthrough strategy. So, as a provocation, here is a very different list of the jobs required for strategy development (Fig. 111). Think through how each of these roles will be filled in your organisation (by an individual or a team), whether there are any gaps and how best they might be filled.

Figure 111 Roles required for strategy development

1. **The Magician** is the creator who conjures solutions from loosely connected ideas and observations. You saw in Chapter 1 how strategic ways of thinking are intuitive, creative and designed to produce synthesis; an integrated perspective on the organisation, a vision of the future you seek to bring about. Strategy is not primarily a matter of calculation and deduction but rather a matter of imagination and commitment. This is the magician's work.

2. **The Executive** decides between the strategic options available and commits the organisation to a particular strategic destination and a set of core methods for getting there. The role of the Executive is usually assumed by the most senior manager or management team. If the strategy is an organisational strategy, the Executive will be the chief executive or the senior leadership team. If the strategy is a functional strategy (e.g. digital, marketing, financial), the Executive will be the leader or leadership team for that part of the organisation. To do this role well, the Executive needs two main types of support – the Advocate and the Analyst.

3. **The Advocate** distils the available strategic possibilities into a manageable number of strategic options for the Executive to decide between. A good Advocate is opinionated. Not in a personally entrenched, unmovable way, but in making the case as strongly as possible for each strategic option by showing it in its best light. Directors of Strategy typically fill the role of Advocate within larger organisations.

4. **The Analyst** is the dispassionate custodian of the strategic evidence base. The Analyst plays both a proactive and a reactive role. The proactive role provides an evidence-based profile of the current situation and foreseeable prospects of the organisation. This evidence-base will be a key determinant of the strategic options proposed by the Advocate. The reactive role analyses the viability of different strategic options being considered. Specifically, the

Executive may need the Analyst to obtain new evidence in order to decide between the options presented by the Advocate. This updates and refines the strategy evidence-base.

5. **The Author** takes the strategic decisions made by the Executive and turns them into clear, persuasive, justifiable communication assets. At its simplest, this means writing the strategy document. This, however, may not be sufficient for all purposes. You may have committed, as part of the strategy production process, to consult stakeholders on the strategy decisions made, before they are finalised. This would require the strategic decisions to be explained, with an emphasis on why these decisions were made and on the basis of what evidence. Strategy will also need to be presented for ratification and endorsement. This would require the strategic decisions to be explained, with an emphasis on how they will benefit the organisation and how progress will be monitored.

6. **The Controller** has the power to accept (or reject) the presented strategy and make it official. By making it official, the Executive is authorised to execute the changes specified in the strategy. This is the typical role of a Board of Directors.

When you come to actually undertake this strategy development scoping, make sure you have also read Chapter 8 on strategy development to give you a much better understanding of the jobs, evidence and decisions you are trying to scope.

7.6 Strategy acceptance scoping

So far you have seen how strategy scoping can be used to set strategy horizons and the aspirations/drivers shaping your new strategy, identify the key strategic decisions that need to be made during strategy development and the jobs that need to be done to make those decisions evidence-based.

Strategy *acceptance* scoping, then, sets out to write acceptance criteria for the decisions and jobs scoped out for strategy development. Setting acceptance criteria is a lot more systematic if you have kept a log of the decisions and outcomes of both horizon scoping and development scoping (Fig. 112).

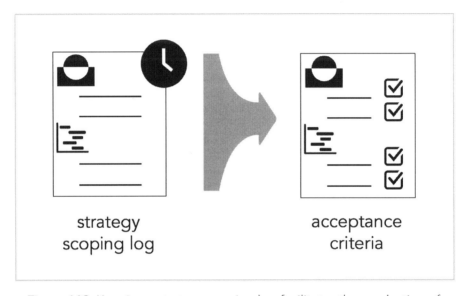

strategy
scoping log

acceptance
criteria

Figure 112 Keeping a strategy scoping log facilitates the production of acceptance criteria for a future strategy

Remember, the criteria you are working on here are not measures of success for the strategy once it reaches its strategy end-date (if it has one). Rather, they are acceptance criteria for the strategy as soon as it has been developed. How do you tell if the strategy you have written is good enough to be launched and made official? This is why you are aiming for acceptance criteria: criteria by which the developed strategy is accepted.

Here, in general terms, are the acceptance criteria for a strategy, at the end of strategy development:

1. **Mission, vision and values.** Do they frame the new strategy well? Does the strategy make more sense with than without them? Alongside the new strategy, do they engage and inspire?

2. **Strategy aspirations.** Is it clear what these aspirations are – do they make sense? Is it clear why they are aspirations? Do you have reason to believe that achieving these aspirations is feasible and, if achieved, will they be beneficial?

3. **Strategy drivers.** Is it clear what they are? Is it clear why they require a strategic response? Do you have reason to believe that responding to these drivers would be beneficial, or perhaps that ignoring them would be risky?

4. **Key decisions.** For each of the key decisions you believe is necessary for strategy development, what criteria can you use to check that the decision made was a good one?

5. **Evidence, analysis and insight.** For each strand of research that you believe is necessary for strategy development, what criteria can be used to check the evidence-gathering and analytic processes were rigorous and the insights produced were robust?

6. **Jobs to be done.** Most of the jobs to be done will already have been evaluated by checking they led to robust insights or good decisions. If any slip through this net, however, how can you set criteria to ensure the jobs were done well?

Along with these elements of horizon scoping and development scoping, strategy acceptance criteria and the use of a strategy log complete the Triple-Loop Model of Strategy Scoping (Fig. 113).

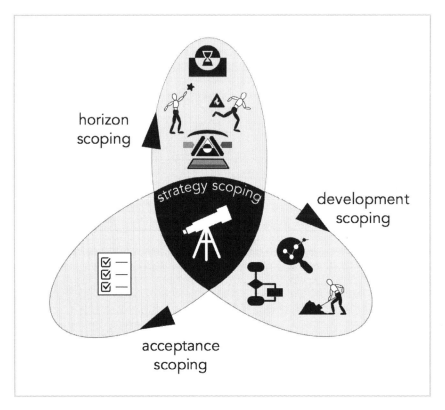

Figure 113 Elements of the Triple-Loop Model of Strategy Scoping

7.7   Record-keeping: the strategy scoping log

The use of a strategy scoping log, whether it be a dedicated document, a series of documents and records, or minutes from scoping-related meetings, can provide the basis for developing acceptance criteria for your forthcoming strategy. It also ensures that due process can be demonstrated, and accountability assured. Figure 114 shows a template for keeping a log of strategy scoping and the associated acceptance criteria required for the strategy to be launched. Figure 115 shows an example of the template filled in for our case study, Artigence.

Figure 114 Strategy scoping log with acceptance criteria for launch

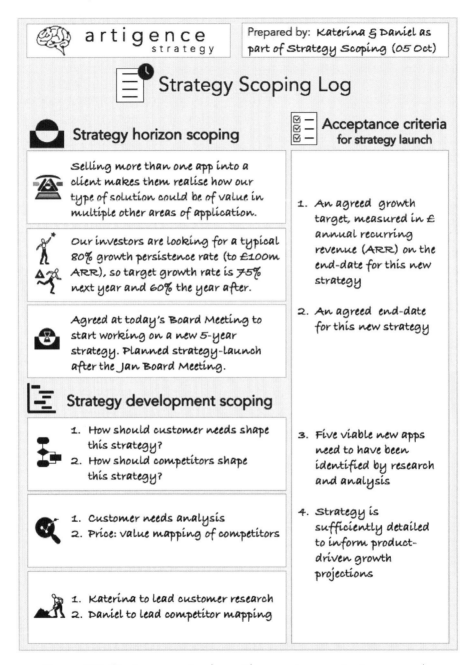

artigence strategy

Prepared by: Katerina & Daniel as part of Strategy Scoping (05 Oct)

Strategy Scoping Log

Strategy horizon scoping

Selling more than one app into a client makes them realise how our type of solution could be of value in multiple other areas of application.

Our investors are looking for a typical 80% growth persistence rate (to £100m ARR), so target growth rate is 75% next year and 60% the year after.

Agreed at today's Board Meeting to start working on a new 5-year strategy. Planned strategy-launch after the Jan Board Meeting.

Strategy development scoping

1. How should customer needs shape this strategy?
2. How should competitors shape this strategy?

1. Customer needs analysis
2. Price: value mapping of competitors

1. Katerina to lead customer research
2. Daniel to lead competitor mapping

Acceptance criteria for strategy launch

1. An agreed growth target, measured in £ annual recurring revenue (ARR) on the end-date for this new strategy

2. An agreed end-date for this new strategy

3. Five viable new apps need to have been identified by research and analysis

4. Strategy is sufficiently detailed to inform product-driven growth projections

Figure 115 Strategy scoping log with acceptance criteria - example

7.8 Strategy scoping outputs

That's it! The strategy scoping process is complete.

The output of strategy scoping is a strategy announcement. In some organisations this will simply be a brief announcement, emphasising the importance of the new strategy for the organisation's future and perhaps the date of its expected launch.

For other organisations, this will herald the start of in-depth consultations, expected to shape the new strategy throughout its development. In this latter case, a strategy announcement document is similar to a Government 'green paper'.[5] Governments including the UK, the European Union, the US, Canada, Australia and Hong Kong produce green papers as outline proposals for legislation, setting out the Government's background thinking on the need for legislation and its tentative, but at this stage uncommitted, suggestions on how that legislation could be framed. A green paper is designed to stimulate debate and discussion and hence to inform Government decision-making about its proposed legislation. It is typically followed by a white paper, which is a more specific and firmly committed proposal for legislation. Recent examples of green papers on strategy from the UK include the Government's Internet Safety Strategy green paper,[6] the Government's Integrated Communities Strategy green paper,[7] and Birmingham City Council's Community Cohesion Strategy green paper.[8] Two universities have also published green papers as part of their strategy production process: The University of Nottingham[9] in the UK and Monash University[10] in Australia.

Figure 116 shows the strategy announcement from Artigence, our case study.

artigence

The next 5 years

At yesterday's Board meeting we committed to the development of a new five-year strategy for Artigence with a planned strategy-launch after the January board meeting. This reflects the amazing performance everyone has contributed to over the past 18 months and our wish to make the best possible decisions for our future as we push forward into our next phase of growth.

This next phase is the classic 'scale-up' problem faced by every fast-growth tech start-up – how we make the leap from this year's annual recurring revenue (ARR) of £10m to get us on the trajectory towards £100m ARR. We have identified the opportunity for product-driven growth. To do this we are going to need to understand both our customers and our competitors like never before. Katerina will be leading customer research and Daniel leading competitor analysis, with a view, at this stage, to identifying five viable new apps.

All-hands meeting this Thursday lunchtime, when we'll start the discussions.

Katerina   Daniel

Co-founders

Figure 116 Artigence strategy announcement

7.9   Summary and key takeaways from Chapter 7

1. Strategy scoping is a **decision-making process** right at the start of strategy production that sets out to inform the scope of the forthcoming strategy and the process by which that strategy will be developed.

2. Strategy scoping has two outcomes:

    a. **A definition of what this new strategy will contain;**

    b. **A definition of what you need to find out** in order to develop the strategy.

3. The **iceberg principle of strategy scoping** suggests that while most of your forthcoming strategy is out of sight and inaccessible, some of it is visible and can be used to scope strategy development.

4. There are four benefits of strategy scoping to strategy development that make it a good investment of time and effort:

    a. **Simplicity** – strategy development becomes simpler, more straightforward and more purposeful;

    b. **Transparency** – strategy development becomes more transparent, improving involvement across the organisation;

    c. **Justifiability** – strategy development becomes less prone to bias, more evidence based, more data-driven and hence a lot easier to explain and justify;

    d. **Engagement** – a simpler, more transparent and more justifiable strategy ultimately leads to more active engagement and willing commitment across the organisation, and hence to strategic success.

5. The **Triple-Loop Model of Strategy Scoping** has three iterative stages: horizon scoping, development scoping and acceptance scoping.

6. **Strategy horizon scoping** identifies what is most likely to be in-scope and out-of-scope for the forthcoming strategy, through:

    a. **situation analysis** – how your current situation relates to your new strategy;

    b. **strategy aspirations and strategy drivers** – what opportunities and obstacles could shape your new strategy;

    c. **strategy time-horizon** – what is the likely lifespan of your new strategy.

7. **Strategy development scoping** tries to work out the key decisions that would be needed to develop the kind of strategy you just scoped out in horizon scoping. If you know the **decisions,** you can work out the **evidence, analysis and insights** needed to inform those decisions. And from this, you can work out the strategy development **jobs to be done.**

8. **Strategy acceptance scoping** sets out to write acceptance criteria for the decisions and jobs needed to develop the new strategy. These will tell you whether your strategy, when it is written, is good enough to become official and be launched.

9. **Record-keeping** – keeping a log of horizon scoping and development scoping ensures due process can be demonstrated and can form the basis for defining acceptance criteria.

10. The output from strategy scoping is a **strategy announcement,** letting the organisation know that work to develop a new strategy is about to commence.

7.10 Let's talk about... strategy scoping

Use these questions to prompt deeper conversations on strategy scoping across your organisation:

1. *Do you, as an organisation, believe you need a strategy scoping process? How else can you inform and define the process by which your new strategy will be developed?*

2. *How structured should your strategy scoping process be? Who ought to be involved? Who ought to be consulted? How will you deal with dissenters / disruptors? How will you reach robust yet meaningful conclusions from the process?*

3. *How does your current situation relate to your new strategy? What opportunities and obstacles could shape your new strategy? What is the likely lifespan of your new strategy?*

4. *What key decisions will be needed to develop your new strategy? What evidence, analysis and insights will be needed to inform those decisions? What strategy development jobs will need to be done? How will you know your strategy is good enough to be launched?*

5. *How thoroughly should you describe your thinking and decision-making processes about your new strategy? How will you document them? Should you, for example, document ideas you considered but then rejected as part of strategy scoping?*

Notes on Chapter 7

(all web content accessed between April and September 2020)

[1] Baxter M 1995 *Product Design: Practical methods for the systematic development of new products.* Chapman & Hall, London. The shipbuilding story was featured on p106.

[2] United States Coast Guard. *How much of an iceberg is under water?* https://www.navcen.uscg.gov/?pageName=iipHowMuchOfAnIcebergIsBelowTheWater

[3] Cambridge English Dictionary. *Horizon.* https://dictionary.cambridge.org/dictionary/english/horizon

[4] O'Donovan D & Rimland Flower N, 2013. *The Strategic Plan is Dead. Long Live Strategy.* Stanford Social Innovation Review. https://ssir.org/articles/entry/the_strategic_plan_is_dead._long_live_strategy

[5] Wikipedia. *Green Paper.* https://en.wikipedia.org/wiki/Green_paper

[6] HM Government, 2017. *The Internet Safety Strategy Green Paper.* https://www.gov.uk/government/consultations/internet-safety-strategy-green-paper

[7] HM Government, 2018. *Integrated Communities Strategy green paper.* https://www.gov.uk/government/consultations/integrated-communities-strategy-green-paper

[8] Birmingham City Council, 2018. *Community Cohesion Strategy for Birmingham Green Paper.* https://www.birminghambeheard.org.uk/economy/community-cohesion-strategy/supporting_documents/Birmingham%20Community%20Cohesion%20Strategy%20Green%20Paper%20%20FINAL.pdf

[9] University of Nottingham, 2018. *Green Paper Consultation.* https://www.nottingham.ac.uk/about/new-university-strategy/green-paper-consultation.aspx

[10] Monash University. *Strategic Plan.* https://www.monash.edu/about/who/strategic-plan

Chapter 8

Strategy development

---

*That rare miracle has again come to pass, a
future has been created out of nothing more
than ink, paper and the imagination.*[1]

This chapter focuses on strategy development, part of the production
stage of the strategy lifecycle (Fig. 117).

Figure 117 The strategy lifecycle model, showing strategy development

It may look like a small part of the entire strategy lifecycle but, for most people, this is where the magic happens. The magic of creating a visionary strategy that is both inspiring and credible. Like most magic, it takes a lot of hard work, built upon a small number of robust yet powerful techniques.

In a sense, this whole book has been building up to this moment. In Chapter 1 you learned about the fundamentals of strategy and how strategy success is one of the most complex things you can ever attempt. Chapters 2 to 6 each set out to reduce that complexity to more manageable dimensions. In Chapter 2 you learned that strategy moved through a lifecycle in which different types of strategic capability are applied at different stages of that lifecycle. In Chapter 3 you discovered core models you could apply across the strategy lifecycle (the House of Strategy Model and the Value Model of Strategy). Chapter 4 showed that strategy could be mapped, systematically and rigorously, using why-how logic. This gives you the capability to connect strategic aspirations with the frontline actions needed to realise them. Chapter 5, on strategy governance, was all about how power and control is exercised in the pursuit of strategy success: power and control that originates at the top of the organisation but must be delegated across the organisation for strategy to be effectively engaged with and committed to. In Chapter 6 you laid the groundwork for strategy measurement and in Chapter 7 you scoped the new strategy's horizons, the work needed to develop the strategy and the criteria you would use to accept the strategy for launch.

So, let the magic begin!

8.1   The Triple-Loop Model of Strategy Development

Strategy development involves iteration through three interconnected loops of activity (Fig. 118).

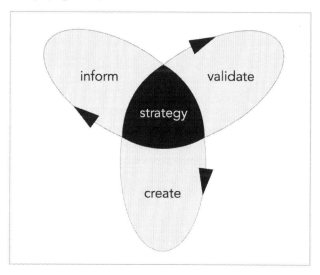

Figure 118 The Triple-Loop Model of Strategy Development

You start with a set of criteria for *validating* your strategy; this may seem counter–intuitive but consider it as the 'brief' for what you are about to develop (you will learn about 'bounded creativity' in Section 8.3). Next you *create* strategy ideas to try to meet those criteria. Validation and creation, however, must be *informed* by data from the outside world to ensure that strategy remains grounded in reality. These three processes are iterative. A linear process is not going to reconcile three interdependent processes. This is especially true when two of them keep adding new information into the mix: the creation of new strategic ideas and new insights arising from research and analysis.

At the centre of the Triple-Loop Model of Strategy Development is a region of synthesis. This is how you craft a single, coherent, concise, meaningful, plausible strategy from the myriad of ideas and insights flying around your three strategy development loops. You have seen in Chapter 1 that your strategy needs to define the desired future state for your organisation, identify the benefits of achieving it and propose the core methods needed to get there (Fig. 119).

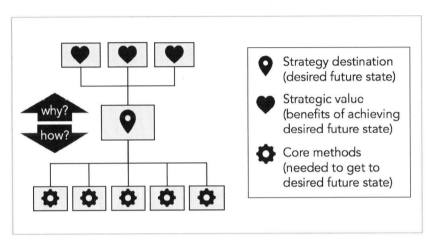

Figure 119   Strategy development outputs

The strategy development process delivers a strategy ready for launch by taking your informed, validated strategy ideas and reviewing them against the design elements that every good strategy should contain (you will see in Section 8.8 how this can be achieved using the Strategy Design Model). At the end of the strategy development process you will have a documented strategy identifying:

1. Strategy destination – where you are trying to get to;

2. Strategy success criteria – how you will confirm that you have reached your destination;

3. The core methods used to get there;

4. The overall benefits to your organisation of reaching this destination.

In addition to this strategy document, documentation is also needed to explain and justify the process by which this strategy was developed.

Effective governance depends on scrutinising and challenging the output (the strategy): is it good enough, innovative enough, and sufficient to reach your destination? Effective governance also depends on scrutiny of the robustness of the process by which the strategy was brought about (i.e. the process of validating, creating and informing strategy development). Finally, the board needs to be comfortable that there is a plan for taking this strategy forward and that the strategy is going to be effectively adopted.

8.2   Strategy validation

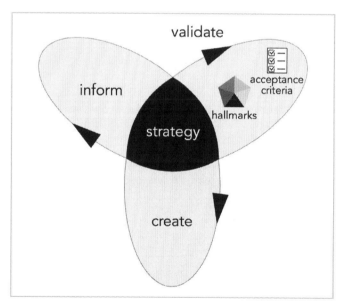

Figure 120 Acceptance criteria and hallmarks of good strategy can be used to validate strategy

There are two different sets of criteria you can use for strategy validation (Fig. 120). The first is the acceptance criteria you defined during strategy scoping (see Chapter 7). These criteria serve two purposes. Firstly, they enable you to decide if the strategy, once developed, is good enough to 'make official' and launch. Secondly, they define the goals your strategy is building towards. Strategy acceptance criteria are specific to the particular strategy you are developing.

The second set of criteria you can use for strategy validation, by contrast, are the 'Hallmarks of Good Strategy' and these apply to any strategy.

Once you have found a way to meet these different sets of validation criteria, the strategy should be good enough. Do no more. Stop messing with it.

8.2.1 The Hallmarks of Good Strategy

There are five hallmarks of good strategy (Fig. 121).

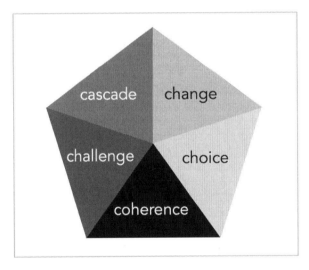

Figure 121 The Hallmarks of Good Strategy

1. **Strategy is about change.** The whole purpose of strategy is to seek commitment across the organisation to a future that is different from the one you would arrive at by continuing on your current course. This change of direction is a defining feature of strategy. If you don't seek change, why do you need a strategy? Change is disruptive,

expensive, hard work and often stressful to those making it happen. It should be sought sparingly and only ever for good reasons. Strategy is not the place to ask everyone to keep up the good work. The Earth needs to continue rotating around the Sun for your strategy to succeed but that doesn't feature in your strategy either!

Strategy being about change is almost a truism, but simply assuming it rather than examining it can make strategy a lot harder to develop and deploy. By being clear that strategy is about change, you can focus attention on aspects of your organisation that actually need to change. No strategy ever needs to cover everything your organisation does. Not even, as one CEO admitted, mentioning every team in the strategy so no-one feels left out. If office accommodation or digital infrastructure are critical to achieving the changes you seek to bring about, they need to be included in the strategy. If not, leave them out.

This, in turn, focuses attention on how much change is sought within a strategy. Clearly, for organisations in desperate circumstances, massive change may be critical for survival. Others, however, may see a bright future for their organisation with only modest change needed to get there. They could continue to invest the majority of their resources in continuing to do what they already do well, leaving only a minority of resources available to drive change. Their strategies, therefore, need to reflect the amount of change they are willing to invest in.

2. **Strategy is about choice.** Michael Porter, known as the 'founder of modern strategy thinking', has championed the fact that strategy is mostly about choice. "The essence of strategy is choosing to perform activities differently than rivals do."[2] Clearly, the closer you get to considering all plausible options, the more likely you are to choose the best. This requires insightful diagnosis. As Richard Rumelt describes it:

"A great deal of strategy work is trying to figure out what is going on. Not just deciding what to do but the more fundamental problem of comprehending the situation." [3]

AG Lafley, former CEO of Procter and Gamble says:

"In my now forty-plus years in business, I have found that most leaders do not like to make choices. They'd rather keep their options open. Choices force their hands, pin them down, and generate an uncomfortable degree of personal risk ... in effect, by thinking about options instead of choices and failing to define winning robustly, these leaders choose to play but not to win." [4]

When it comes to the mechanics of making strategic choices, Rumelt's advice is to look for the levers of competitive advantage. He gives the example of Stephanie, a local shop owner trying to fend off competition from a nearby supermarket. She had a multitude of choices available to her including staff changes (regular, friendly staff who'd get to know the locals), stock changes (fresh organic produce or discounted Asian products for the local student population) and a variety of discounts and promotions. It was only when she decided to focus on 'serving the busy professional who has little time to cook' that her choices became simpler and more obvious. Rumelt describes this as a 'guiding policy' – an "overall approach for overcoming the obstacles highlighted by the diagnosis".[5]

3. **Strategy is about coherence.** According to Roger Martin:

"Strategy is ... one integrated set of choices: what is our winning aspiration; where will we play; how will we win; what capabilities need to be in place; and what management systems must be instituted?" [6]

Rumelt suggests:

> *"Unlike a stand-alone decision or a goal, a strategy is a coherent set of analyses, concepts, policies, arguments, and actions that respond to a high-stakes challenge."* [7]

He goes on to say:

> *"To have punch, actions should coordinate and build upon one another, focusing organizational energy."* [8]

Achieving coherence is difficult, especially across different parts of the organisation. Donald Sull, from the MIT Sloan School of Management, asked managers how frequently they could count on others to deliver on their promises. 84% said they could depend on their boss and their own direct reports all or most of the time, but this figure dropped to 59% when it ran to individuals in other functions or departments within the organisation. [9]

The solution to this coherence challenge is to link the aims and actions of different parts of an organisation to a common strategic purpose to ensure everyone is pulling in the same direction. This, of course, is the basis of strategy mapping, where why-how logic ensures built-in coherence of strategic goals and the SaNity Check Model validates your strategy to ensure its internal consistency (see Chapter 4). You will see how this works in the Artigence case study, later in this chapter.

4. **Strategy is about challenge.** Rumelt is emphatic about the importance of identifying the challenges underlying strategy:

> *"A good strategy does more than urge us forward toward a goal or vision. A good strategy honestly acknowledges the challenges being faced and provides an approach to overcoming them."* [10]

"Bad strategy may actively avoid analyzing obstacles because a leader believes that negative thoughts get in the way." [11]

"Strategic challenges [are the factors exerting] a decisive influence on an organisation's likelihood of future success." [12]

The main strategic challenges to consider are often external to the organisation. What changes are happening in the marketplace, to customers, competitors and suppliers? What political, economic, social and technological changes are foreseeable? In an environment that is Volatile, Uncertain, Complex and Ambiguous (VUCA factors),[13] scenario planning can form a critical role in identifying challenges and their likely impact on the organisation.[14]

5. **Strategy is about cascade.** If, as you saw above, strategy seeks to bring about a commitment to change across the entire organisation, it is essential that the strategy 'reaches' all the change-makers across the entire organisation. This happens by what Lafley and Martin call a strategy cascade[15] (see Chapter 4 on strategy mapping). The strategic choices made on behalf of the entire organisation cascade down through business units and departments, shaping the strategic choices they, in turn, make; "the choices at the top of the cascade setting the context for the choices made below, and the choices at the bottom influencing and refining the choices above."[16] As an example, they describe how Procter and Gamble have an overall corporate strategy, which helps shape a sector strategy (e.g. beauty care), which helps shape a category strategy (e.g. skin care), which helps shape a brand strategy (e.g. Olay).

Figure 122 gives a framework for validating your strategy ideas against the hallmarks of good strategy and can be used to judge whether one strategy idea is better or worse than another in a structured, systematic way. A case study using this framework can be found at the end of this chapter (Section 8.11).

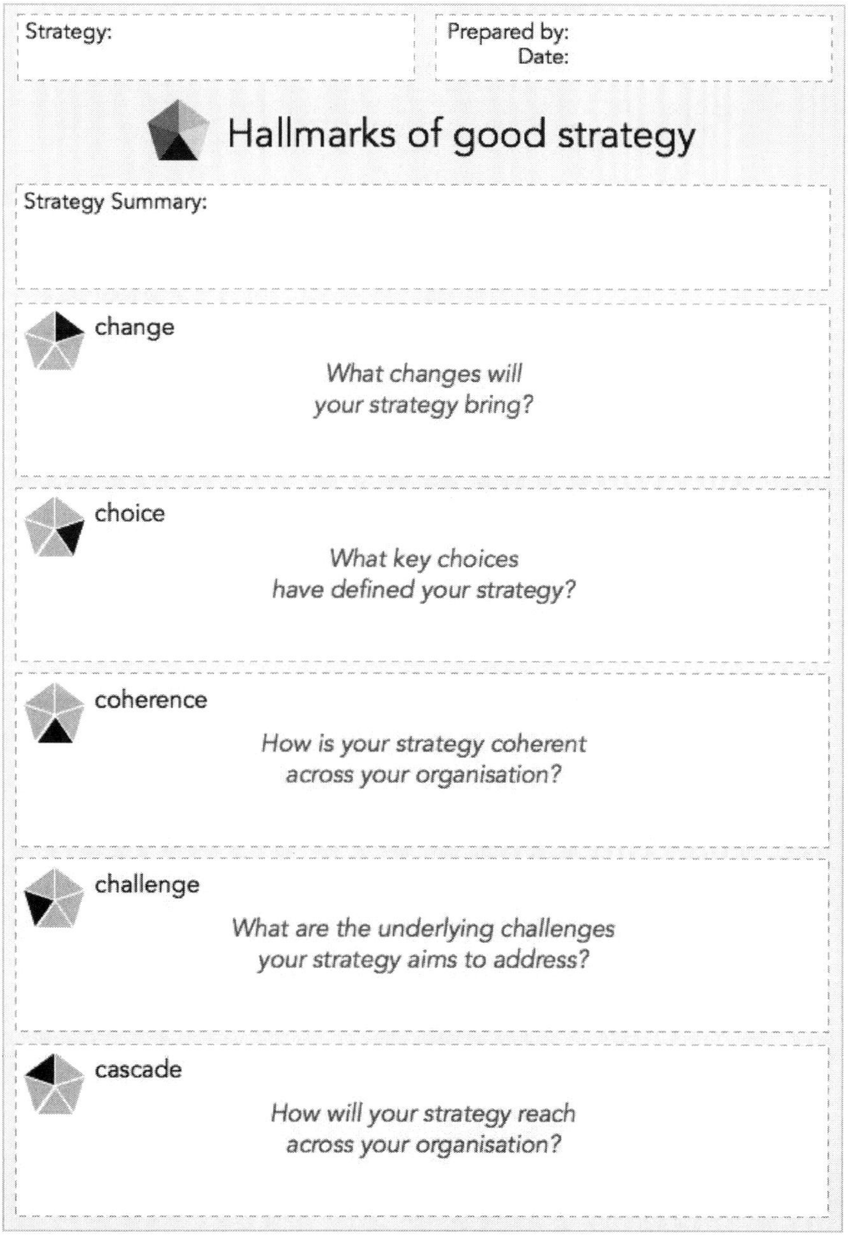

Figure 122 Hallmarks of good strategy checklist template

8.3   Creative thinking

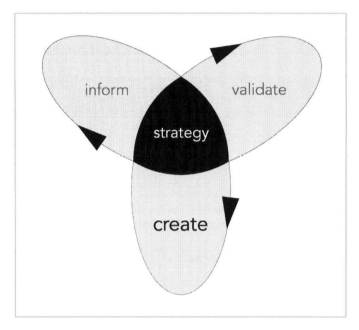

Figure 123 The create loop of strategy development

The second activity involved in the Triple-Loop Model of Strategy Development is the creative imagination of strategic ideas (Fig. 123). In a recent Harvard Business Review article,[17] New York University Professor, Adam Brandenburger, suggested that using strategy tools, especially the more rigorously analytical ones, such as Porter's Five Forces[18] and competitor mapping,[19] is better for understanding business context than dreaming up ways to re-shape it.

> *"Game-changing strategies… are born of creative thinking: a spark of intuition, a connection between different ways of thinking, a leap into the unexpected."[20]*

This fits with what you learned in Chapter 1 from Herbert Simon, Nobel prize winning economist and psychologist: strategy is not part of the "natural sciences [which] are concerned with how things are", but rather is part of the sciences of the artificial, which are "concerned with how things ought to be." [21]   The process of *doing* strategy is about devising "courses of action aimed at changing existing situations into preferred ones" – in other words it is a design process.

Design involves two distinct types of thinking, as first described in 1956[22] by J P Guilford, one of the founders of the psychology of creativity.[23] These are *divergent thinking* followed by *convergent thinking*.

8.3.1   Divergent thinking (from the word diverge, meaning to move apart) is the ability to think of lots of ideas. Guilford identified four key characteristics of divergent thinking:[24]

1.   *Fluency* – the ability to produce a great number of ideas or problem solutions in a short period of time;

2.   *Flexibility* – the ability to simultaneously propose a variety of approaches to a specific problem;

3.   *Originality* – the ability to produce new, original ideas;

4.   *Elaboration* – the ability to systematise, organise and further develop the details of an idea in your head.

8.3.2   Convergent thinking (from the word converge, meaning moving closer together) is often thought of as simply selecting the best or the correct idea produced during divergent thinking. This, however, is an over-simplification. Part of convergent thinking, as the name suggests, is the bringing together, the combining, the hybridisation or the synthesis of multiple individual ideas - this is *creative convergence* and is much more creative than simply idea selection.

Design is, therefore, a combination of divergent and convergent thinking. Think of a wide range of strategic possibilities and then merge, combine and synthesise them until you have a set of interconnected core ideas, around which you can build a strategy.

8.3.3 Bounded creativity – From what has just been said, you might imagine that the aim of divergent thinking is to produce lots and lots of ideas. Whilst the volume of ideas is important, it is not all that is important. Divergent thinking requires you to think of lots of ideas *matching a given set of criteria*. This is not just creativity. It's bounded creativity[25] and that's a lot harder.

A substantial body of research has shown that bounded creativity follows the Goldilocks principle:[26] creativity is boosted by some constraints but hampered by too many constraints. Design is, therefore, an iterative cycle of setting constraints, thinking of lots of ideas matching those constraints, converging on the best ideas and then re-evaluating and refining the constraints (Fig. 124).

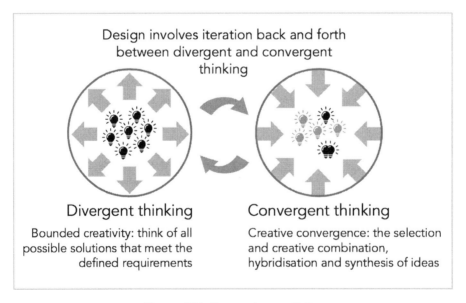

Figure 124 Strategic creativity

8.4   Framing as a method of creative thinking

The creative part of strategy development is enabled by a method called 'framing' (Fig. 125).

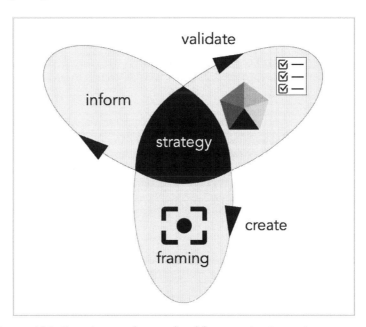

Figure 125 Framing as the method for creative input into strategy development

Let's start to explore the concept of framing with a parable originating in the Buddhist scripture Udana[27] that tells the tale of a group of blind men discovering an elephant for the first time (Fig. 126).[28]

> *The first man, having found the elephant's tusk, said the elephant was just like a spear.*
> *The second, touching the trunk, said it was like a fat snake.*
> *The third, touching one of the elephant's legs, said it was like a tree trunk.*
> *The fourth, at the elephant's tail, said the elephant was just like a rope.*

Figure 126 The parable of the four blind men and the elephant

To Buddhists, this parable shows that no individual can fully understand the teachings of the Buddha. For strategy development, we are going to use it to introduce a different lesson: the psychology of framing. You'll return to the elephant parable after this classic psychology experiment.

Amos Tversky and Daniel Kahneman, the founding fathers of behavioural economics, conducted a study in 1981 in which students were asked about how best the US should prepare for an outbreak of a new disease in Asia.[29] One group of students were asked which of the following options they would favour:

1. If Program A is adopted, 200 people will be saved.

2. If Program B is adopted, there is 1/3 probability that 600 people will be saved, and 2/3 probability that no people will be saved.

Just to be clear, the 'utility' outcome of both is identical – both programmes will save 200 people. It is just that program A states this categorically. Program B states this probabilistically. Despite these identical outcomes, 72% chose option A and only 28% chose option B.

A different group of students were then given the following options:

1. If Program C is adopted 400 people will die.

2. If Program D is adopted there is 1/3 probability that nobody will die, and 2/3 probability that 600 people will die.

The 'utility' outcome here is also identical – 400 people are going to die. Yet, in this case, only 22% chose option C and 78% chose option D, the reverse of the first experiment. So, programs A and C were presented as simple facts: 200 people will be saved or 400 will die. Programs B and D presented the same outcomes in terms of probability. In one case the factually-presented option was preferred (200 people will be saved). In the other case the factually-presented option was avoided (400 people will die). Why? The key to understanding these results is how we perceive and act in response to risk. When deciding about good news, we play safe. If 200 people are going to be saved, let's be sure they are actually saved – we pick the factually-presented option. When deciding about bad news, we are happy to take a chance. If 400 people are going to die, you'll go with the probability. As Tversky and Kahneman conclude "choices involving gains are often risk averse and choices involving losses are often risk taking."[30]

This is a great example of the psychological power of framing. Just as the blind men got very different impressions of what an elephant was, so we can all be nudged into very different impressions of what are, in fact, identical alternatives, by the way they are framed.

Sarah Kaplan, Professor of Strategic Management at the University of Toronto, studied the role of framing in strategic decision-making inside a telecommunications firm over an eight-month period.[31] Using ethnographic research techniques,[32] she interviewed key managers, attended meetings and was copied-in on all emails and documents as key strategies emerged within the firm. She was able to identify individuals who held different 'frames', meaning they held different views of both what the problem was and what the best solution was. These individuals formed shifting coalitions with others holding similar views (having similar frames) as the decision-making progressed. Kaplan describes, in detail, the 'framing contests' that took place as different individuals and groups tried to persuade others that their frame was the right frame. Depending on the social skills of the 'contestants' and the strength of the evidence they had accumulated, people would change their allegiance to a particular frame. When enough people aligned behind one specific frame, the group as a whole were well on the way towards a strategic decision. To try to win one of the framing contests, a slide presentation grew to 110 slides and then continued to grow to 238 slides before the framing contest was won.

This shows clearly the psychological, social and political forces at work in framing strategy development. This is a fact of life and no tools or processes will make these forces go away. You can, however, strive to make strategy framing more explicit. You can try to ensure the framing contests are more to do with strategic prospects and less to do with the social skills of the contestants. You can aspire to make strategic decision-making more transparent and the framing that led to those decisions better defined.

8.5   The framing methodology

Thus far, you have seen framing as a method of changing the context in which an issue is presented. So, each blind man came into contact with the elephant in a way that suggested it was a very different type of object. Had they been able to re-frame the situation, perhaps by walking around the elephant touching its tusks, trunk, legs and tail in sequence, they might have come a lot closer to conceptualising a single, very large animal with a diverse collection of body parts. Similarly, you can use framing to re-contextualise the strategy you are striving to develop, and in doing so, inject sources of creativity into your thinking. Here is a simple example.

Begin with an analysis of the Strengths, Weaknesses, Opportunities and Threats (SWOT) for your organisation (Fig. 127):

- *Strengths*: what do you do well right now? What resources do you have? What systems and procedures work well? How are you distinctive? How are you seen positively by others?

- *Weaknesses*: what areas need improvement? What resources or procedures are you lacking? How are you viewed negatively by others or seen as weak compared to your competitors?

- *Opportunities*: What opportunities will your strengths, or weaknesses, afford you in the future? Are there trends, developments or policy changes external to your organisation to take advantage of? Are there opportunities for small gains as well as big wins?

- *Threats*: What threats will your strengths and weaknesses expose you to? Are there trends, developments or policy changes that might damage your organisation? What challenges could you face from changes in your competitors, marketplace, supply chain, customer-base or technology?

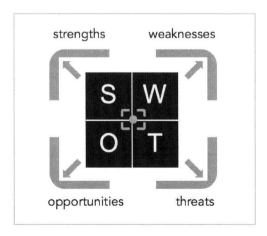

Figure 127 SWOT analysis framing for creative input into strategy development

On the template for 'SWOT frame-stretching' (Figure 136 given in Section 8.6) fill the boxes marked current strengths / weaknesses and future opportunities / threats; identifying two for each will be fine, for now. You are now going to *frame-stretch* them.

Work around the template to imagine what your strategy might contain if focused entirely on, in turn, your strengths, weaknesses, opportunities and threats. By doing so, you stretch your strategy in different directions, by framing it in different contexts. This is divergent thinking (Fig. 128).

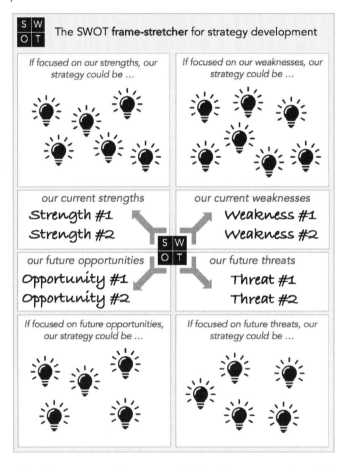

Figure 128 Generating ideas using SWOT frame-stretching (divergent thinking)

A second meaning of the word 'frame' reveals you can use the concept of framing for convergent thinking as well. A frame is an 'enclosing border' around a picture, a door, a window or the lenses in a pair of glasses.[33] Since one of the key roles of strategy is to distinguish between what you choose to do and what you choose not to do, a frame can be a useful metaphor to demarcate what is included within strategy and what is excluded. Section 8.6 provides a 'frame-setter' template to be used alongside the 'frame-stretcher' for SWOT analysis. In completing the frame-setting template, you differentiate between what's included in strategy and what's excluded, whilst imagining your strategy is focused on just your strengths, weaknesses, opportunities or threats. You can use the ideas you generated in frame-stretching as a basis for this exercise. This is convergent thinking; the selection and creative combination, hybridisation and synthesis of ideas (Fig. 129).

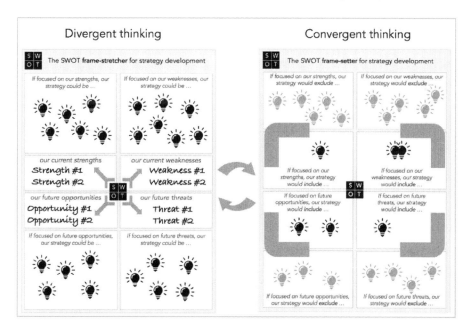

Figure 129 Frame-stretching (divergent thinking) and frame-setting (convergent thinking)

This frame-stretcher and frame-setter approach can be used with a wide variety of strategy models (Fig. 130) helping you to re-frame your strategy in different ways, and then both generate and refine creative strategy ideas bounded by these different frames. Whilst developing a new strategy, you can use several of these models to try to maximise your creative input into the process.

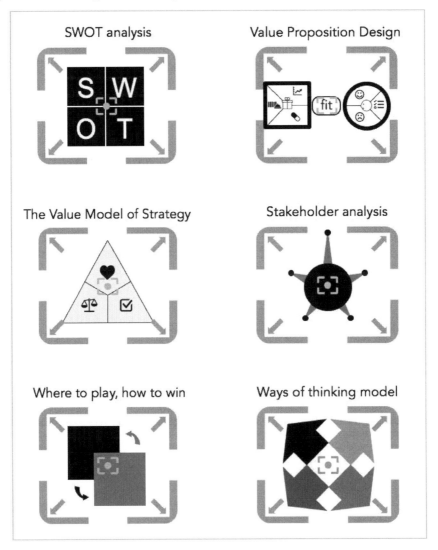

Figure 130 Strategy models for frame-stretching and frame-setting

Thomas Howard, Associate Professor at the Technical University of Denmark, aggregated data from several industrial studies and found that "the rate of idea generation during brainstorming decreases slowly and steadily after 30 minutes, with a dramatic decrease in idea quality after just 20 minutes ... the introduction of stimuli into the brainstorm sessions was beneficial and helped to maintain idea frequency and quality."[34] So, as a guide, only use these framing models in brief (less than 1 hour) sessions. If, after that time, you feel the issue remains unresolved or more could be gained from it, you probably need to add data (research and analysis), add new people (to gain fresh perspective) or re-frame the issue, using a different model (such as the ones you are about to discover). It is unlikely you will make further progress just by spending longer on it.

Having already looked at framing for SWOT analysis in the example above, let's look now at how you can use the other five models in Figure 130 for strategy frame-stretching and subsequent frame-setting. Templates for all these framing exercises are given in Section 8.6, after the descriptions of the models below.

8.5.1 Value Proposition Design framing

Originally from Alex Osterwalder and Yves Pigneur's wonderful book *Business Model Generation*,[35] this Value Proposition Design model[36] explores the 'jobs' a customer needs to get done and the gains and pains associated with these jobs right now. In their language, a job is not an occupation. It is a customer need that a product or service can fulfil. They describe customer jobs as "the things your customers are trying to get done in their work or in their life. A customer job could be the tasks they are trying to perform and complete, the problems they are trying to solve, or the needs they are trying to satisfy."[37] The customer jobs a mobile phone might satisfy, for example, might be functional (to make phone calls, be woken up in the morning, take photos etc.), emotional (to keep in contact with friends and family, to stop worrying about being late etc.) or social (to look good or appear successful).

The Value Proposition Design model then explores new products and services that could be offered to harness the gains or relieve the pains associated with these jobs. A match between customer needs and the products and services offered indicates product-market fit.

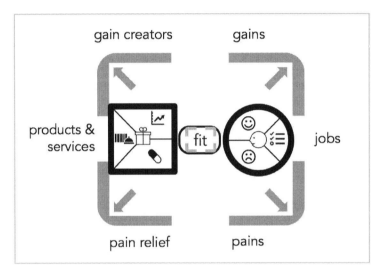

Figure 131 Value Proposition Design framing for creative input into strategy development

To use this model in strategy frame-stretching (Fig. 131), focus first on customer jobs. Which customer jobs do you, as an organisation, enable, facilitate or support? How could your strategy change that? Could you widen the range of customer jobs you facilitate? Could you focus them more sharply? Flip them so you focus on the same jobs but for a different customer, or the same customer but different jobs. Then re-frame, so you are focused on gains – what benefits, what joy, what delight does your customer get from your organisation? Could you give more of it? Could you provide it in a different way? Could you make it last longer? Re-frame on to customer pains. Can you, as an organisation, relieve your customers pain more effectively? In a faster-acting way? Does your customer suffer pains that you don't currently address? Then finally, re-frame on to your products and services. In light of your focus on customers and their gains and pains, how could your strategy change your product and service offering? Extend the range? Change its positioning / branding? Deliver in different ways? Remember, when using this example, you must not slip into redesigning one of your products. Keep focused on strategy. What does Value Proposition Design tell you about your whole organisation, and its future direction? You can then move on to frame-setting, where you consider what your strategy would include and exclude if focused on the different areas you have identified by frame-stretching. Templates for frame-stretching and frame-setting using the Value Proposition Design model are given in Section 8.6.

8.5.2 The Value Model of Strategy framing

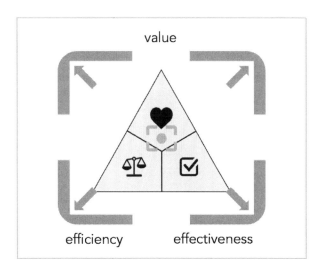

Figure 132 Value Model of Strategy framing for creative input into strategy development

You discovered the Value Model of Strategy in Chapter 3, if you want to go back and refresh your memory. Using this model for strategy framing (Fig. 132) forces you to think deeply about the value your organisation offers and what value you get back in return. Does the value you deliver enable your customers to make money? Or make their lives easier? What value do you deliver to the world?

Once you have some ideas about value, you turn your attention to what it means to be effective in delivering that value. What would it take to have excellent effectiveness? What about world-class effectiveness? Then finally turn to efficiency. What do you have to 'spend' (what resources do you need) to be really effective in delivering value? How could that be improved and what would world-class efficiency look like? Templates for frame-stretching and frame-setting using the Value Model of Strategy are given in Section 8.6 and you will see framing using the Value Model of Strategy applied to our Artigence case study in Section 8.11.

8.5.3 Stakeholder analysis framing

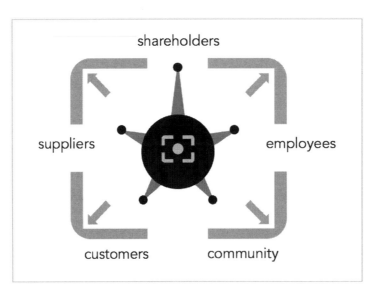

Figure 133 Stakeholder analysis framing for creative input into strategy development

Your first task here is to define your key stakeholders for purposes of strategy analysis. Whose interests do you want to have driving the content of your new strategy? Graham Kenny, CEO of Australian consultancy Strategic Factors, suggests strategy should be based upon the interests of the following key stakeholders in the organisation: owners, customers, employees and suppliers.[38] Here, however, you will use five stakeholders: shareholders, customers, employees, suppliers and community (Fig. 133). The 'community' stakeholder represents the broad social impact your organisation might have at local, national and global level. Now adapt your frame-stretcher and frame-setter templates (given in Section 8.6) for this stakeholder analysis. For frame-stretching, what could your strategy be if focused on shareholders, customers, employees, suppliers or community? For frame-setting, if focused on shareholders, customer, employees, suppliers or community, what would your strategy include and what would it exclude?

8.5.4 'Where to play, how to win' framing

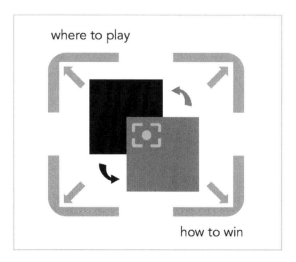

Figure 134 Where to play, how to win framing for creative input into strategy development

The 'where to play, how to win' model comes from AG Lafley and Roger Martin's excellent book *Playing to Win: How Strategy Really Works.*[39] Strategy, they claim, is about making specific choices to win in the marketplace. Two of those key choices are:

1. Where to play – where will you compete, which geographies, product categories, consumer segments and channels?

2. How to win – what is your value proposition and competitive advantage?

Used in strategy framing (Fig. 134) this model forces you to think how your strategy could potentially change your market positioning. Could you, for example, enter different geographies or different product categories? Could you target different customer segments or reach them through different channels? And could you find new ways to win, wherever you choose to play? How can you optimise your product, service, price or distribution to beat your competitors? Templates for framing exercises using 'where to play, how to win' are given in Section 8.6.

8.5.5 'Ways of thinking' model framing

Adam Brandenburger, whose ideas you learned about in Section 8.3 on creative thinking, suggests four ways of thinking to unlock breakthrough strategic ideas,[40] as shown in Figure 135.

1. *Contrast*: what conventional wisdom can you question? Here are a few historical examples: movies that used to be picked up and returned to a local Blockbuster store were disrupted by Netflix's mail-order and then streaming model. Money that used to be transferred from one bank to another was then disrupted by PayPal's person-to-person money transfer. Taxis and taxi drivers that used to be heavily regulated and licensed by city authorities were disrupted by Uber.

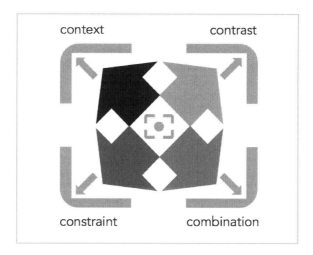

Figure 135 'Ways of thinking' framing for creative input into strategy development

2. *Combination:* which products and services that traditionally have been separate, can be connected? The company Tencent combined a social media platform and a mobile payment system within WeChat. Apple is combining mobile technology with health monitoring in the Apple Watch.

3. *Constraint:* turn limitations into opportunities. A lovely example, cited in Brandenburger's article,[41] comes from Audi who set out to win the Le Mans 24 Hours race but concluded they couldn't make their cars go faster than the competition. This about-as-bad-as-it-gets limitation was turned to their advantage by forcing them to develop diesel-powered race-cars which required fewer pit-stops. Audi went on to win three Le Mans races in a row between 2004 and 2006.

4. *Context:* How can far-flung industries, ideas or disciplines shed light on your more pressing challenges? One of the all-time classics has got to be George de Mestral who put burdock seeds under a microscope to investigate what it was about them that made them stick to his dog and his clothes so effectively. The answer led him

to the invention of Velcro. Similarly, the low-tack adhesive developed by Dr Spencer Silver at 3M in 1968 was seen as a 'solution without a problem' until, in 1974, a colleague of Dr Silver's, Arthur Fry, came up with the idea of using the adhesive to secure his bookmark in his hymn book; and so the Post-it Note was born.[42]

You can explore the 'ways of thinking' model for frame-stretching and frame-setting using the templates given in Section 8.6.

8.6   Templates for frame-stretching and frame-setting

The following pages contain templates for frame-stretching (divergent thinking) and frame-setting (convergent thinking) for the creative use in strategy development of the six strategy models described in Section 8.5:

1. SWOT analysis (Fig. 136 and Fig. 137)

2. Value Proposition Design (Fig. 138 and Fig. 139)

3. Value Model of Strategy (Fig. 140 and Fig. 141)

4. Stakeholder analysis (Fig. 142 and Fig. 143)

5. 'Where to play, how to win' (Fig. 144 and Fig. 145)

6. 'Ways of thinking' model (Fig. 146 and Fig. 147).

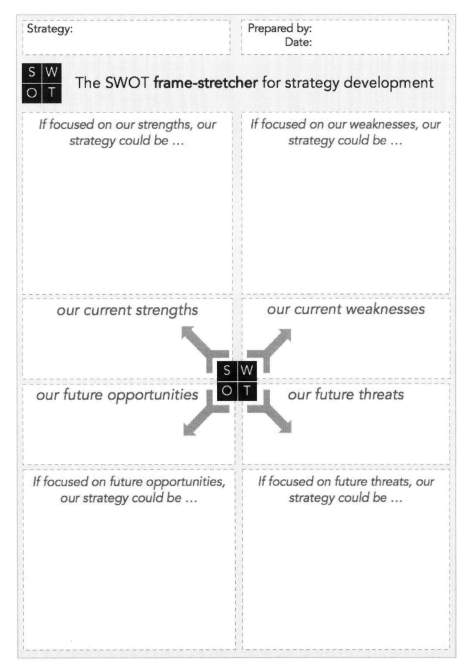

Figure 136 The SWOT frame-stretcher for strategy development

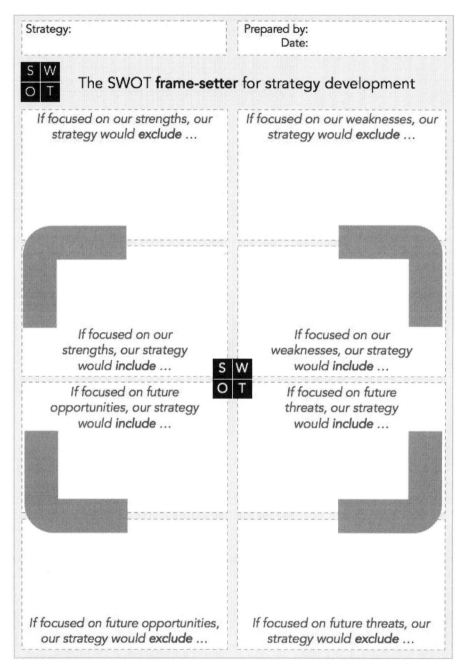

Figure 137 The SWOT frame-setter for strategy development

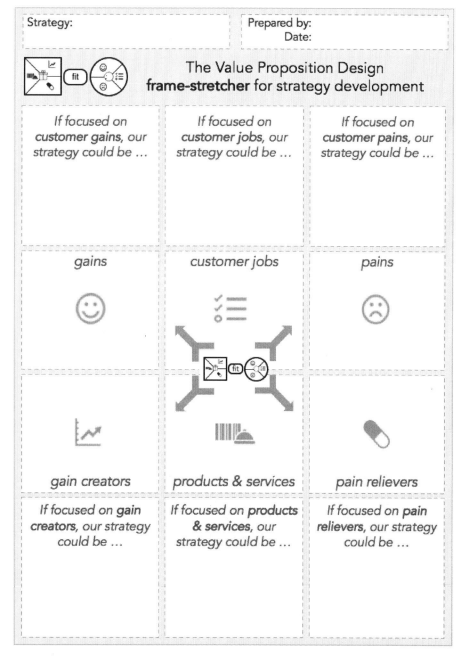

Figure 138 The Value Proposition Design frame-stretcher for strategy development

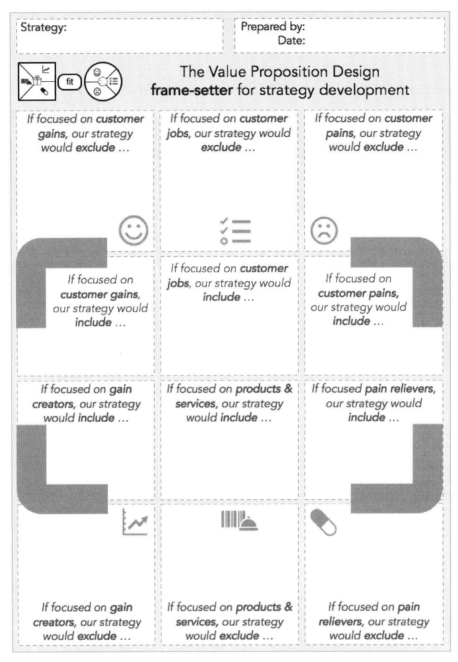

Figure 139 The Value Proposition Design frame-setter for strategy development

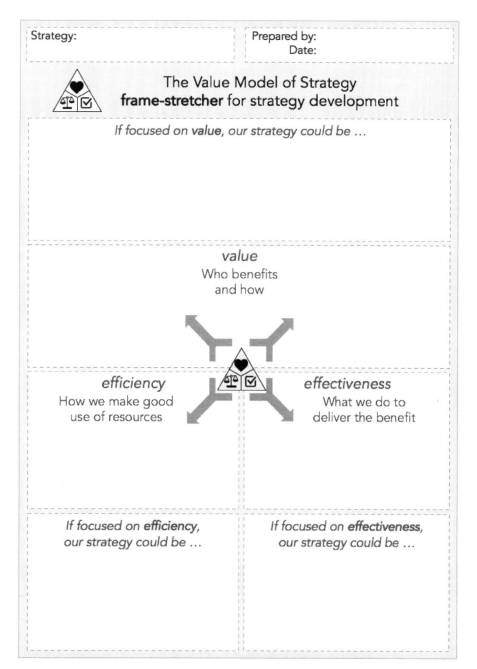

Figure 140 The Value Model of Strategy frame-stretcher for strategy development

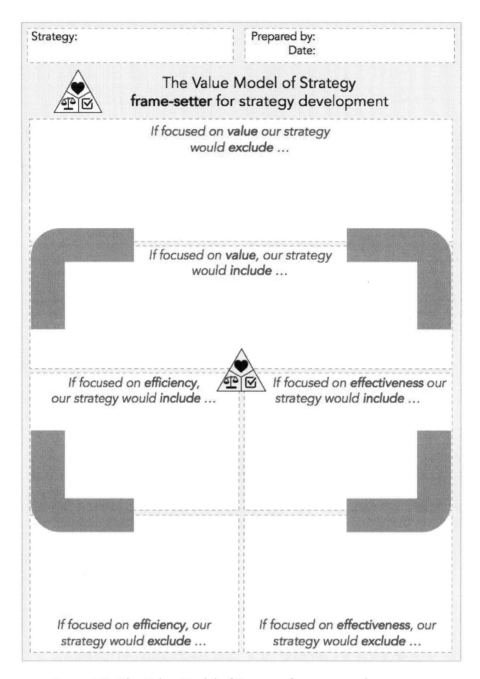

Figure 141 The Value Model of Strategy frame-setter for strategy development

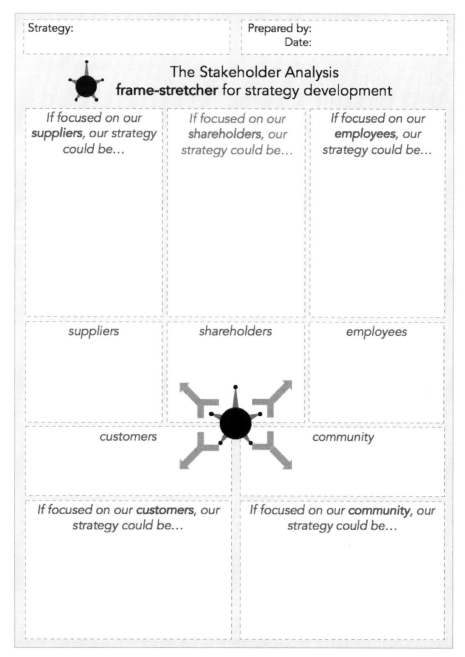

Figure 142 The Stakeholder Analysis frame-stretcher for strategy development

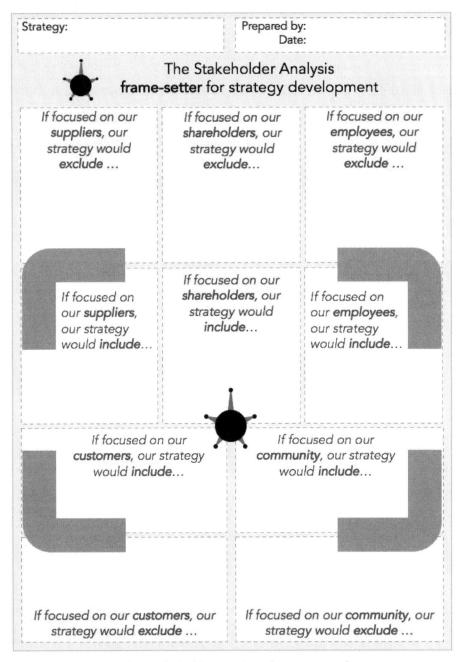

Figure 143 The Stakeholder Analysis frame-setter for strategy development

Strategy:	Prepared by: Date:

The Where to Play, How to Win
frame-stretcher for strategy development

*If focused on **where to play**, our strategy could be …*

where to play
where will we compete, which geographies, product
categories, consumer segments and channels?

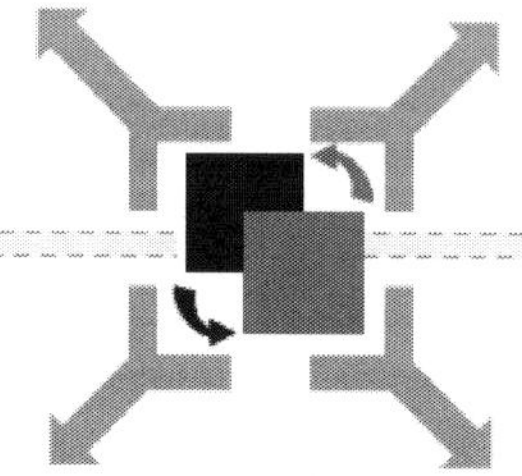

how to win
what is our value proposition and competitive advantage?

*If focused on **how to win**, our strategy could be …*

Figure 144 The 'Where to play, how to win' frame-stretcher for strategy
development

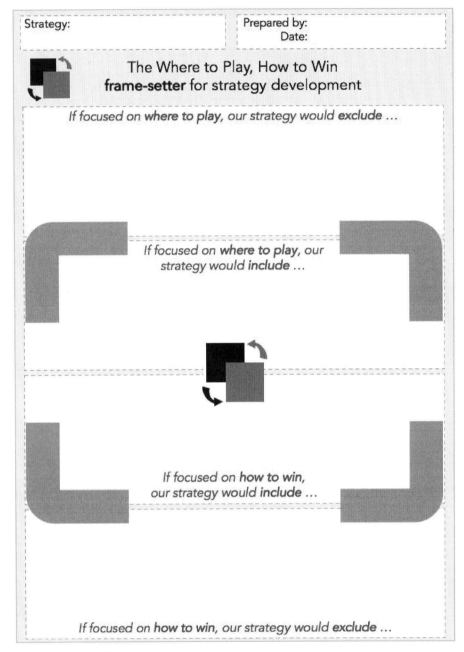

Figure 145 The 'Where to play, how to win' frame-setter for strategy development

Strategy:	Prepared by: Date:

The Ways of Thinking
frame-stretcher for strategy development

*If focused on **context**, our strategy could be …*	*If focused on **contrast**, our strategy could be …*

context
how can other industries, ideas or disciplines shed light on your challenges?

contrast
what conventional wisdom can you question?

constraint
how can you turn limitations into opportunities?

combination
which products / services, that are currently separate, can be connected?

*If focused on **constraint**, our strategy could be …*	*If focused on **combination**, our strategy could be …*

Figure 146 The 'Ways of thinking' frame-stretcher for strategy development

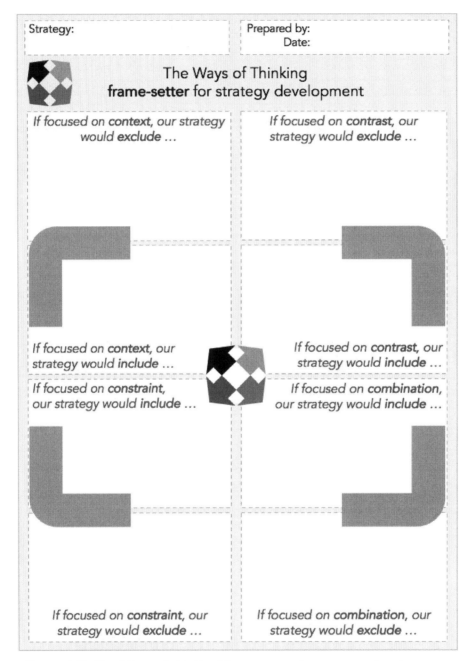

Figure 147 The 'Ways of thinking' frame-setter for strategy development

8.7   Informing the strategy development process

Having explored how to create and validate strategic ideas, you now need to consider the final loop in the strategy development model. Strategy development cannot happen solely in the strategist's head; it must be informed by data from the outside world. Data which needs to be researched, analysed, interpreted and turned into strategic insights and Key Performance Indicators (KPIs – see Chapter 6 on strategy measurement).

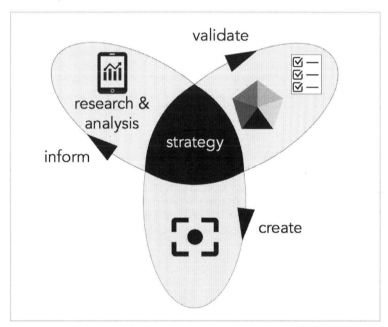

Figure 148 Strategy development needs to be informed by research and analysis

Of course, adding research insights into strategy development is a lot easier said than done. The particular insights you need will depend upon the strategic ideas you have created, and the questions raised by their validation. In addition, the strategic ideas you create will be shaped by the research insights gleaned so far. This brings us back to the notion that strategy development must be a looping, iterative process in order to fully refine the resultant strategy (Fig. 148).

In general, however, strategy will need to be informed by research and analysis in three areas: customers, competitors and capabilities.

1. **Customer research** – examples include:

   a. *Research to better understand customers*: for example, customer needs analysis, customer task analysis, ethnographic research.

   b. *Customer 'response' research*: this approach prompts the customer for their response to one or more objects, images or descriptions. This can be used to evaluate brand preferences, discover what they like and dislike about product features, test their response to proposed prices or ask what they think of new product ideas.

   c. *Market analysis*: research focused on how best to categorise and cluster groups of customers together. This could include media profiling to target advertising better, geographic profiling to plan retail expansion or customer segmentation to personalise emails and website content to interests and preferences.

2. **Competitor research** – examples include:

   a. *Price-value mapping*: a simple scatter graph showing how different products vary in price along one axis and value along the other axis.

   b. *Porter's Five Forces Analysis*:[43] An economic analysis of the positioning of competitors in the marketplace, in terms of:

      i. *Rivalry* – few competitors with little rivalry tend leads to stronger market positioning and larger margins;

ii. *Supplier Power* – the more you depend on a small number of powerful suppliers, the less bargaining power you have with them;

iii. *Buyer Power* – few buyers making large orders increases your dependency on them and hence their purchasing power over you;

iv. *Threat of Substitution* – the more your products and services can be swapped out by alternatives, the less power you have in the marketplace;

v. *Threat of New Entry* – the more readily new businesses can enter your market, the more likely you are to find yourself facing new competitors.

3. **Capabilities research** – examples include:

a. *Digital transformation audit:* how could digital technology enable you to add value or drive operational efficiencies?

b. *Innovation review:* how capable are you currently at innovation? How does your track record compare to your industry peers?

8.8   The Strategy Design Model

So, you have created, validated and researched lots of strategy ideas and your strategy is starting to take shape. How, then, do you make sure that the strategy features all the elements that are needed? Imagine it is a vehicle you are designing instead of a strategy. There are several design features you would want to know it had in place, to be sure it was fit-for-purpose. Propulsion, steering and brakes would be a good start. What, then, is the equivalent set of design features that makes strategy fit for purpose? The Strategy Design Model provides the answer (Fig. 149). This model comprises eight interlinked elements that every good strategy should be designed to feature.

Figure 149 The Strategy Design Model

1. **Destination** – where you are striving to get to. What is your "winning aspiration?"[44] What is the important end you are striving to reach?[45]

2. **Methods** – what are the handful of core activities that are critical for you to reach your destination?

Destination and methods are the essence of strategy. They are what strategy is designed around. Your strategy also needs to be designed so that its goals are appropriately aligned, innovative and prioritised, and that strategy success is measurable:

3. **Alignment** – the logic connecting actions to outcomes. If everyone in your organisation is pulling in the same direction, you will achieve more and achieve it quicker than if they are pulling in different directions.

4. **Innovation** – the cultivation of new ways of thinking and working. How much innovation does the strategy demand? How will you build the organisational capability and culture to achieve it?

5. **Priority** – the identification of what really matters. Peter Drucker, known as the 'founder of modern management'[46] says "The worst thing is to do a little bit of everything. It is better to pick the wrong priority than none at all."[47]

6. **Performance** – data indicative of meaningful progress. "What gets measured, gets managed!"[48] Whilst this may be true, it is not always a good thing if the changes that matter most are the hardest to measure (e.g. aspects of culture change within an organisation). The measurement of progress serves two purposes: firstly, it justifies continued commitment to the strategy and secondly it informs course-correction and fine-tuning of strategy adoption.

Finally, your strategy needs to be designed to be adaptable and adoption-ready:

7. **Adaptability** – resilience and agility combined. According to Rita Gunther McGrath, author of the best-selling *The End of Competitive Advantage,*[49] "the traditional approach of building a business around a competitive advantage and then hunkering down to defend it … no longer makes sense."[50] "Instead, organizations need to forge a new path to winning: capturing opportunities fast, exploiting them decisively, and moving on even before they are exhausted."[51] A key element of strategy is defining how the organisation is going to respond to change, how it is going to move fast and take advantage of new opportunities as they arise.

8. **Adoption** – active engagement, willing commitment. The success of every strategy depends on the support it can recruit from the individuals needed to bring about change, which is why we call it adoption: less push, more pull. Putting people at the centre of

strategy design ensures their involvement, commitment and active engagement. The governing body and senior leadership need to adopt the strategy and ensure their decisions both support the strategy and avoid eroding or undermining it. Front-line employees and key stakeholders (customers, suppliers, business partners etc.) need to think and work in ways conducive to making the changes sought by the strategy.

By putting the Strategy Design Model at the heart of strategy development, you ensure that your strategy has all the design elements it needs. This completes the Triple-Loop Model of Strategy Development (Fig. 150).

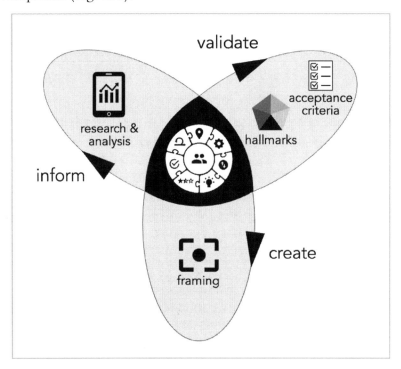

Figure 150 The Strategy Design Model as part of the Triple-Loop Model of Strategy Development

Figure 151 gives a checklist for the elements from the Strategy Design Model.

Strategy:	Prepared by:
	Date:

Strategy Design Checklist

Strategy Summary:

Destination	What is your "winning aspiration?"
Where you are striving to get to	What is the important end you are striving to reach?

Methods	What are the handful of core activities
Core activities to reach your destination	that are critical for you to reach your destination?

Alignment	Are your goals aligned so that everyone
The logic connecting actions to outcomes	is pulling in the same strategic direction?

Innovation	How much innovation does the strategy
The cultivation of new ways of thinking and working	demand? How will you build the capability and culture to achieve it?

Priority	Have you prioritised your goals?
The identification of what really matters	Do your priorities add up to strategic success?

Performance	Are your goals measurable? Will your
Data indicative of meaningful progress	measurements enable fine-tuning of your strategy or a change of course if necessary?

Adaptability	Is your strategy capable of responding to
Resilience and agility combined	change? Will you be able to move fast to take advantage of new opportunities?

Adoption	Does your strategy have the support of
Active engagement, willing commitment	the individuals needed to bring about change?

Figure 151 Strategy Design Checklist

8.9   Strategic decision-making

You've been through the process. You may have looped through it several times. You have designed and synthesised. All the elements are in place. You have validated. You have a strategy. Or, at least you think you have. All that is left is to decide finally that this IS actually your strategy and commit to it. How does that work?

The first thing to say is that having a strategy that meets your acceptance criteria, ticks all the hallmarks of good strategy and derives logically from the insights you have obtained from research and analysis is a remarkable achievement – well done! You have made it through the odyssey of strategy development and come out at the end with a result. A true hero's journey.

It should be emphasised that the validation criteria you set yourself within the Triple-Loop Model of Strategy Development are already a high bar for strategy acceptance. For most purposes, this should be sufficient. There is, however, one further final stage of best practice you might wish to consider.

Daniel Kahneman is a Nobel prize winning behavioural economist and best-selling author of *Thinking, Fast and Slow*.[52] When he warns that there are some really bad ways of making strategic decisions, and then offers advice on how to do it better, you probably need to listen.

Kahneman, with co-authors Dan Lovallo and Olivier Sibony begin their article[53] by comparing strategy decisions with recruitment decisions. They point out that the most common way of interviewing candidates for a job is by means of unstructured interviews. This question and answer format, which may cover a defined set of issues but does so in an informal, conversational way, leads to "biased evaluations that have very little predictive value" according to extensive research.[54]

They suggest that there are three key psychological problems with unstructured interviews:

1. As interviewers, we develop *quick and sticky mental models* of people on the basis of limited evidence early in the process and only adjust these models slowly, giving first impressions a disproportionate effect out our decision;

2. Our mental models tend to have *excessive coherence* – they are simpler and more coherent than reality. This comes about partly because we tend to ask questions to confirm what we already expect;

3. Our evaluations have *biased weighting* – we don't give all the bits of information the weight they deserve, because we will discount some important bits of information and give great weight to factors that ought to be irrelevant.

As a result, many organisations, including Amazon, Google and McKinsey have changed their recruitment processes to structured interviews, using what Kahneman et al call the Mediated Assessment Protocol (MAP). This works by:

1. defining the assessments in advance;

2. ensuring that all assessments are done independently by multiple people, using fact-based assessments where possible;

3. making the final evaluation after all the mediating assessments are complete.

The same applies to strategic decision-making. Done in an unstructured way, it is subject to huge biases and is likely to appear a lot more coherent than it actually is – especially to the person who wrote it!

Here is how you should follow Kahneman et al's protocol for strategy development, with some accompanying comments about the value and challenges along the way. The aim is to provide final validation for your new strategy by showing that several independent assessors prefer this strategy over an alternative.

Step #1 The process requires you to have two viable strategies to compare. This may be a struggle; it is great that you made it through all the validation checks with one strategy intact, but two? That's unlikely. So, instead you could compare your preferred strategy with the best of the strategy ideas you rejected. Now you are no longer deciding which of the two strategies to run with, but you are giving your preferred strategy a final acceptance test.

Step #2 Decide on the assessment criteria in advance – these can mostly come from your acceptance criteria and hallmarks of good strategy. Check they are as fact-based as possible and improve them in this respect if necessary.

Step #3 Recruit your strategy assessors. Three is probably a good number. Try to ensure they are all well informed about the organisation, its core business, its competitors and the opportunities and obstacles it faces.

Step #4 Get your assessors to undertake their assessments, using the assessment criteria provided. They should do this independently and uninfluenced by the assessment of others.

Step #5 Bring your assessors together to make their final evaluation of the strategy, based on their individual, fact-based assessments.

Taking this final step to evaluate your strategy can ensure that you avoid biased evaluations that can get in the way of strategy success.

8.10 The practicalities of strategy development

You have learnt a lot of the theory behind strategy development, so now to the practicalities. What follows is a summary of how you put strategy development into practice. You begin by taking the strategy acceptance criteria from strategy scoping. You add generic hallmarks of good strategy and you end up with a robust set of validation criteria to check if any strategy you create is good enough to launch. You then start creating strategy ideas, by framing and re-framing your thoughts about strategy. Specifically, you work through divergent (idea-generating) thinking by frame-stretching and then convergent (idea-selecting and -combining) thinking by frame-setting. As strategy ideas develop, research and analysis provides the insight to inform validation and inspire creativity. Vague disconnected ideas about strategy start to be pulled together through the Strategy Design Model. The destination they seek becomes clearer, the core methods of reaching that destination come into focus. The innovation involved becomes clearer. Some ideas emerge of how strategic success could be measured.

8.10.1 The 'candidate' strategy

Gradually you will approach the point where you have a candidate for the new strategy. It's not complete yet, but you can see what type of strategy it would be if more work was done on it. Now's the time to move to validation. How well does it fit the acceptance criteria you produced in strategy scoping? Does it meet each of the hallmarks of good strategy? This validation work should reveal gaps in your strategic thinking, weaknesses in the design of your strategy or perhaps simply unanswered questions. Could you resolve these with research and analysis? Do you need another round of creative re-framing?

8.10.2 Strategy development log

Take care to log each step in your strategic thinking, as you progress, just as you did with your strategy scoping log. This may be in the form of a dedicated document (Fig. 152) or included in the minutes of meetings where progress on strategy development is considered.

Ideally, for each step in your thinking, you should note down:

1. *Your starting point.* At the beginning of this step what did you know, what were you thinking, what were you anticipating?

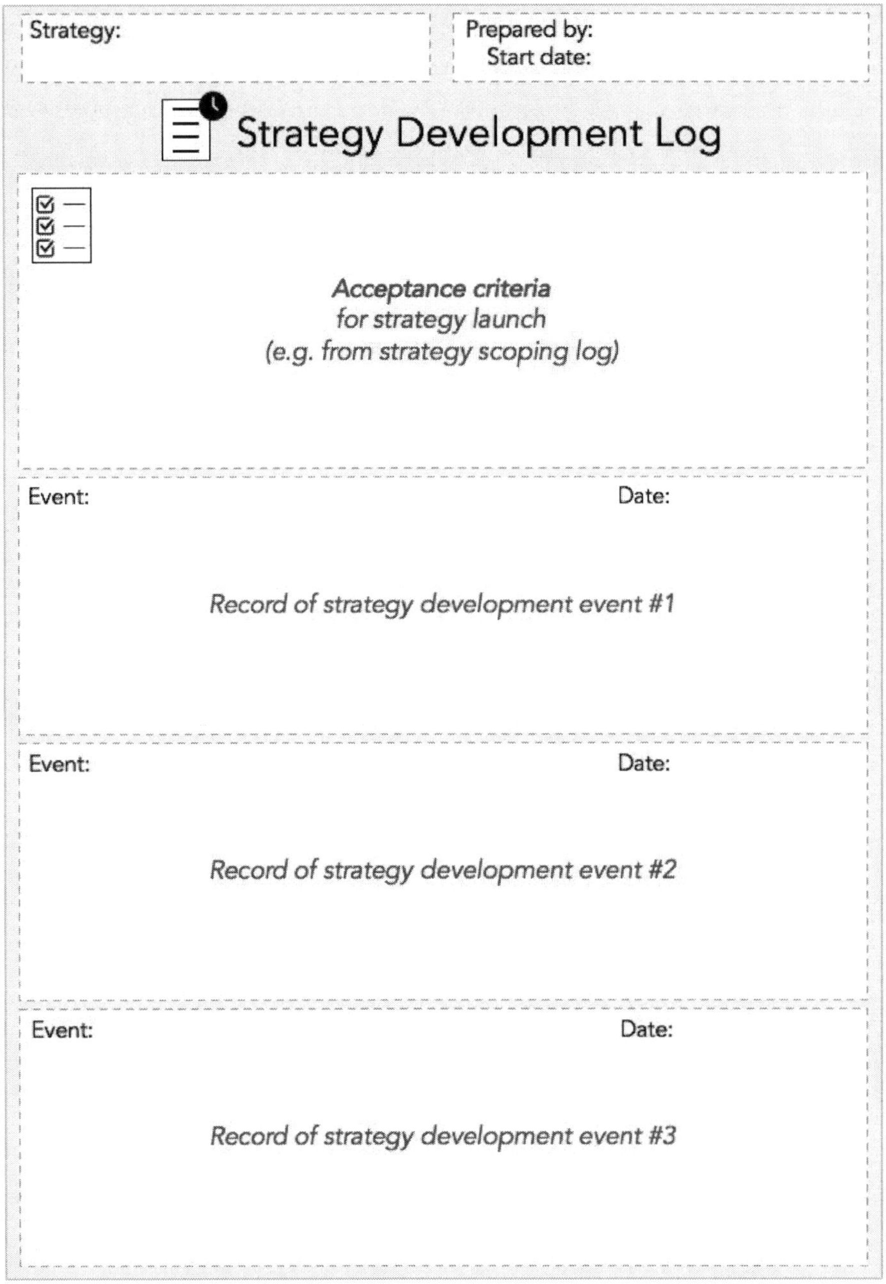

Strategy:	Prepared by:
	Start date:

📄 Strategy Development Log

☑ —
☑ —
☑ —

Acceptance criteria
for strategy launch
(e.g. from strategy scoping log)

Event: Date:

Record of strategy development event #1

Event: Date:

Record of strategy development event #2

Event: Date:

Record of strategy development event #3

Figure 152 Strategy Development Log

2. *What you did.* Research? Analysis? Creative thinking? Validating your conclusions so far? Challenging prior assumptions? Throwing everything in the bin and starting again?

3. *Your end point.* What insights did you glean? What new ideas did you generate? What conclusions did you reach? What questions remain? What should the next step be?

As you loop back and forth between creating and validating your strategy, you may realise that the acceptance criteria you came up with in strategy scoping need to be changed. This is fine, and in a research-intensive strategy development process, almost inevitable, as you learn what your strategy could or should be. What you need to take great care to avoid is changing the acceptance criteria simply to make your favoured approach to strategy acceptable. So, be especially careful to log any changes to these acceptance criteria. Be clear about what they were to begin with, what you now propose they are changed to and why. What makes you think the new acceptance criteria are better? In what way are they more favourable to the interests of the organisation? How would the organisation's interests suffer or be at risk if the acceptance criteria remained in their original form?

8.10.3 Strategy launch

At the end of the strategy development process you will have a documented strategy identifying:

1. Strategy destination – where you are trying to get to;

2. Strategy success criteria – how you will confirm that you have reached your destination;

3. The core methods used to get there;

4. The overall benefits to your organisation of reaching this destination.

Having committed to this new strategy you need to ensure that it is ratified by the board, as agreed in strategy governance (see Chapter 5). Then all that remains is to prepare the assets for strategy launch. For a small organisation this may simply be a printed document, PowerPoint and a speech by the Chief Executive. For a larger organisation, it could involve a PR campaign and an internal marketing campaign with all the digital and print assets these require.

8.11 Case study: Artigence strategy development

Artigence entered strategy development with four clear strategy acceptance criteria from strategy scoping (what the new strategy needed to feature to be accepted and launched). The new strategy must:

1. have an agreed end–date;

2. have an agreed growth target to be reached by this strategy end–date, measured in £ Annual Recurring Revenue (ARR);

3. involve the identification of five viable new apps from research and analysis;

4. be sufficiently detailed to inform product-driven growth projections.

Strategy development began by frame-stretching their initial strategy ideas, using the Value Proposition Design model (Fig. 153). They then used the results of this for frame-setting (Fig. 154).

Had it been up to Katerina, they would have missed this step altogether and jumped straight into market research. Whenever Daniel believed in a process, however, he stuck to it. So, they worked through the frame-stretcher / frame-setter process. It didn't come up with anything unexpected, but it did immerse them in a 'range extension' strategy more deeply than they would have done otherwise. Without this, they would not have been primed to see its fatal flaw when it arose.

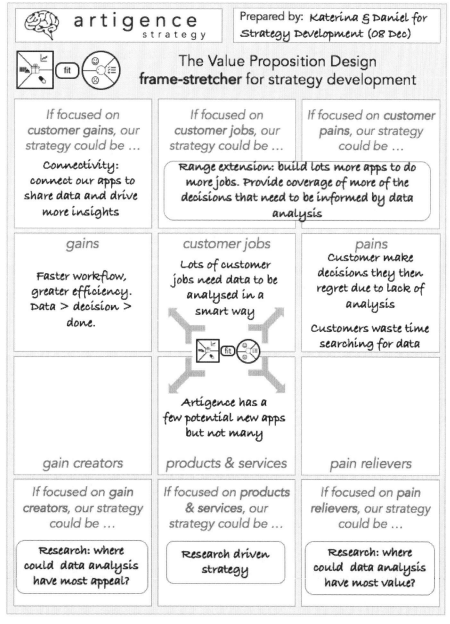

Figure 153 Value Proposition Design frame-stretcher for Artigence

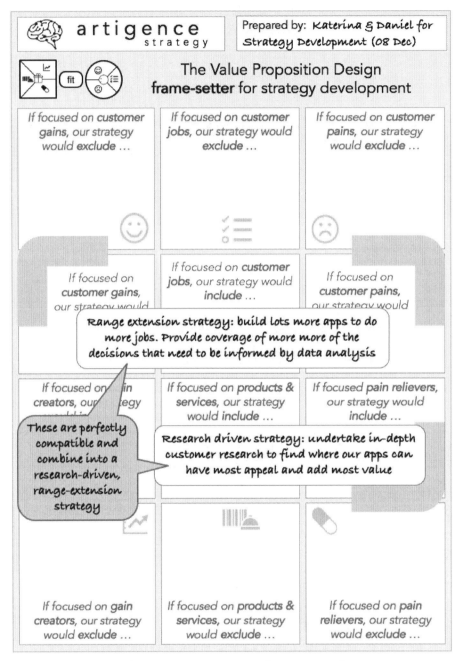

Figure 154 Value Proposition Design frame-setter for Artigence

Nobody was in any doubt that customers had lots of potential applications for smart data apps. Customers who were already using one of Artigence's apps were especially vocal in explaining how they could use the same type of solution in many other aspects of their work. This was the driver for their strategy idea to extend their range of smart data apps and to use customer research to identify which areas of application were most promising. They just needed to convince themselves (and subsequently, the board) that there were a handful of obvious, high-demand apps they could develop to launch this range extension strategy. They began the research.

Now, bear in mind, this research was intended to identify a handful of viable opportunities for new apps. It was not designed to question whether building new apps was a good idea. Artigence was a successful business. Their past couple of years' growth was faster than anyone had imagined. All they needed to do was to do more of the same. Or so they thought.

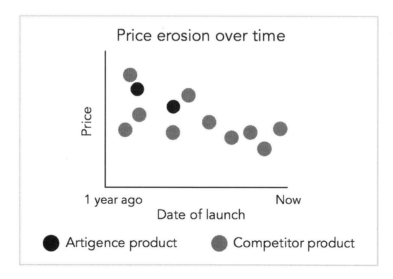

Figure 155 Artigence competitor research and analysis showing price erosion over time

The research, as expected, revealed lots of unmet needs for new data apps. What was less expected was the rate of new entrants into the smart data apps marketplace. Even more unexpected than that was what this was doing to prices (Fig. 155). Most of the new market entrants appeared to be selling clones of top-selling apps for knock-down prices (Fig. 156). Daniel, who read philosophy as an undergraduate, emailed Katerina about the results, ending with "Life for a start-up in an undifferentiated market is nasty, brutish and short". [55]

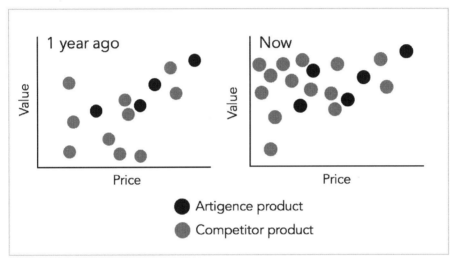

Figure 156 Artigence competitor analysis showing change in Price-Value

They needed to get back to first principles and re-think what it was they offered and how they could maintain differentiation and add more value for their customers. They chose to frame-stretch again but this time using the Value Model of Strategy. They needed to dig deep into what value they offered, to whom and how they could maximise their differentiation from all of these low-price competitors. The results of this new frame-stretcher are shown in Figure 157.

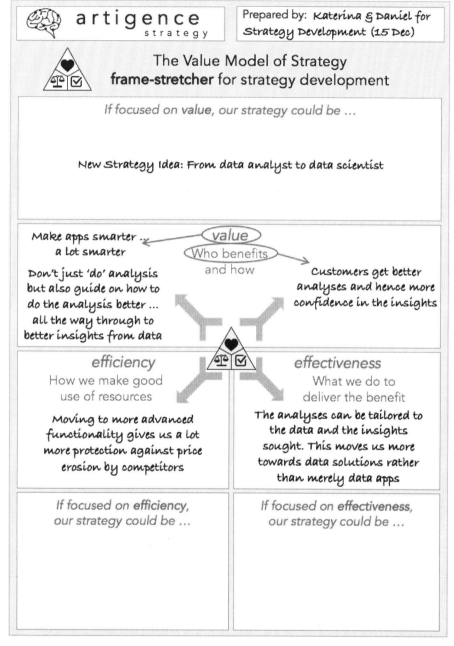

Figure 157 Value Model of Strategy frame-stretcher for Artigence

This frame-stretching quickly led to a new strategy idea. The breakthrough came when Daniel invited Bashir, who he had recently employed as a software engineer, to join the session. Bashir was a good software engineer, who coded well. He was also consistent in his comments that Artigence really ought to make their apps smarter. After Daniel had taken him through the idea of frame-stretching and the Value Model of Strategy, Bashir jumped straight in.

"Value, yes, value is a great way to look at it. The greatest way to add value to data is to analyse it in smart ways. Not always in the same way, regardless of the data and the answers we're looking for. That's kinda dumb! But maybe some sort of super-app could decide how a bunch of front-line apps worked... how they select and organise the data, which analytical tools they use and which results and insights they surface. That's what a smart data person would do."

It was Katerina's response to Bashir that captured this new strategic idea. "We need to give our apps a promotion. They're no longer data analysts, they're now data scientists."

As these thoughts were recorded in the frame-setter (Fig. 158) the 'data-analyst-to-data-scientist' idea grew stronger and stronger. They realised it would be loved by the many clients (small and large) who had tried, but not succeeded, to build a data science capability in-house. That would give Artigence a great defence against price erosion.

This change in strategy meant some of their original acceptance criteria from strategy scoping were no longer relevant – e.g. identify five viable new apps from research and analysis. A replacement acceptance criterion was added: test the 'data-analyst-to-data-scientist' idea by mocking-up marketing assets and product pages featuring Artigence's new proposition.

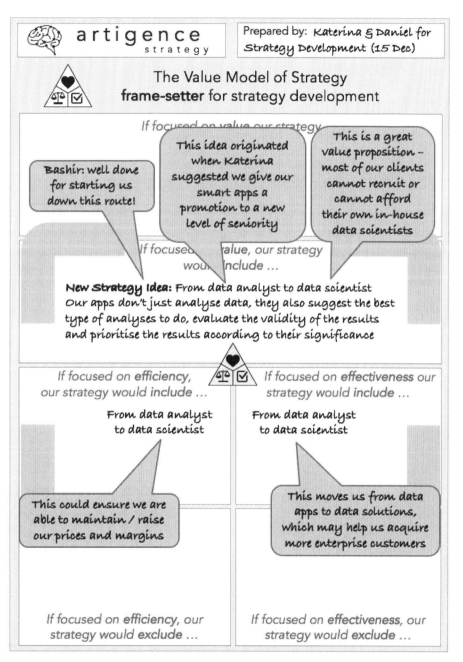

Figure 158 Value Model of Strategy frame-setter for Artigence

8.11.1 Artigence financial projections for strategy development

This new strategy idea enabled the Artigence team to move forward with the financial projections that were always going to be critical for their new strategy. As a software-as-a-service (SaaS) company with subscription-based customer accounts, their financial projections would be in terms of Annual Recurring Revenue (ARR) and Average Revenue Per Account (ARPA). Their two investor-shareholders had both signed up to the Series A funding round on the basis of a growth strategy that is quite typical for tech start-ups. It is based on the principle of revenue growth persistence.[56]   This states that fast-growing companies (particularly fast-growing SaaS companies) should grow a little bit slower than they did last year. Yes, slower - that's not a typo! But just a little bit slower. Here's the reasoning.

For any company to be fast-growing means it must have discovered a significant gap in a market (e.g. Apple with the first iPhone) or possibly invented a whole new market (e.g. Netflix with streaming video, AirBnB with home-sharing). Such companies often grow astonishingly quickly, sometimes many hundred per cent growth per year. Both Amazon and WhatsApp reported early stage growth of 1400% in a year.[57] This is fine when companies are in start-up mode, but when they reach a certain size (often around £10M annual revenue, as Artigence is) they need to move from start-up to scale-up. Here, growth needs to be sustained, not explosive. It also needs to guide them towards a soft-landing into market saturation, when revenue growth will cease, unless a new breakthrough innovation launches them on to a new growth curve. Hence the idea of achieving revenue growth persistence.

Successful high-growth companies, in their scale-up period have been found on average to achieve a growth persistence rate between 80% and 85%. Artigence's investors signed up on the basis of an agreed target of 80% growth persistence. What this means is that the growth rate next year will be 80% of the growth rate this year. Artigence is on track to hit £9.9M revenue this year; a 97% growth rate over last year. Their target of 80% growth persistence means they would grow at 78% next year (80% of 97% = 78%) and 62% the year after (80% of 78% = 62%). This will give them a projected £100M revenue with a 25% growth rate six years from now (a year after the current strategy ends). By happy coincidence, these revenue and growth figures are the perfect sweet spot for stock market floatation via an Initial Public Offering (IPO).[58]

So, revenue growth persistence is *the* critical performance indicator for Artigence's shareholders. For a fast-growing company, however, a 'growth rate' that looks like its declining over time may not be readily recognised by everyone as a good thing. To demonstrate the progress that this strategic KPI represents, it can also be expressed in terms of revenue (ARR in Artigence's case). The table in Figure 159 was presented to the board as part of the strategy sign-off process – it showed the headline revenue (ARR) targets as well as:

1. the *revenue growth rate* from which the revenue targets were calculated;

2. the revenue *growth persistence* rates from which the revenue growth rates were calculated.

artigence Strategy success KPIs							
	Current year	Yr 1	Yr 2	Yr 3	Yr 4	Yr 5	Yr 6
Annual Recurring Revenue (ARR) target	£10M	£17M	£28M	£42M	£59M	£79M	£99M
Revenue growth	97%	78%	62%	50%	40%	32%	25%
Growth persistence	80%	80%	80%	80%	80%	80%	80%

Figure 159 Strategy success KPIs presented to the Artigence Board

This was designed to give the board robust assurance that their growth persistence rate was locked into the strategy, whilst enabling it to be presented more straightforwardly as a revenue target. Figure 160 shows how the 'success-defining KPI' of £79m ARR at the end of 5 years was included in the Artigence Strategy document, for circulation across the company.

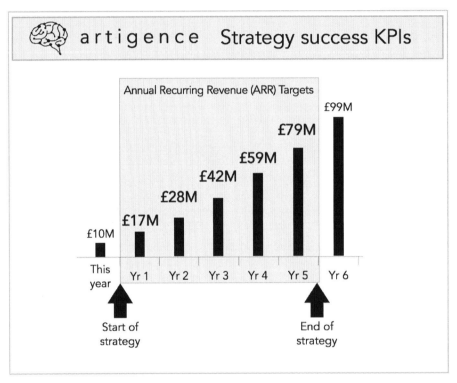

Figure 160 Strategy success KPIs for Artigence

The next refinement needed for the Artigence strategy was to sense-check these growth numbers in terms of the number of new customers needed. This, in turn, needed assumptions to be made about how much revenue each customer would generate. Figure 161 shows the growth in small- and medium-sized business (SMB) customers, assuming Average Revenue Per Account (ARPA) remained static.

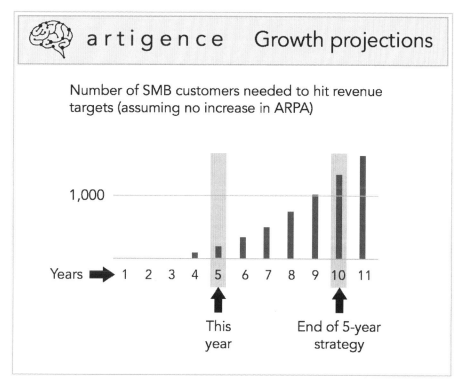

Figure 161 Artigence growth projections - SMB customers only

Although not impossible, this would have been a massive stretch for the sales team. A more promising sign was that Artigence had started to attract enterprise customers. Until 12 months ago, all customers had been SMBs (<1,000 employees and <£10M turnover). As expected, enterprise customers generate a lot more revenue than SMB customers; twice as much, this year so far. So, the sales projections in Figure 162 show a big push towards enterprise customers.

These seemed to be much more feasible sales targets and also fitted beautifully with the 'data-analyst-to-data-scientist' transition. Artigence would move away from selling apps to selling *solutions*.

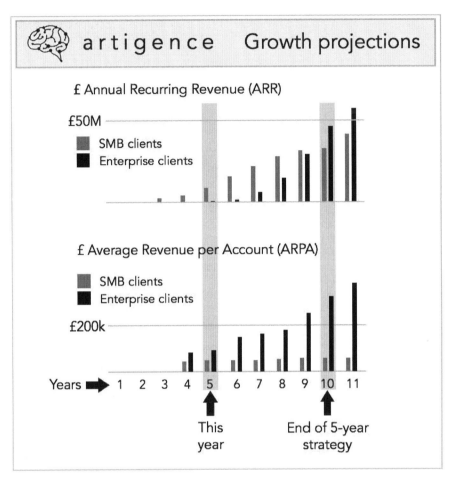

Figure 162 Artigence growth projections emphasising enterprise sales

8.11.2 Artigence market research for strategy development

Market research was needed to support these projections and to meet the new strategy acceptance criterion (test the 'data-analyst-to-data-scientist' idea by mocking-up marketing assets and product pages featuring Artigence's new proposition).

The proposition was mocked up in marketing and sales assets and shown to a small sample of current and prospective enterprise clients. The results are shown in Figure 163. The mocked-up assets were well-received and hence the acceptance criterion was deemed to have been met.

Figure 163 Results of market research to meet strategy acceptance criteria

One additional thing that this market research confirmed was that the data-scientist approach took quite a bit of explanation and persuasion. This prompted lengthy discussions about how much of a barrier to sales this might be. The solution, they concluded, was to move to a content-led,[59] inbound marketing approach.[60] This approach attracts customers to independently express their interests in products and services having learned about them from engaging and persuasive content, such as blog articles, social media and company web content. This would also work well with a move into the enterprise market. Figure 164 shows the strategy map that the Artigence team ended up with at the end of strategy development.

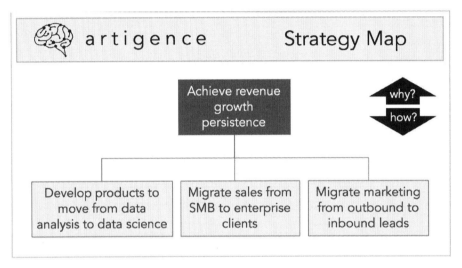

Figure 164 Strategy map for the new Artigence strategy

8.11.3 Artigence's critical-to-success KPIs

You learnt about 'critical-to-success KPIs' in Chapter 6 on strategy measurement. The first critical-to-success KPIs to be defined for Artigence were for the strategy's core methods. One such method was *to migrate marketing from outbound to inbound leads.* Research revealed that other successful SaaS companies acquire the majority of their new customers from inbound leads: Artigence chose to have an ultimate aim of 67% of their new customer revenue being attributed to inbound leads. Their research also revealed many companies underestimate the amount of time needed to build up sales from inbound leads. They decided it was more important to get this right than to get it done quickly, so they kept their timescales conservative. Figure 165 shows the growth curve they applied to new customer revenue from inbound leads. The growth curve matures at its ultimate level of 67% beyond the current strategy. This meant that by the end of the current strategy in 5 years' time, 50% of new customer revenue should be from inbound leads. This became their first 'critical-to-success' KPI.

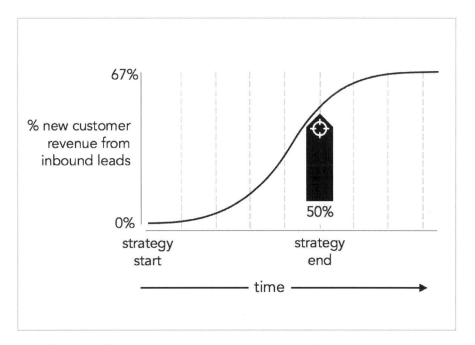

Figure 165 Growth in new customer revenue from inbound leads

8.11.4 Design and validation of Artigence's strategy

Having identified high-level strategic KPIs, Artigence then used the Strategy Design Checklist (Fig. 166) to ensure their new strategy had all the necessary elements in place. As a final validation, the Artigence founders also worked through the Hallmarks of Good Strategy (Fig. 167).

artigence strategy

Prepared by: **Katerina & Daniel** for **Strategy Development** (18 Dec)

Strategy Design Checklist

Strategy Summary:
Artigence will move from apps that operate as 'smart data analysts' to apps that operate as 'smart data scientists'

Destination	Achieve revenue growth persistence. This is a great destination – it is a well-established standard for SaaS businesses, easy to define and aligned with shareholder goals
Methods	1. Develop new products ... 2. Move to enterprise sales ... 3. Move to inbound leads ... Destination says nothing about how to get there – these methods are critical to the strategy
Alignment	Checked the Sufficiency and Necessity of destination and core methods (using SaNity model) - they seem to work fine
Innovation	There's a lot of innovation in this strategy, certainly enough, but could it be too much? We propose three new senior appointments to maximise our likelihood of success
Priority	This will be dealt with in Strategy Adoption
Performance	At the highest level, this strategy is easily measured – did we hit our growth target or not?
Adaptability	This strategy will demand the highest levels of adaptability, as we change both our core product offering and our customer profile
Adoption	This strategy will almost certainly be welcomed by the Artigence team – they'll be very excited about it

Figure 166 Artigence's Strategy Design Checklist

artigence strategy

Prepared by: Katerina & Daniel for Strategy Development (15 Dec)

 Hallmarks of good strategy

Strategy Summary:

Artigence will move from apps that operate as 'smart data analysts' to apps that operate as 'smart data scientists'

 change

This is a substantial change from our current direction of travel. We will move to a higher value offer and be better equipped to combat price erosion. We will need to develop our skill-set across the organisation and spend more of our time working on smarter versions of our current apps.

 choice

During strategy development we pivoted our thinking from developing away from building a wider range of inter-connected apps to the data scientist strategy. This was a choice but only because we concluded the initial idea was non-viable.

 coherence

The data scientist strategy has great coherence. It is a positioning and branding statement but with technical depth. Its coherence is one of its strongest features

 challenge

The 'data scientist' strategy is a huge challenge. For us to have a sufficient overview of an organisation to be able to architect its data and strategise its analysis is at least a five-year challenge. There are, however, small steps we can get done quickly e.g. an app to select analytic methods, validate analysis and prioritise insights.

 cascade

The data scientist strategy is well-suited to cascading through the organisation – the original idea was prompted by a relatively recent hire. It is easy to grasp and works well as a front-line-decision enabler.

Figure 167 Artigence's analysis of the hallmarks of good strategy

The analysis in the Strategy Design Checklist and Hallmarks of Good Strategy allowed the team to take a step back and get some perspective on the new strategy. In recording the results, it became possible to scrutinise each element, and one issue in particular concerned them. The destination was 'Achieve revenue growth persistence'. This focus on money and revenue growth was essential for the board and the shareholders, but it wasn't going to inspire the team or delight prospects and customers. Katerina and Daniel realised they hadn't put enough emphasis on 'purpose beyond profit'. Returning to the Value Model of Strategy (Fig. 168) made them see that this could be accommodated quite simply. The same strategy could be seen as delivering value in two distinct ways; one focused on profit, the other on purpose beyond profit – making data science more accessible in order to have more people making better decisions based on stronger evidence, and hence solving the world's problems quicker and more efficiently. The decision was made to launch the strategy with this purpose-beyond-profit message.

Figure 169 shows the messaging that was used to launch the new strategy to the team, and the Strategy Development Log that captured the development process can be seen in Figure 170.

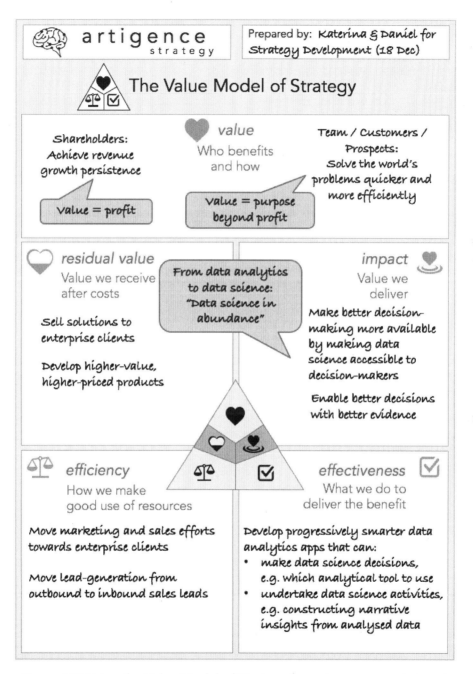

Figure 168 Using the Value Model of Strategy to analyse purpose beyond profit

Data science in abundance

Just imagine how much better the world would be if more of the decisions of communities, of businesses and of governments were more evidence-based. So many of the challenges facing us might never have arisen. Even if they had, their resolution could have been quicker and more efficient.

Over the next five years, Artigence aims to lead the world in making data science accessible to decision-makers. We'll make our data analytics apps progressively smarter and smarter until they start making data science decisions (e.g. which analytical tool to use) and undertaking data science activities (e.g. constructing narrative insights from analysed data). As we do this, we also aim to move our marketing and sales efforts more towards enterprise clients and move our lead-generation from outbound to inbound sales leads.

Our strategy is available to read at team.artigence.com/strategy and over the next few weeks we will be getting you all involved in conversations about strategy adoption.

All-hands meeting this Thursday lunchtime: let's fire the starting gun on this new strategy!

Katerina   Daniel

Co-founders

Figure 169 Artigence's strategy launch

artigence strategy

Prepared by: Katerina & Daniel for Strategy Development (18 Dec)

 Strategy Development Log

 Strategy acceptance criteria (from strategy scoping log)

1. An agreed target growth in annual recurring revenue
2. An agreed end-date for this new strategy
3. 5 viable new apps identified by research and analysis
4. Product-driven growth projections

 Frame-stretcher / setter: Value Proposition Design

- Range extension strategy: build lots more apps to do more jobs. Provide coverage of more of the decisions that need to be informed by data analysis
- Research driven strategy: undertake in-depth customer research to find where our apps can have most appeal and add most value

 Strategy research and analysis

- Increasing competition with some application areas becoming commoditised and suffering dramatically falling prices
- Previous strategy idea of range extension no longer valid

 Frame-stretcher / setter: Value Model of Strategy

- New strategy idea: from data analyst to data scientist
- Much better in many ways – but needs growth projections and change to strategy acceptance criteria

 Strategy acceptance criteria (updated)

1. An agreed target growth in annual recurring revenue
2. An agreed end-date for this new strategy
3. Proven market test of mock-up marketing and sales assets
4. Product-driven growth projections

 Growth projections

- 80% growth persistence rate only possible with increase in enterprise clients – move to sell solutions rather than apps

 Market-testing new strategy

- Mock-ups well received by enterprise clients and prospects
- Market test makes clear this new strategy needs careful and detailed explanation

Figure 170 Artigence strategy development log

8.12 Summary and key takeaways from Chapter 8

1. **Strategy development involves iteration** through three interconnected loops of activity:

    a. **Validation** that your strategy is fit-for-purpose as defined in its acceptance criteria;

    b. The **creation** of strategic ideas to meet those validation criteria;

    c. **Informing** your strategic thinking with research and analysis from the outside world.

2. **Strategy validation** uses two sets of validation criteria:

    a. **Strategy acceptance criteria**, defined during strategy scoping;

    b. **Hallmarks of good strategy**, which specify that:

        i.   Strategy is about change;

        ii. Strategy is about choice;

        iii. Strategy is about coherence;

        iv. Strategy is about challenge;

        v.   Strategy is about cascade.

3. The creativity loop of strategy development involves both **divergent thinking** and **convergent thinking** within the constraints of **bounded creativity**.

4. **Strategy framing** is a key part of strategy development and a variety of frame-stretching and frame-setting tools can enhance the range and quality of strategic ideas.

5. **Strategy needs to be informed** by research and analysis in three areas: **customers, competitors** and **capabilities.**

6. The **Strategy Design Model** can be used to check that your strategy-in-development has all the elements required to make it practical, adoptable, adaptable and impactful.

7. The **Mediated Assessment Protocol** (MAP) can be used to decide between alternative strategy candidates.

8. **Record-keeping** – keeping a log of strategy development ensures that pivotal events and strategy acceptance criteria can be scrutinised and justified.

9. Your completed strategy needs to define:

   a. The **desired future state** for your organisation (strategy destination)

   b. The **benefits of reaching this desired future state** (strategic value)

   c. The **core methods** by which you intend to reach this strategy destination.

   d. The **strategy success criteria** you will use to confirm when you have reached your destination.

10. The output from strategy development is **strategy launch,** which takes the completed and ratified strategy to the point of strategy adoption.

8.13 Let's talk about... strategy development

Use these questions to prompt deeper conversations on strategy development across your organisation:

1. *How structured should your strategy development process be? Which processes and tools do you use?*

2. *How do you manage the 'brief' against which you validate a new strategy? How 'fixed' is it from the start of strategy development? How do you change it, if at all? How do you make sure it doesn't constrain your strategy development too much or too little?*

3. *Are you creative enough in your strategy development? How do you manage too few, or too many, creative ideas? Who should be contributing strategy ideas?*

4. *How do you inform your strategy development? How do you get data? How do you know when you have got enough data? When do you stop research and analysis?*

5. *How will you document the strategy development process? How do you ensure accountability for the decisions made? How will you ensure the right strategy is being launched?*

Notes on Chapter 8

(all web content accessed between April and September 2020)

[1] Adapted from Salinger JD, 1951. *Catcher in the Rye.* Little, Brown and Company, New York.

[2] Porter ME, 1996. *What is Strategy?* Harvard Business Review, 31 October 1996.

[3] Rumelt R, 2011. *Good Strategy Bad Strategy: The Difference and Why it Matters.* Profile Books, NY. p79.

[4] Lafley AG, 2013. *Strategy as Winning.* In Lafley AG and Martin RL, 2013. *Playing to Win: How Strategy Really Works.* Harvard Business Review Press, Boston. p48.

[5] Rumelt R, 2011. *Good Strategy Bad Strategy: The Difference and Why it Matters*. Profile Books, NY. Chapter 5 The Kernel of Good Strategy, subsection on Guiding Policy.

[6] Martin RL, 2013. *Don't Let Strategy Become Planning*. Harvard Business Review. 5 February 2013.

[7] Rumelt R, 2011. *Good Strategy Bad Strategy: The Difference and Why it Matters*. Profile Books, NY. p6.

[8] Rumelt R, 2011. *Good Strategy Bad Strategy: The Difference and Why it Matters*. Profile Books, NY. p87.

[9] Sull D, Homkes R and Sull C, 2015. *Why Strategy Execution Unravels — and What to Do About It*. Harvard Business Review, March 2015.

[10] Rumelt R, 2011. *Good Strategy Bad Strategy: The Difference and Why it Matters*. Profile Books, NY. p4.

[11] Rumelt R, 2011. *Good Strategy Bad Strategy: The Difference and Why it Matters*. Profile Books, NY. p7.

[12] The Baldrige Glossary. http://www.baldrige21.com/BALDRIGE_GLOSSARY/BN/Strategic_Challenges.html

[13] Bennett N and Lemoine GJ, 2014. *What VUCA really means for you*. Harvard Business Review, Jan-Feb 2014.

[14] Roxburgh C, 2009. *The Use and Abuse of Scenarios*. McKinsey Strategy & Corporate Finance, November 2009. https://www.mckinsey.com/business-functions/strategy-and-corporate-finance/our-insights/the-use-and-abuse-of-scenarios

[15] Lafley AG and Martin RL, 2013 *Playing to Win: How Strategy Really Works*. Harvard Business Review Press, Boston

[16] Lafley AG and Martin RL, 2013 *Playing to Win: How Strategy Really Works*. Harvard Business Review Press, Boston. p15.

[17] Brandenburger A, 2019. *Strategy needs creativity*. Harvard Business Review, March–April 2019.

[18] Wikipedia. *Porter's Five Forces Analysis* https://en.wikipedia.org/wiki/Porter%27s_five_forces_analysis

[19] D'Aveni R, 2007. *Mapping Your Competitive Position*. Harvard Business Review, November 2007.

[20] Brandenburger A, 2019. *Strategy needs creativity*. Harvard Business Review. March–April 2019. p58.

[21] Simon HA, 1996. *The Sciences of the Artificial*. 3rd Edition. MIT Press, Cambridge, Massachusetts.

[22] Guilford J P, 1956. *The Structure of the Intellect*. Psychological Bulletin, 53(4), 267–293. Summarised in Barlow CM, 2000. Guilford's Structure of the Intellect. http://www.cocreativity.com/handouts/guilford.pdf

[23] Makov S, 2017. *Joy Paul Guilford – One of the founders of the Psychology of Creativity*. https://geniusrevive.com/en/joy-paul-guilford-one-of-the-founders-of-the-psychology-of-creativity/

[24] New World Encyclopedia, 2018 *J.P. Guilford*. https://www.newworldencyclopedia.org/entry/J._P._Guilford

[25] Baskerville R, Kaul M, Pries-Heje J, Storey VC and Kristiansen E, 2016. *Bounded Creativity in Design Science Research*. Proceedings of the 2016 International Conference on Information Systems (ICIS) cited at https://aisel.aisnet.org/icis2016/ISDesign/Presentations/5/ and available online at https://aisel.aisnet.org/cgi/viewcontent.cgi?article=1141&context=icis2016

[26] The Goldilocks principle is explained on Wikipedia at https://en.wikipedia.org/wiki/Goldilocks_principle. Two Harvard Business Review articles have shown that creativity is boosted by constraints but hampered by too many. They are Richardson A, 2013. *Boosting Creativity Through Constraints*. Harvard Business Review, 11 June 2013 and Acar OA, Tarakci M and van Knippenberg D, 2019. *Why Constraints Are Good for Innovation*. Harvard Business Review, 22 November 2019.

[27] Bhikkhu T (translator), 2012. *Tipitaka, Udana 6.4* https://www.accesstoinsight.org/tipitaka/kn/ud/ud.6.04.than.html

[28] Wikipedia, *Blind Men and an Elephant*. https://en.wikipedia.org/wiki/Blind_men_and_an_elephant

[29] Tversky A and Kahneman D, 1981. *The Framing of Decisions and the Psychology of Choice*. Science 211: 453-458.

[30] Tversky A and Kahneman D, 1981. *The Framing of Decisions and the Psychology of Choice*. Science 211: 453-458. p453.

[31] Kaplan S, 2008. *Framing Contests: Strategy Making Under Uncertainty*. Organisational Science 19 (5): 729–752.

[32] Wikipedia, *Ethnography*. https://en.wikipedia.org/wiki/Ethnography

[33] Miriam Webster Dictionary. *Frame*. https://www.merriam-webster.com/dictionary/frame

[34] Howard TJ, Culley SJ and Dekoninck, EA, 2011. *Reuse of ideas and concepts for creative stimuli in engineering design*. Journal of Engineering Design, 22(8), 565-581.

[35] Osterwalder A and Pigneur Y, 2010. *Business Model Generation: A Handbook for Visionaries, Game Changers and Challengers*. John Wiley and Sons Inc, New Jersey.

[36] Osterwalder A, Pigneur Y, Bernarda G, Smith A and Papadokas P, 2014. *Value Proposition Design*. John Wiley and Sons Inc, New Jersey.

[37] Osterwalder A, Pigneur Y, Bernarda G, Smith A and Papadokas P, 2014. *Value Proposition Design*. John Wiley and Sons Inc, New Jersey. p12.

[38] Kenny G, 2011. *Strategic Planning and Performance Management: Develop and Measure a Winning Strategy*. Routledge, Abingdon, UK. p14.

[39] Lafley AG and Martin RL, 2013. *Playing to Win: How Strategy Really Works*. Harvard Business Review Press, Boston, Massachusetts.

[40] Brandenburger A, 2019. *Strategy needs creativity*. Harvard Business Review. March–April 2019.

[41] Brandenburger A, 2019. *Strategy needs creativity*. Harvard Business Review. March–April 2019. p66. The book cited, featuring the Audi Le Mans example is Morgan M and Barden A 2015. *A Beautiful Constraint: How To Transform Your Limitations Into Advantages, and Why It's Everyone's Business*. John Wiley and Sons Inc, New Jersey.

[42] Wikipedia. *Post-it Note*. https://en.wikipedia.org/wiki/Post-it_Note

[43] Wikipedia. *Porter's Five Forces Analysis* https://en.wikipedia.org/wiki/Porter%27s_five_forces_analysis

[44] Martin RL, 2013. *Don't Let Strategy Become Planning*. Harvard Business Review. 5 February 2013.

[45] Rumelt R 2011. *Good Strategy Bad Strategy: The Difference and Why it Matters*. Profile Books, NY. p11.

[46] Denning S, 2014. *The Best of Peter Drucker*. Forbes Magazine. 29th July 2014. https://www.forbes.com/sites/stevedenning/2014/07/29/the-best-of-peter-drucker/#3dcad5c05a96

[47] Drucker P, 2011. *Management*. Abridged and revised edition of the original 1974 *Management: Tasks, Responsibilities, Practices*. Routledge, NY. p114.

[48] "What gets measured gets managed" is frequently attributed to Peter Drucker but, in fact probably originates in the thinking of Lord Kelvin – see https://athinkingperson.com/2012/12/02/who-said-what-gets-measured-gets-managed/

[49] McGrath RG, 2013. *The End of Competitive Advantage: How to Keep Your Strategy Moving as Fast as Your Business*. Harvard Business Review Press, Boston.

[50] Kinni T, 2014. *Rita Gunther McGrath on the End of Competitive Advantage*. Strategy + Business Spring 2014, Issue 74. https://www.strategy-business.com/article/00239?gko=ede47

[51] McGrath RG, *The End of Competitive Advantage*. https://www.ritamcgrath.com/books/the-end-of-competitive-advantage/

[52] Kahneman D, 2011. *Thinking, Fast and Slow*. Allen Lane, London.

[53] Kahneman D, Lovallo D and Sibony O, 2019. *A Structured Approach to Strategic Decisions: Reducing errors in judgment requires a disciplined process*. MIT Sloan Management Review, 60 (3): 67-73.

[54] Kahneman D, Lovallo D and Sibony O, 2019. *A Structured Approach to Strategic Decisions: Reducing errors in judgment requires a disciplined process*. MIT Sloan Management Review, 60 (3): 67-73. p68.

[55] Thomas Hobbes wrote the *Leviathan* during the English Civil War and argued that strong government was needed to avoid a 'state of nature' in which 'the life of man was solitary, poor, nasty, brutish and short'. Leviathan Chapter VIII Of the Natural Condition of Mankind

[56] The original research on growth persistence rates for SaaS companies was published by Vitus A 2012. *Predictable Growth Decay in SaaS Companies*. https://www.scalevp.com/blog/predictable-growth-decay-in-saas-companies. A more recent interpretation and discussion is in O'Driscoll R 2018. *Understanding the Mendoza Line for SaaS growth*. https://techcrunch.com/2018/02/09/understanding-the-mendoza-line-for-saas-growth/

[57] Bishop M, 2014. *How Fast Can a Company or Industry Grow?* https://medium.com/@FutureBash/how-fast-can-a-company-or-industry-grow-e4a047d075a5

[58] Verjee A, 2018. *SaaS IPO Benchmarking | ARR at IPO.*
https://medium.com/@amanverjee/saas-ipo-benchmarking-arr-at-ipo-48bf5811f619

[59] Perricone, C. *The Ultimate Guide to Content Creation.* Hubspot.
https://blog.hubspot.com/marketing/content-creation/

[60] Hubspot. *What Is Inbound Marketing.* Hubspot.
https://www.hubspot.com/inbound-marketing

Chapter 9

Strategy adoption

The secret to strategy adoption is good communication between senior leadership and change-makers across the organisation, informed by the expertise on both sides, and conducted in psychological safety.

You now have a strategy – congratulations! The first stage of the strategy lifecycle, strategy production, is complete. There are many labels for the part of the strategy lifecycle that follows strategy production. Strategy implementation. Strategy deployment. Strategy execution. Such labels raise two issues. The first is that they make it look as though, once the hard work of producing the strategy is done, strategy success will just happen, almost on its own. It just needs to be *deployed*. It merely needs *implementation*. It requires only *execution*, as per the instructions that the strategy itself contains. The second, somewhat related, issue is that it looks as though strategy is something done by leaders to followers. It makes the front–line teams appear to be passive recipients. All of which, of course, is nonsense. It is once the strategy is written that the hard work begins. Aspirations need to be translated into actions. Actions need to be delegated, and possibly delegated again and again in a large organisation. Resources need to be prioritised. Targets need to be set and then checked to ensure they aggregate up to strategic success. New ways of working need to be devised. Innovation needs to be conjured into existence. Strategic success needs to be squeezed from the organisation (or individual), drop by drop. So, strategy doesn't just need to be implemented, deployed or executed. It needs to be *adopted*. This involves not just *strategic planning*, but *engagement and commitment* across the entire organisation (Fig. 171). The outcome of strategy adoption is a strategic plan, detailing the actions necessary to bring about the strategic change you seek, how these actions have been delegated and prioritised, and the targets that have been set to demonstrate progress towards strategy success.

Figure 171 The strategy lifecycle model showing strategy adoption

9.1   The importance of strategy adoption

There are two ways to explain the importance of strategy adoption:

1. *Strategy failure rates.* Lots of strategies fail, and this failure is often attributed to poor strategy adoption.

2. *It shapes organisational culture.* Whilst a negative culture can inhibit strategy adoption, ensuring engagement and commitment with strategy can itself have a positive effect on the culture within organisations.

9.1.1 Strategy failure rates

Search online for 'strategy failure' and you will find some dramatic headlines from respected authorities. According to Nitin Nohria, Dean of the Harvard Business School, "The brutal fact is that about 70% of all change initiatives fail," [1] According to Walter Kiechel, Editorial Director of Harvard Business School Publishing, "… fewer than 10 percent of effectively formulated strategies were successfully implemented."[2] Although quoted widely, it has never been clear where such figures originated.[3] A better-quantified approach comes from a meta-analysis of research on strategy failure rates by Carlos Candido and Sergio Santos, Economists from the University of the Algarve in Portugal (Fig. 172).[4]

Figure 172 Failure rates for strategy implementation

A meta-analysis is an aggregated analysis of several independently published research papers (meta-analysis means analysis of analyses). Failure was interpreted as either:

1. that a new strategy was formulated but not implemented;

2. that a strategy was implemented but with poor results.

In their paper, Candido and Santos argue that the failure rate reduces over time due to better understanding and application of strategy, yet the data published from 2000 onwards still gives a median failure rate of 44%. So, it is clear that a lot of strategies don't deliver what they promise.

9.1.2 The development of organisational culture

Also quoted widely but of uncertain origin is the phrase "Culture eats strategy for breakfast". [5] This is often taken to mean that culture is somehow superior to strategy or even, perhaps, that organisations with a strong culture can get away with having a poor strategy or no strategy at all. Let's explore this in more depth.

A dictionary definition of 'culture' is 'the ideas, customs, attitudes and social behaviour of a particular people or society'.[6] Organisational culture, therefore, will be the ideas, customs, attitudes and social behaviours typical of an organisation. A positive organisational culture[7] will have good communication, a clear sense of purpose, opportunities for growth and development, reward and recognition for good work, feelings of trust and adherence to clear values. A toxic organisational culture[8] will be hyper-competitive, giving rise to lots of conflict and distrust, will show fear of authority, often expressed in a feeling of pressure to over-work. It will also be characterised by low morale and particular habits, such as 'covering', where individuals feel they have to hide their true identity to fit in.[9]

From this, it is clear that a strong organisational culture will be conducive to strategy adoption, even though the data doesn't look great for this happening. Many organisations face a crisis of engagement. Globally, only 15% of employees are "highly involved in and enthusiastic about their work and workplace."[10] In the US, the figure is better, at 34%, but still not great. [11] Two critical issues seem to hold the solution.

Firstly, employees need to find their work *purposeful*. A recent survey by PWC's consultancy, Strategy&, found that only 28% of employees felt fully connected to their company purpose and only 34% thought they strongly contributed to their company's success.[12]

Secondly, academic Teresa Amabile and psychologist Steven Kramer found that making employees feel they were making 'tangible progress towards meaningful goals' was the thing that motivated them most at work: more than praise, more than reward and more than promotion. They called it the Progress Principle.[13]

What better way to help employees feel their work is purposeful and to make them believe they can make tangible progress towards meaningful goals than to get them engaged with, and committed to, a new strategy? So, whilst it is easy to see how culture is important for strategy adoption, this shows strategy adoption is also important for the development of a positive organisational culture.

One related finding that is important to note here is that research has also shown that middle managers are critical to strategy success. In one change program within a large telecoms company, 117 individual projects were funded: 80% of those proposed by senior executives failed; 80% of those proposed by middle managers succeeded.[14] Another study looked at 56 randomly-selected companies in multiple sectors, within which they found that only 32% of the large-scale change and innovation efforts succeeded. A hallmark of these successful programmes was that mid-level managers, two or more levels below the CEO, were involved. These middle managers led change initiatives by "working the levers of power up, across and down through their organizations."[15]

9.2   The 'H' Model of Strategy Adoption

Strategy adoption depends on the active engagement and willing commitment of change-makers. The 'H' Model of Strategy Adoption is designed to explain this more fully. Your first step in learning about this model is recognising that strategy is, by necessity, owned by senior leadership to begin with. Not because senior leadership are the only people capable of creating a strategy, nor even, necessarily, the best people in the organisation to do so. This is simply a matter of strategy governance. The board has the constitutional authority to approve the future direction of the organisation. Once they have approved the strategy, they delegate power to senior leadership to take the necessary action to bring about the outcomes defined in the strategy. These outcomes, however, cannot be delivered by senior leadership alone. They need front-line teams to deliver strategic change. Thus, as shown in this simplified version of the 'H' Model (Fig. 173), strategy adoption requires the active engagement and willing commitment of both senior leaders and front-line teams to the strategy.

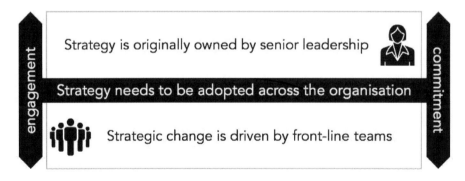

Figure 173 A simplified version of the 'H' model of strategy adoption

Figure 174 reveals the nature and content of the strategy originally owned by senior leadership: a good strategy specifies a destination and defines a handful of core strategic goals by which that destination will be reached.

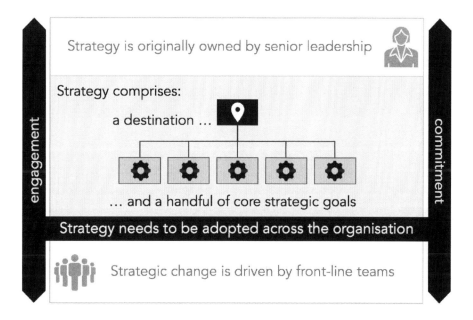

Figure 174 The 'H' Model of Strategy Adoption, showing what a good strategy comprises

This strategy then needs to be adopted across the organisation, so that strategic change can be driven by front-line teams. This requires the handful of core strategic goals to be elaborated (Fig. 175). You do this by asking the question 'How are we going to achieve each of these core goals? What methods will we use?' These are strategy mapping questions and can be tackled using the why–how logic you learned about in Chapter 4 and which you will see exemplified later in this chapter in the Artigence case study.

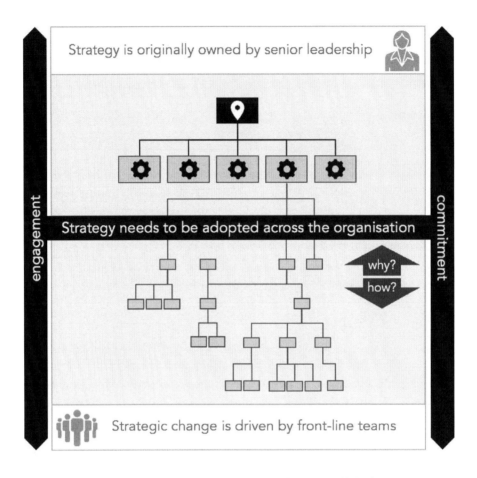

Figure 175 Strategy adoption requires each of the handful of core strategic goals to be elaborated using strategy mapping

The best answers to most of these strategy mapping questions will come from the combined efforts of both senior leadership, who can provide strategic context on why these particular core goals were selected, and front–line teams who can provide practical context on the best methods to achieve them. This combined approach can be accomplished through 'adoption conversations' which provide a way of elaborating strategic goals beyond the handful of core goals that featured in the strategy (Fig. 176).

Figure 176 Strategy adoption enabled by adoption conversations

Stepping through your handful of core strategic goals, you need to resolve how best to achieve each of them. The first step is working out who needs to be involved. Start with the people you see as critical contributors to whichever core strategic goal you are focused on. Senior leadership explains what each core strategic goal means and why it was considered an essential method of reaching your stated strategic destination. Any ideas from the leadership team on how this particular goal could be achieved should also be shared. Then members of the frontline teams will provide context. What, of all the activities that are already being done, could contribute to this new goal? Of any new activities proposed to achieve the goal, have any been tried before and, if so, with what result? Then explore, given the goal being tackled and the potential methods of achieving it, who else should be brought into these conversations.

It is worth noting that these strategy adoption conversations need to begin *within* the senior leadership team. Unless this team is very small, individuals within it will have been involved to different degrees in the development of the new strategy. It is vital, therefore, that the entire senior leadership team enters into strategy adoption fully engaged and committed amongst themselves.

9.2.1 Rules for Adoption Conversations

In some organisations, these adoption conversations may occur naturally and comfortably. Such organisations will be characterised by having little social distance[16] between leadership and front-line teams and having regular in-depth conversations. For many organisations, however, adoption conversations will come less naturally. Here are the rules suggested by Ed Morrison and colleagues in their book *Strategic Doing* for any conversations about strategy. [17]

1. **Have rules for these conversations and make them explicit.** Whilst it is all too easy to assume that implicit rules are shared, they may not be. Introducing a rule after it has been broken is tantamount to reprimanding the rule-breaker. Better to introduce them up front. This also makes everyone more aware of the rules and hence more likely to comply with them, for example rules on confidentiality, timings, use of everyday language or when it is okay to interrupt.

2. **Be clear from the start about intentions, purpose and outcomes.** When setting up these adoption conversations, state your intentions (e.g. "I am responsible for ensuring our new strategy is effectively adopted across the organisation and would like to discuss with you how you and your team can contribute, and what ideas you have about ensuring the strategy's success."). Be clear also about the specific purpose of each meeting and what outcomes you seek. Seek feedback from other participants on your proposed intentions, purpose and outcomes.

3. **Make time for the conversation.** Both the quantity and the quality of the time are important. It is hard to judge how much time it will take to resolve an issue. One solution is to set aside a generous amount of time for an initial meeting and then arrange subsequent meetings to complete the conversation, if necessary. That time should be uninterrupted. Interruptions disrupt conversations for far

longer than the interruption itself lasts. Conversational flow is broken, attention is distracted, and ideas may be lost.

4. **Group size.** Having a diversity of experience, ideas and opinions can enrich the conversation, but having too many people involved makes it harder for each to be properly heard. Also, the bigger the group, the more some people will feel inhibited to contribute. Research cited in the *Strategic Doing* book suggests around five to seven people is the ideal group size.

5. **Psychological safety.** How confident people feel about taking risks, admitting vulnerabilities and speaking up to higher authorities is part of organisational culture and cannot be switched off and on for individual meetings. Nevertheless, adoption conversations should be explicit about their commitment to psychological safety, and should reassure participants that:

    a. their voice will be heard – one way to achieve this is to be clear that the conversation will respect 'equity of voice' – everyone will be expected to talk for a similar amount of time;

    b. their knowledge and experience will be respected;

    c. their contribution will be valued;

    d. it is their ideas that will be judged, not them as individuals;

    e. all criticism will be constructive.

6. **Conversational leadership.** Good, productive conversation needs to be guided and facilitated. If the conversation drifts towards irrelevancies, it needs to be nudged back on course. If it delves too deep, it needs to be brought back from the detail. If it becomes too abstract, it needs to be grounded. And, of course, the rules need to be adhered to. All without dominating the conversation, shutting any individual down or compromising psychological safety. For

·some, conversational skills and conversational leadership skills may need to be developed before adoption conversations begin.

How these adoption conversations work is shown in Figure 177.

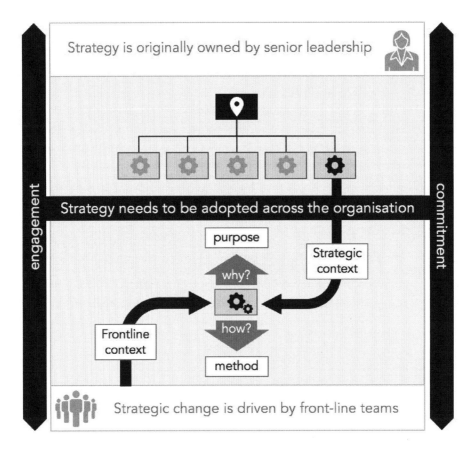

Figure 177 The why-how logic of strategy mapping is enriched by both strategic context and frontline context

Each of the core strategic goals will be elaborated into sub–goals which define the methods to be used to achieve their 'parent' core goal. Each of these sub goals will be defined by a combination of the why–how logic of strategy mapping and the context provided by the adoption conversations between senior leadership and front-line teams.

A template to facilitate this process is shown in Figure 178. This
template would be completed for each of the core strategic goals.

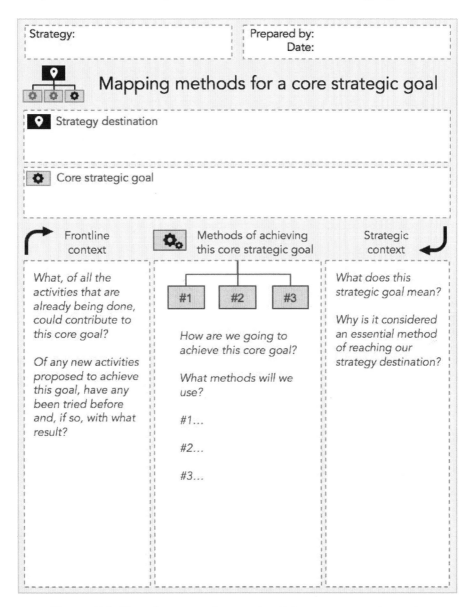

Figure 178 Template mapping methods for core strategic goals

Figure 179 shows this template completed for one of the strategic goals in our Artigence case study.

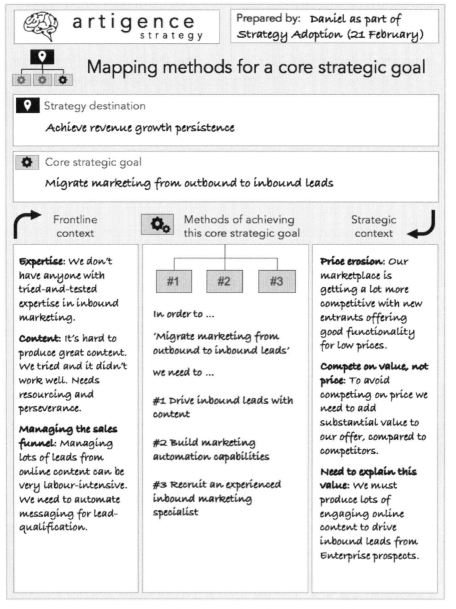

Figure 179 Artigence's completed template for strategy elaboration of one of its core strategic goals

By elaborating each of the core strategic goals, to define the methods needed to achieve them, you will map out your entire strategic plan to show all of the changes needed across the organisation to bring about strategic success.

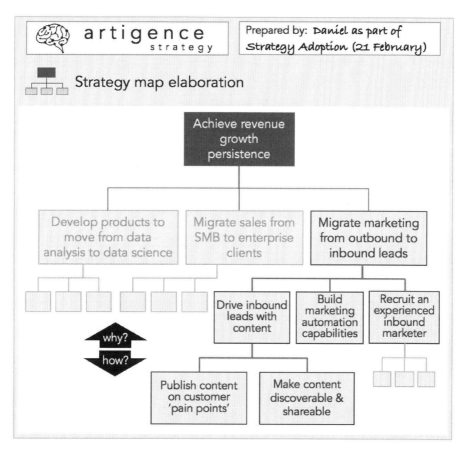

Figure 180 Elaborated strategy map for one of Artigence's core methods

Figure 180 shows the elaborated strategy map for the 'inbound leads' core method of Artigence's strategy. This shows the three sub-goals that define 'how to' *migrate marketing from outbound to inbound leads,* derived from the template in Figure 179 above. Then it shows one of these sub-goals elaborated: how Artigence is going to *drive inbound leads with content* is by *publishing content on customer 'pain points'* and by *making content discoverable and shareable.*

Having produced an elaborated strategy map, the next step is to validate it using the SaNity Check Model you learned about in Chapter 4 on strategy mapping. Doing so checks the sufficiency and necessity of goals in the strategy map (Fig. 181).

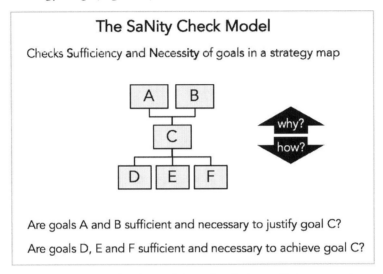

Figure 181 The SaNity Check Model to check the sufficiency and necessity of goals in a strategy map

As shown in Figure 182, and as is so often the case with strategy mapping, SaNity checking does a lot more than validate the map. It has created a whole new strand of the strategic plan. Here's how.

When, using the SaNity Check Model, the Artigence team asked themselves "why are we *publishing content on customer 'pain points'*". It was immediately obvious that the answer was more than *driving inbound leads.* It could also help re-brand and re-position them. Okay, so *publishing content on customer 'pain points'* serves two purposes. But that wasn't quite enough. There was more to this whole issue, which after quite a bit more discussion, made them realise they could establish themselves as an authority in data analysis, or data science or maybe data–informed business decision-making – the precise area of expertise wasn't important for now. What was important was that by making themselves authoritative, they could position themselves as a trusted advisor to enterprise clients. And this, of course, put them in a great position to guide these clients towards data solutions that Artigence could supply.

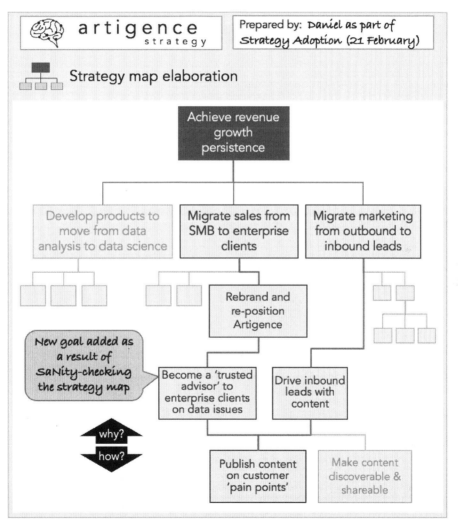

Figure 182 The SaNity Check process produces a whole new strand in the strategic plan

9.3   Understanding engagement and commitment

You may already have an intuitive sense of what it means to be engaged and committed and how that differs from being unengaged and uncommitted (Figure 183), but it is important to have a more systematic understanding as well.

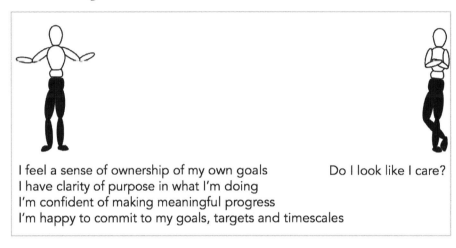

I feel a sense of ownership of my own goals   Do I look like I care?
I have clarity of purpose in what I'm doing
I'm confident of making meaningful progress
I'm happy to commit to my goals, targets and timescales

Figure 183 Engaged and committed ... or not!

Engagement and commitment can be explained in terms of:

1. *goal ownership and goal connections*, between your goals and the goals of others;

2. having a *meaningful sense of purpose;*

3. having a feeling of being able to make *tangible progress* towards that meaningful purpose.

9.3.1 Goal ownership and goal connections

For you to feel engaged and committed to strategy, you must understand your role in achieving strategy success, regardless of where that role sits within the organisation. You need clarity about your strategic goals. You need to feel a genuine sense of ownership of those goals, not feel like they have been imposed upon you. You also need to understand how your goals connect to other people's goals. What do the people in adjacent teams need to achieve for your goals to have their full strategic impact? How do your goals impact the likelihood of success of others?

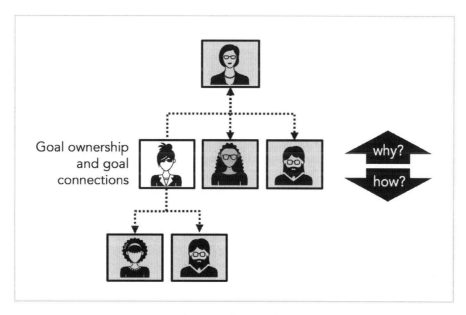

Figure 184 Goal ownership and goal connections

Figure 184 shows how these relationships are represented in a strategy map. Your goal, shown with the white background, enables your boss to achieve her goal (as you will see in a moment it will not always be your boss, someone else may own the goal above yours). The two of you need to be able to work together because she is the owner of the immediate purpose of your goal and her success depends on your success. Her success also depends on the success of the owners of the two goals next to yours – likely to be your peers within a team. So, you and your two peers need to work together to make sure you don't get in each other's way, you support each other as needed and the right synergies arise out of your work towards your respective goals.

You will also have delegated goals to others – the two goals beneath yours. The success of your goal depends on their success. You will see the person that owns one of the goals beneath yours also owns one of the goals next to yours. Let's imagine he has some specific skill that complements your own skills, which is why the two of you work together so well as colleagues. It just so happens that one of the methods of achieving your goal requires someone with the very skills your colleague has, so he agrees to take ownership of the sub-goal under your goal. This doesn't transform you into his boss. You are still colleagues. It is just that goals cascade across organisations in a much richer and more interconnected way than could ever be represented by a hierarchical line management structure. A strategy map doesn't tell you how to manage these various interpersonal working relationships, but it does reveal how goals and goal owners need to work together to contribute towards strategic success.

9.3.2   A meaningful sense of purpose

If you have clear goals, if you feel ownership of those goals and if they are meaningful and hold significance for you, they should give you a sense of *immediate purpose*. If these goals are connected effectively, you should have a clear line of sight between your own goals and the organisation's strategic goals. This gives you a sense of *strategic purpose* (Fig. 185).

9.3.3   Making tangible progress

Provided your goals feel like they are attainable, they will enable you to see how progress can be made. *Tangible progress towards meaningful goals* is, as you discovered in section 9.1.2, the most powerful motivator and greatest driver of engagement in the workplace (Fig. 186).

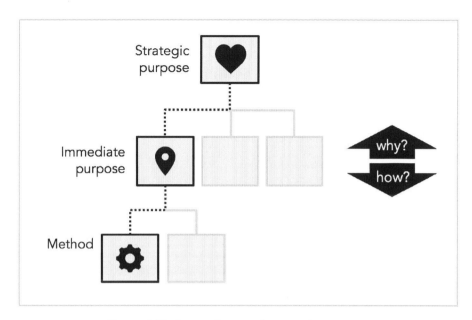

Figure 185 Immediate and strategic purpose

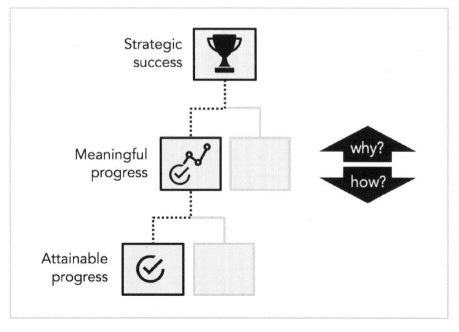

Figure 186 Tangible progress towards meaningful goals

9.4   Supporting strategy adoption

As ought to be clear by now, the secret to strategy adoption is good quality communication between senior leadership and the change-makers across the organisation, informed by the respective expertise on both sides, and conducted in psychological safety. No process is powerful enough on its own to make this happen; the models and frameworks presented so far are designed to be enablers. The following model is, however, designed to check if strategy adoption has been effective.

If you think back to Chapter 5, you discovered that effective strategy governance blended executive governance with working governance. Executive governance is what empowers the executive to make the changes mandated in the strategy; working governance is how this mandate-to-change is translated into action by means of planning and the engagement and commitment of change-makers across the organisation. Just imagine you get the right balance between the formalisation of authority and engagement and commitment. What have you just created? A great organisational culture for strategy success!

Okay, it isn't always that simple. If you start with a toxic culture across the entire organisation, even the most brilliant strategy will not be enough to turn that around. In less extreme circumstances, however, there is a strong case to be made that the effective implementation of strategy governance, as defined in this book, establishes the organisational culture in which strategy needs to take root.

In the most positive imaginable culture for strategic success, every individual and team contributing to that success should feel that:

1. they are engaged and committed to their strategic goals and hence to strategy success;

2. their engagement and commitment is reciprocated by support from the organisation to enable them to succeed.

The Goal Adoption Support Model can be used by anyone across the organisation to check that their own strategic goals are effectively supported. It can further be used by senior leadership as a 'health-check' on the effectiveness of strategy adoption, by highlighting areas where the organisation supports the adoption of strategic goals well, and where it does not.

Figure 187 shows the eight elements that support each strategic goal.

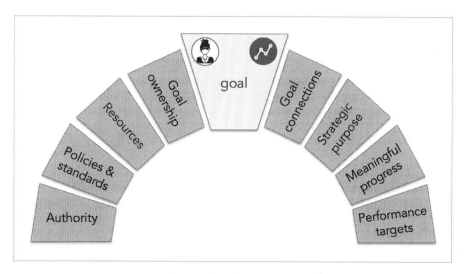

Figure 187 The Goal Adoption Support Model

1. **Authority** – are the lines of authority clear for your goal?

    a. ✓ - Your direct line managers (i.e. your manager, your manager's manager etc.) have the necessary authority to enable you to make your contribution to strategic success. You have a clear idea of RACI (Responsible, Accountable, Consulted, Informed) roles, and how they support your goal.

    b. X - Your contribution to strategic success depends on people or outcomes that are line-managed by other parts of the organisation (not your line managers). You are unable to define RACI roles, or your goal is unsupported by them.

2. **Policies and standards** – is your goal supported by policies and standards?

   a. ✓ - Your goal is supported and enabled by current policies and standards.

   b. X - Current policies and standards may get in the way of your contribution to strategic success.

3. **Resources** – do you have the resources needed to achieve your goal?

   a. ✓ - You have the budget and other resources (technology, staff, data etc.) necessary for you to achieve your goal.

   b. X – Insufficient budget / resources may get in the way of achieving your goal.

4. **Goal ownership** – do you understand the details of your goal and what is required of you to achieve it?

   a. ✓ - You are comfortable with your ownership of this goal. You understand how the goal is described and what it sets out to achieve. You have the knowledge and skills to be able to make a success of this goal.

   b. X – You have concerns about your ownership of this goal.

5. **Goal connections** – do you understand the interdependencies of your goal with others across the organisation?

   a. ✓ - You understand how this goal connects to, and has interdependencies upon, other goals, owned by other people and teams. You are comfortable that you have, or can, establish good enough working relationships with these other goal owners to ensure your goal contributes to strategic success.

   b. X – You have concerns about the interdependencies of your goal to its connected goals.

6. **Strategic purpose** – do you understand how your goal contributes to strategic success?

   a. ✓ – You understand how your goal connects to strategic success.

   b. X – You have concerns about how your goal connects to strategic success.

7. **Meaningful progress** – are you confident that progress on your goal will be meaningful?

   a. ✓ – You understand what you need to do to make progress on this goal and feel this will be tangible progress towards something meaningful to you and the organisation.

   b. X – You have concerns about how meaningful any progress will be.

8. **Performance targets** – do you have relevant, specific and achievable performance targets for this goal?

   a. ✓ – You understand why the performance targets related to your strategic goal have been set as they have. You accept that they are intended to serve two purposes: i) providing tangible, challenging and achievable measures of progress for your work and ii) defining the contribution you need to make to overall strategic success.

   b. X – You have concerns about your performance targets.

Figure 188 translates the Goal Adoption Support Model into a checklist that can be ticked off by individuals for their own strategic goals, with prompts of what to consider for each element of the model.

| My goal: | Prepared by: |
| | Date: |

Goal Adoption Support Checklist

Do you have everything you need to achieve the strategic goal
delegated to you? If you answer no (X), make sure you note down why.

Authority

✓ or X   *Are the lines of authority clear for your goal?*

☐

Policies and standards

✓ or X   *Is your goal supported by policies and standards?*

☐

Resources

✓ or X   *Do you have the resources needed to achieve your goal?*

☐

Goal ownership

✓ or X   *Do you understand the details of your goal and what is required of you
to achieve it?*

☐

Goal connections

✓ or X   *Do you understand the inter-dependencies of your goal with others
across the organisation?*

☐

Strategic purpose

✓ or X   *Do you understand how your goal contributes to strategic success?*

☐

Meaningful progress

✓ or X   *Are you confident that progress on your goal will be meaningful?*

☐

Performance targets

✓ or X   *Do you have relevant, specific and achievable performance targets for
this goal?*

☐

Figure 188 The Goal Adoption Support Checklist

9.5   From strategy map to strategic plan

Figure 189 shows, in strategy map format, your goals for the strategy adoption phase of the strategy lifecycle.

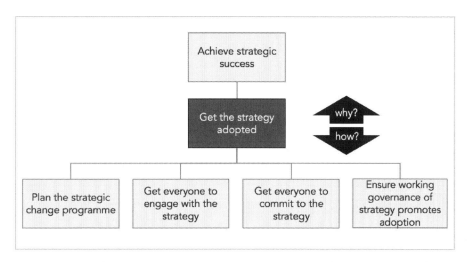

Figure 189 Planning, engagement, commitment and governance within strategy adoption

You have already seen in this chapter the need to get everyone engaged with, and committed to, the strategy. You also need to ensure that arrangements for working governance of strategy don't get in the way of strategy adoption, and, ideally, promote it. Once these are in place, you are ready to build the strategic plan.

The strategy map you have just created provides the logical structure underpinning your strategic plan. This is a great first step in strategic planning. You now understand the key dependencies and interdependencies (where goals serve multiple purposes) underlying your strategic plan. Such robustness is hard to achieve without strategy mapping and provides a strong foundational framework for building the remaining detail of your strategic plan. This includes *goal delegation, goal prioritisation, risk assessment, goal target-setting* and *time-slicing.*

You have seen in Chapter 5, that strategic risk is an ongoing issue throughout the strategy lifecycle, requiring governance provisions to monitor and review it. Risks identified when the strategy was written will have changed by the time the strategic plan is finalised and will change again throughout strategy adaptation. Due to this changing nature of risks, risk assessment will be considered as part of strategy adaptation in Chapter 10.

9.5.1 Goal delegation

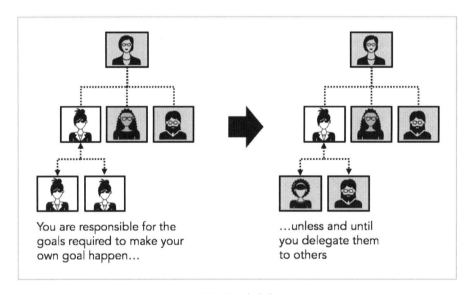

You are responsible for the goals required to make your own goal happen...

...unless and until you delegate them to others

Figure 190 Goal delegation

Goal delegation may prove to be a formality after all of the adoption conversations you have just had, but it is an important formality. Your adoption conversations should have evolved to include everyone who needed to be involved and, hence, who ought to have goals delegated to them. Following these adoption conversations, goal delegation shouldn't come as a surprise to anyone. Goal delegation is important because distributed goal ownership is the foundation for all strategy adoption. By goal ownership, we don't mean a name being attached to a goal on paper only. Goal ownership means active engagement and willing commitment to the achievement of that goal. To try to ensure that goal ownership continues to be delegated all the way to frontline teams, a simple rule is recommended: if you have a goal delegated to you, you are responsible for, and will be held accountable for, it and all its sub-goals and sub-sub-goals until you delegate these goals to someone else. This means that you are responsible for all of the actions that are required to make your own goal happen, unless and until you have delegated responsibility for those actions to someone else (Fig. 190).

9.5.2 Goal prioritisation

It is all too easy to dismiss goal prioritisation, especially when you are considering the handful of core strategic goals. Clearly, they are all important! Yet, consider the dangers of failing to prioritise clearly enough. Antonio Nieto-Rodriguez, a seasoned executive at several global corporations, warns in a Harvard Business Review article on prioritisation what will happen if organisations give equal priority to goals such as improving both customer satisfaction and operational efficiency.[18] All this does is leave staff unclear about their best course of action when one option favours efficiency and the alternative favours customer satisfaction. RyanAir, according to Nieto-Rodriguez, is one of the few companies to leave their employees in no doubt on this issue – operational efficiency takes preference over customer satisfaction.

So, you need to make sure that the prioritisation of goals is made clear. Take care also not to confuse the two possible meanings of priority. To say something has a higher priority can mean it is more *important*: it should be done in preference or should have more time, effort and resources dedicated to it. Alternatively, a higher priority might be more *urgent* and should simply be done first. In the remainder of this discussion, you will take priority to mean importance. Within the context of strategy mapping, designating something as more urgent is better dealt with in target-setting, which you will come on to next.

Figure 191 shows the Cascade Model of Goal Prioritisation. It is derived from the Analytic Hierarchy Process (AHP), devised by the late Thomas L. Saaty, a mathematician and Professor at the Joseph M. Katz Graduate School of Business, University of Pittsburgh. Originally published in 1977,[19] Saaty went on to publish over two dozen books on the subject.[20] AHP combines thinking from both maths and psychology and is now established as one of the most robust and systematic processes for complex decision-making. It has, for example, been used by Microsoft to quantify the quality of software systems, by the University of Cambridge to decide offshore plant locations and by the American Society of Civil Engineers to assess risk in cross-country petroleum pipelines.[21]

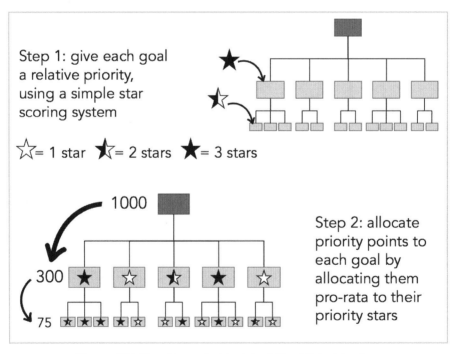

Figure 191 The Cascade Model of Goal Prioritisation

Much of the process of AHP focuses on deconstructing a decision into a cascade of its constituent elements - just as strategy can be cascaded into its elements using strategy mapping. To start the Cascade Model of Goal Prioritisation, you need to pick a goal in your strategy map. If you wish to prioritise the entire strategy map, pick the primary goal, although you could pick any goal and prioritise only the goals beneath it. To prioritise your goals, a three-point or five-point priority scoring system typically works fine. Saaty's original version of the Analytic Hierarchy Process had a nine-point scoring system, with the facility to go into even finer detail, if necessary. For the present example, you will use a three-point system indicated by stars. As shown in Figure 191, you give the goals either a one, two- or three-star priority. Next, you allocate priority points by cascading them down the strategy map. Give your start-goal an arbitrary number of priority points – make sure the number of points is around 50 times the number of goals you are distributing them to – in this case 17 goals, so 1,000 points is fine (Figure 192).

You cascade these priority points down through the strategy map by allocating them in proportion to the star rating of each goal. In the row of goals under the primary goal, for example, you have five goals with, from left to right, three stars, one star, two stars, three stars and two stars respectively. The total number of stars across the row is, therefore, ten (3+1+2+3+3=10). So, a three-star goal gets 3/10ths of the 1,000 points, a one-star goal gets $1/10^{th}$ of the 1,000 points etc. Figure 192 shows how priority points continue to cascade down through the strategy map. As a result of this priority cascade, you start to get some striking differences from your initial three-point priority scoring system. The two goals circled in Figure 192 have nearly an eight-fold difference in priority, which is remarkable, when your original scoring system had only a three-fold difference to begin with.

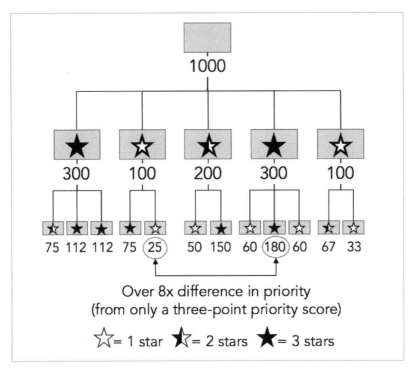

Figure 192 Cascading priority points across a strategy map

9.5.3 Target-setting and time-slicing

You were introduced to strategy measurement in Chapter 6. You now need to look at the practicalities of target setting as part of strategic planning for the case study, Artigence. At the end of Chapter 8 Artigence defined their success-defining KPI; they aimed to achieve £79M annual recurring revenue (ARR) by the end of the strategy (5 years from its launch). They also defined their first critical-to-success KPI: 50% of new customer revenue should be from inbound marketing leads by the end of their 5-year strategy.

You have already seen how to 'elaborate' a strategy using the why-how logic of strategy mapping to connect strategic goals. Similarly, you can connect together and align multiple *measurements* of strategy in order to identify 'critical-to-success' KPIs. Figure 193 demonstrates this using the strategy map built for the Artigence case study in Chapter 8. The figure shows the part of the map concerned with *migrating marketing from outbound to inbound leads*, and the targets that might be needed for each goal.

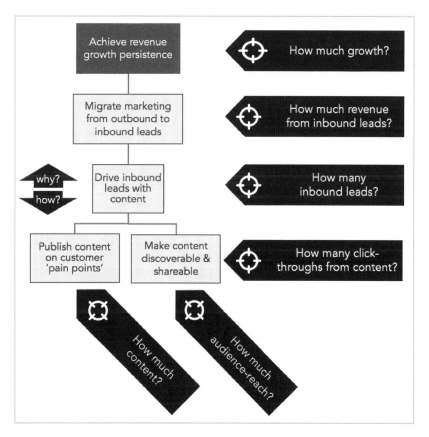

Figure 193 KPIs from Artigence's strategy map

The strategy map says Artigence is going to:

1. *achieve revenue growth persistence* by *migrating marketing from outbound to inbound leads;*

2. *migrate marketing from outbound to inbound leads* by *driving inbound leads with content;*

3. *drive inbound leads with content* by *publishing content on*

customer 'pain points' and *making that content discoverable and shareable.*

Given this logical arrangement of goals, it is relatively straightforward to see that there needs to be some sort of cascade of KPIs for setting and tracking their performance. So, for example, if Artigence have a revenue target derived from a growth persistence rate, they can ask how much of that revenue should come from inbound leads. From Artigence's financial projections the target for this 'critical-to-success' KPI (inbound-lead-driven-revenue) was defined as 50% of new customer revenue from inbound leads by the end of the strategy. From this they can research (or guesstimate and subsequently refine) an inbound lead conversion rate and average order value to give them a target for the number of inbound leads needed to achieve the 'inbound-lead-driven-revenue' target.

The Cascade Model of KPIs proposes that wherever you have a strategy map, you can cascade KPIs over that map, thereby revealing the logical connection between the individual KPIs (Figure 194).

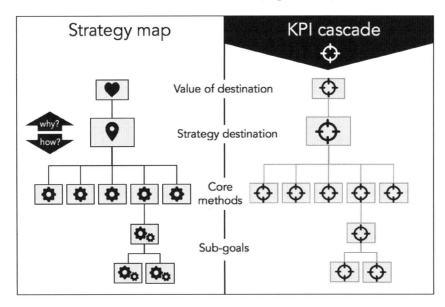

Figure 194 The Cascade Model of KPIs

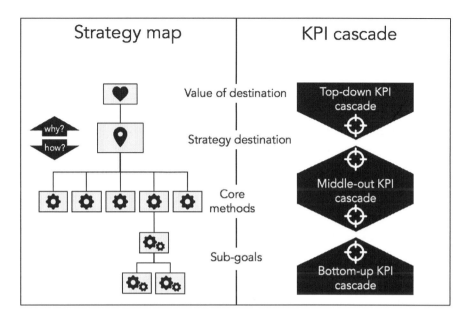

Figure 195 KPIs don't always need to be cascaded in one direction

As illustrated in Figure 195, there is no reason for this cascading process to be limited to any single direction. It could start at the top of the strategy map and work down, start at the bottom of the map and work up or even start in the middle and work out.

Coming back to the practicalities of Artigence, Katerina and Daniel had several adoption conversations with the marketing and sales teams to 'elaborate' the core method, i.e. to find ways to *migrate marketing from outbound to inbound leads*, which led to the goal *drive inbound leads with content*. Their first conclusion was that this part of the strategy needed to be tested and proven in steps.

Step 1: they needed to prove that they could build what they described as a 'content engine'; a group of people capable of producing a regular stream of engaging content that would generate marketing leads. This, they thought, could be tested by the third quarter of next year (year 1 of the strategy).

Step 2: they needed to find out if the marketing leads generated in this way could actually be converted into customers. This would take longer, to allow for the sales cycle; the period of time that elapses between a prospect deciding they want to buy something and them deciding what to buy and placing the order. The end of year 2 of the strategy was their aim here. By time-slicing the strategic plan in this way, they could then work out what targets to put in place to check they were on track to meet the main critical-to-success KPI (50% of new customer revenue from inbound leads) by the time the strategy ended in 5 years' time (Figure 196).

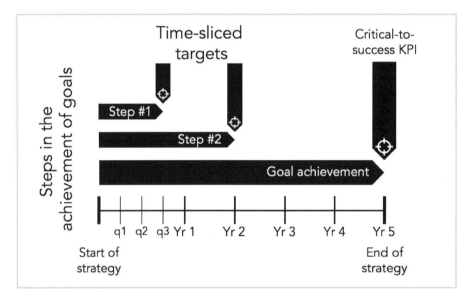

Figure 196 Steps in the progress of goals time-slices targets

Having time-sliced the targets, the next step was to put numbers to them. Step 2 required them to prove that inbound leads could be converted into customers. From their previous projections on overall annual recurring revenue (ARR), by the end of Year 2 of the strategy, they needed to have ARR of £28M (Fig. 197). This is a rise of £11M of new customer revenue from the previous year (£17M at the end of Year 1).

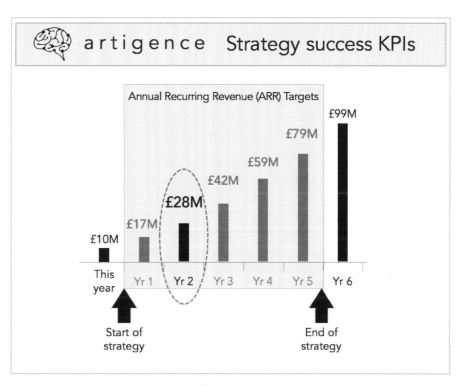

Figure 197 Target ARR for Artigence at the end of Year 2

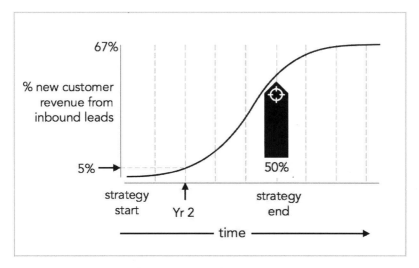

Figure 198 Estimate of proportion of Artigence new customer revenue coming from inbound leads at the end of Year 2 of their 5-year strategy

The question they then needed to answer was, how much of that £11M increase in ARR needed to come from inbound leads?

From the growth curve showing the percent of sales coming from inbound leads over the course of their 5-year strategy (Fig. 198), Artigence was able to estimate that 5% of this new customer revenue needed to come from inbound leads. By the end of year 2 of the strategy, therefore, £550k of new customer revenue needs to have come from inbound leads (5% of £11M = £550k).

The Step 1 target (to prove that they could build what they described as a 'content engine') took a little more work. Katerina produced a marketing and sales funnel for inbound leads (Fig. 199), identifying at each stage of the funnel the percentage of people who, according to Artigence's data, moved on to the next stage. In order to generate £550k of new customer revenue by the end of Year 2 of the strategy, Katerina worked out that they would need to have had 36,000 visitors, 8% of whom (2,880) converted into marketing leads and so on (decreasing in line with the percentage at each stage of the funnel) until 8 eventually became customers. This, at an Average Order Value (AOV) of £68,750, would achieve the target of £550k revenue. By the third quarter (Q3) of Year 1 of the strategy, they would, therefore, need to prove they were capable of producing a regular stream of engaging content that would generate marketing leads. In order to have 8 customers from inbound leads at the end of Year 2, it was felt that 2 new customers ought to be on their way to conversion by Q3 of Year 1. Remember the Step 1 target is nothing to do with sales or revenue; this target is about generating enough content to drive enough marketing leads to be able to convert 2 customers, even if they have not actually committed to purchase by Q3 of Year 1. Working up through the marketing and sales funnel from 2 customers, the target, therefore, is to have attracted 9,338 visitors, and converted 747 of them into marketing leads by Q3 of Year 1.

Marketing and sales funnel		q3 Year 1	Year 2
8%	Visitors	9,338	36,000
15%	Marketing-leads	747	2,880
25%	Sales-qualified-leads	112	432
25%	Pitch-delivered	28	108
30%	Price-quoted	7	27
	Sale-confirmed	2	8
	Average order value (AOV)		£68,750
	New revenue from inbound leads		£550k

Figure 199 Marketing and Sales Funnel for Artigence's inbound marketing

These targets, along with the documented delegation, prioritisation and target-setting of all the other goals identified as necessary to reach the core strategy goals, form the basis of Artigence's strategic plan – the ultimate output of the adoption stage of the strategy lifecycle. By ensuring the active engagement and willing commitment of all the change-makers involved, the strategic plan is the vehicle that will ultimately deliver strategy success.

9.6   Summary and key takeaways from Chapter 9

1. Strategy adoption involves **strategic planning**, and the **active engagement and willing commitment** of people across the organisation

2. Strategy adoption is important to foster an **organisational culture** conducive to strategic success. As a result, your strategy will have less chance of becoming one of the 44% of strategies that fail.

3. Engagement and commitment can be secured by ensuring employees:

   a. find their work **purposeful**.

   b. make '**tangible progress towards meaningful goals**' (the 'Progress Principle')

   c. have **ownership of their goals** and understand the **connections** between their goals and the goals of others.

4. Research suggests that the **engagement and commitment of middle managers** is particularly critical to strategic success.

5. **The 'H' Model of Strategy Adoption** depicts how authority for strategic change moves from senior leaders to change-makers across the organisation. It explains how the **elaboration of strategic goals** and **adoption conversations** are key enablers of successful strategy adoption.

6. **Adoption conversations about strategy can be difficult**, so giving careful thought about how to handle them is important. The following rules can help:

   a. Have **explicit rules** for adoption conversations;

   b. Be clear from the start about **intentions, purpose and outcomes**;

   c. **Make time** for the conversation;

   d. Choose an appropriate **group size**. 5-7 participants is ideal;

   e. Ensure the '**psychological safety**' of participants;

   f. Appoint a **leader** to guide and facilitate adoption conversations.

7. Once the strategy map has been elaborated to the point of defining the strategic goals of front-line teams, it needs to be **validated**. The **SaNity Check Model** provides a systematic way of doing so.

8. The **Goal Adoption Support Model** enables you to check that the adoption process has actually given individual strategy goal owners all they need to achieve their goal.

9. **Strategic planning** includes goal delegation, goal prioritisation, risk assessment, goal target-setting and time-slicing.

10. **Goal delegation** is important because distributed goal ownership is the foundation for all strategy adoption.

11. The **Cascade Model of Goal Prioritisation** can be used to attribute relative importance to strategic goals.

12. The **Cascade Model of KPIs** proposes that wherever you have a strategy map, you can cascade KPIs over that map, thereby revealing the logical connection between the individual KPIs.

13. **Time-sliced targets** can be used to check that you are on track to meet your success-defining and critical-to-success KPIs.

9.7   Let's talk about... strategy adoption

Use these questions to prompt deeper conversations on strategy adoption across your organisation

1. How engaged in the roll out of strategy have your middle managers and front-line teams been in the past? Did that work okay? Would you want to do things differently next time around?

2. *How systematic would you want to be in elaborating your strategic goals? Could you map your core strategic goals out all the way to front-line teams and then validate the logic of all the goal connections?*

3. *Do all of your major strategic goals have clear owners? Do the owners know they are strategic goal owners? Do they act like strategic goal owners? In general, are you good enough at managing the ownership of strategic goals?*

4. *How much 'psychological safety' do you offer as an organisation? Does everyone feel they can speak truth to power? Is everyone confident enough to take risks in their work? Are you tolerant of failure? Are you comfortable with the culture surrounding strategy?*

Notes on Chapter 9

(all web content accessed between April and September 2020)

[1] Nohria N and Beer M, 2000. *Cracking the Code of Change.* Harvard Business Review, May / June 2000.

[2] Keichel W, 1982. *Corporate Strategists under fire.* Fortune Magazine 27 December 1982, p38.

[3] Jones P, 2018. *Do 9 out of 10 strategies really fail? I don't think so!* https://www.excitant.co.uk/do-9-out-of-10-strategies-fail/

[4] Candido CFJ and Santos FP, 2015. *Strategy implementation: What is the failure rate?* Journal of Management and Organization. 21 (2): 237–262.

[5] Quote Investigator, 2017. *Culture Eats Strategy for Breakfast.* https://quoteinvestigator.com/2017/05/23/culture-eats/

[6] Oxford English Dictionary. *Culture.* https://www.lexico.com/definition/culture

[7] Several blog posts have identified the traits of positive organisational culture, including LBMC Employment Partners, 2019. *Characteristics of a Positive Workplace Culture*. https://www.lbmc.com/blog/characteristics-positive-workplace-culture/; Rozen M 2016. *The Seven Characteristics Of Successful Company Cultures*. https://www.huffpost.com/entry/the-seven-characteristics_b_11339884

[8] McKee A, 2019. *Keep Your Company's Toxic Culture from Infecting Your Team*. Harvard Business Review, 29 April 2019.

[9] McKee A, 2019. *Keep Your Company's Toxic Culture from Infecting Your Team*. Harvard Business Review, 29 April 2019. p2.

[10] Gallup, 2017. *The State of the Global Workforce*. https://www.gallup.com/workplace/238079/state-global-workplace-2017.aspx

[11] Gallup, 2018. *Employee Engagement on the Rise in the U.S.* https://news.gallup.com/poll/241649/employee-engagement-rise.aspx

[12] PwC Strategy&, 2019. *The Crisis of Purpose*. https://www.strategyand.pwc.com/gx/en/unique-solutions/cds/approach/research-motivation/the-crisis-of-purpose-infographic.pdf

[13] Amabile T and Kramer SJ, 2011. *The Progress Principle: Using Small Wins to Ignite Joy, Engagement, and Creativity at Work*. Harvard Business Review Press.

[14] Hu Q, 2001. *In Praise of Middle Managers*. Harvard Business Review, September 2001.

[15] Tabrizi B, 2014. *The Key to Change is Middle Management*. Harvard Business Review. October 2014.

[16] Wikipedia. *Social Distance*. https://en.wikipedia.org/wiki/Social_distance.

[17] Morrison E, Hutcheson S, Nilsen E, Fadden J and Franklin N, 2019. *Strategic Doing: Ten Skills for Agile Leadership*. John Wiley and Sons Inc, Hoboken NJ.

[18] Nieto-Rodriguez A, 2016. *How to Prioritize Your Company's Projects*. Harvard Business Review. December 13, 2016.

[19] Saaty TL, 1977. *A scaling method for priorities in hierarchical structures*. Journal of Mathematical Psychology 15 (3): 234-281.

---

[20] Saaty TL, 2016. *Resume.* https://www.informs.org/content/download/368376/3848037/file/Thomas_Saaty_CV_2016.pdf

[21] Wikipedia. *Analytic Hierarchy Process.* https://en.wikipedia.org/wiki/Analytic_hierarchy_process

Chapter 10

Strategy adaptation

Recognise risks.
Understand uncertainty.
Mitigate harm and exploit opportunities.

Strategy adaptation is the third and final stage of the strategy lifecycle and features processes that demand both resilience and agility of the organisation as it strives to reach its strategy destination (Figure 200).

Figure 200 The strategy lifecycle model highlighting strategy adaptation

Strategy adaptation means adjusting and refining a strategy in response to on-going insights from strategic KPIs and to changing circumstances, whether that be the actions of a competitor or a global pandemic. Most of the lifespan of a strategy is spent in strategy adaptation. If you look at the Artigence case study, their strategy was 5 months in strategy development, 2 months in strategy adoption and 58 months in strategy adaptation (Figure 201). Adaptation, therefore, is the default state for strategy. Production and adoption are *transitional* stages in which you create the strategy and work out how to get it planned, engaged with and committed to across the organisation. Once these are accomplished, you then need to pursue strategic success whilst continuously adapting to changing circumstances.

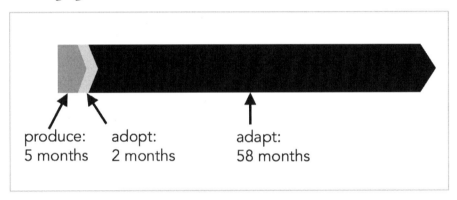

Figure 201 Time spent by Artigence in different stages of the lifecycle

In this chapter, you will begin by addressing the conundrum of strategy adaptation – why bother having a strategy if you are going to change it all the time? Then you will delve deeper into the concept from first principles – what exactly is strategy adaptation, what are its component parts and what does it set out to achieve? You will learn about the resilience and agility required for strategy adaptation, how to identify strategic risk, and then how to prioritise and adapt to that risk. Finally, you will explore ways to understand and anticipate the future in order to build strategic adaptability.

10.1 The conundrum of strategy adaptation

A key feature of strategy is its endurance. As you discovered in Chapter 1, strategy is a big investment involving lots of people that acts as a constant, long-term navigational beacon to align action and guide decisions across the organisation. Except now you are hearing that strategies adapt in response to changing circumstances. This reveals a conundrum: how can strategy be a constant, long-term navigational beacon yet still adapt in response to changing circumstances?

The answer lies in the Separation Model of Strategy, you first learned about in Chapter 2 (shown again in Figure 202).

Strategy defines the destination that the organisation has committed to reach and this remains constant and unchanged over the lifetime of the strategy. The *strategic plan* defines who is going to do what by when to make progress towards the strategic destination. This needs to adapt to changing circumstances.

Figure 202 The Separation Model of Strategy

As you may have realised, this has avoided the thorny issue of core methods, to which there is no easy and universal answer. Core methods are the handful of high-level actions by which you aim to get to your strategic destination. They are part of strategy. There is no point in defining a destination without a credible and coherent account of how that destination will be reached. This is what 'grounds' strategy and prevents it from being merely fantasy or whim. So, does this mean that a strategy's core methods are beyond the reach of strategy adaptation? To which the answer is 'sort of'.

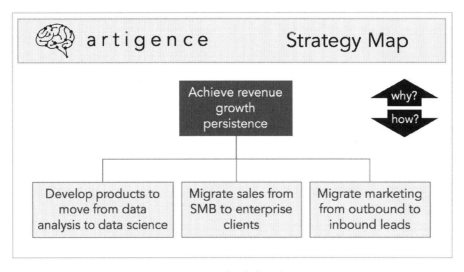

Figure 203 Artigence high-level strategy map

Consider the Artigence case study. Their strategy destination, which is all about revenue growth persistence, has three core methods: moving from data analytics apps to data science solutions, moving from smaller clients to enterprise clients and moving from outbound to inbound marketing (Fig. 203). Now, imagine circumstances change so much that they decide the only way they can hit their revenue growth target is by reverting to their existing data analytics apps and selling lots of them to their current, smaller clients by slashing prices and advertising heavily. This isn't strategy adaptation; this is a whole new strategy. On the other hand, they might discover that they cannot 'migrate' from outbound to inbound marketing but instead need to do both: they need inbound marketing *as well as* outbound. This would probably be seen as a modest strategy adaptation. The extent to which the core methods of strategy can be adapted without triggering a strategy review, leading to a new strategy, is a judgement call. As discussed in Chapter 5, this judgement is a matter of strategy governance and how the judgement is made ought to be covered in the Strategy Governance Charter (Section 5.5).

10.2 Strategy adaptability = resilience + agility

The next big question about strategy adaptation is, 'what is it that you need to do in order to adapt a strategic plan to cope with changing circumstances?' To understand this, you need to dig deeper into two different change-enablers that can be employed to adapt strategy: resilience and agility.

Resilience is the ability to withstand challenges, shocks or stresses without impairment *or* the ability to yield and recover. This definition is a hybrid derived from:

1. Psychology, where resilience refers to the psychological ability to adapt well to difficult circumstances (e.g. family or economic circumstances);[1]

2. Environmental science, where resilience means the ability of a country or eco-system to continue to function in the face of challenges (e.g. pollution, climate change), without impairing their long-term prospect;[2]

3. Materials science, where resilience is the ability of a material to absorb energy when it is deformed elastically and release that energy upon unloading.[3]

To be agile is to be able to move quickly and easily;[4] to be nimble, lithe or spry;[5] to be alert and able to think quickly and clearly.[6] An agile organisation is one that adapts to new and emerging circumstances through innovation. In their excellent book, *Building the Agile Business Through Digital Transformation*, consultants Neil Perkin and Peter Abraham suggest[7] that organisational agility is typically associated with:

1. an incremental approach to innovation (e.g. working in sprints);

2. collaborative, cross-functional, failure-tolerant ways of working;

3. a strong focus on customer needs, with repeated customer testing as work progresses.

Defined like this, it is tempting to think of agility and resilience as "two sides of the same coin"[8] or even that they "go together like two lions protecting the entrance to the sacred place."[9] The question is, however, are they different? Is there one route to strategy adaptation or two? The answer comes from an unexpected source: the concept of yin and yang in ancient Chinese philosophy.[10]

The concepts of 'yin and yang' are representative of a dualist view of the world and hence have lots of different contrasting pairs of ideas associated with them. Linguistically they are complex terms, but a credible case can be made for associating them with the dark / cloudy / shaded side (yin) and the light / bright side (yang) of a hill or mountain. Other associations include (in yin then yang order): feminine/masculine, moon/sun and earth/sky. The association of interest here is that yin means passive and yang means active.

Figure 204 shows how this applies to resilience and agility.

Resilience

1. To toughen or harden systems and processes to withstand the pressures of changing circumstances

2. Enabling systems and processes to yield to the pressures of changing circumstances AND recover quickly and completely

Yin   Yang

Passive   Active

Agility

1. Rapid, innovative response to a challenge or opportunity

2. Alert to opportunities for to change

3. Quick and nimble to initiate innovation

4. Iterative, flexible, purposeful path to find solutions

Figure 204 Connecting Yin and Yang to Resilience and Agility

10.2.1 Enhancing strategic resilience

Enhancing strategic resilience can involve either 'hardening' or 'softening' how your organisation responds to the challenges, shocks or stresses it encounters. Hardening your organisation and its systems and processes makes it able to withstand the pressures of changing circumstances. This can be done by over-specification, by having built-in redundancy or ready-to-roll contingency plans. This is the underlying principle of fail-safe IT systems or a retailer having more than one distribution centre covering key regions. This can also be done by design – you design your systems to work normally under a wider range of more extreme circumstances. At the most extreme, just five hours after the first plane hit the World Trade Centre on 9/11, the first American Express staff arrived at their back-up centre across the Hudson River in New Jersey. 3,800 of their colleagues had been working in the World Trade Centre, 11 of whom tragically lost their lives. By the end of the next business day, the back-up centre team was well on their way to resuming normal service.[11]

Softening your systems and processes makes them yield elastically to stress and bounce back without impairment. Encouraging cross-functional collaboration across the organisation and having diffused power and accountability has been found, for example, to lead to greater levels of resilience because local teams are more able to independently work out new ways of working if their standard operating procedures cease to work as intended.[12]

Resilience is, therefore, like preventative medicine. It inoculates organisations against changing circumstances. When something unexpected threatens to derail the strategy, resilience is intended to help the organisation cope because of the preparation previously put in place. At the time of the coping response, people engaged in the strategy are passive. The systems and processes around them will either withstand the challenge or will yield and bounce back once the challenge has abated. Clearly, building that resilience in the first place is not passive. But, once built, it should enable strategic adaptation without further intervention.

10.2.2 Enhancing strategic agility

Agility, by contrast to resilience, is active. It is therapeutic medicine. It tackles changing circumstances in real time, mobilising the capabilities prepared and practised previously.

In his book *Agile Transformation*, long-time independent consultant, Neil Perkin makes the point that characteristics of organisations which are conducive to scaling and to efficient operations at scale are often what stifle innovation.[13] These might be typified as large teams working in single discipline groups, with strong policies and standards, consistent ways of working, and strict quality and performance standards. He goes on to say, "Small multi-disciplinary teams empowered by digital technologies can generate a disproportionate amount of change and value".[14]

For large organisations, therefore, the first challenge for enhancing strategic agility is how to conjure small multi-disciplinary teams from your existing organisational structure with the time, resources and authority to adapt your strategic plan. This is a key capability needed to underpin strategic agility.

Three other agile capabilities also need to be developed.

1. *Surveillance capability* to ensure that sense can be made of your current situation. What is happening around the strategy? Have you, yourselves, made progress in one aspect of strategy which has had knock-on consequences on other aspects? Are you struggling with parts of the strategy and need to try a different approach? Have any of your competitors noticed what you are doing and responded in ways you need to take account of? Are there changes happening in the wider world that might impact your strategy? Building this situational awareness requires a mix of people, data and processes to build enough surveillance capability to inform you on the potential need for strategic agility.

2. *Commitment capability* to ensure impactful decision-making. The challenge that comes with the surveillance capability you have just built is that it will tend to generate a lot of data. Some will turn out to be utterly irrelevant and some will turn out to be the critical insight that plucked strategic success from the jaws of strategic catastrophe. Sophisticated and efficient decision-making is needed to distinguish between the two, underpinned by commitment to agile action to ensure impact of these decisions.

3. *Responsiveness capability* turns commitment to action into a reality, ensuring that timely change is made. In some cases, the decision to be agile will require the team that was working in one way to switch to working in a different way. This may be hard for the team to learn about the new ways of working, try them out, find they need refinement and get them working effectively and efficiently. Harder

still is when a decision is made that an agile response is needed but no-one has a ready answer on what change needs to be implemented. This is where you need to create the small multi-disciplinary team, described in the introduction to this section.

The three agile capabilities you've just discovered will be revisited later in this chapter: they make up the three sides of the Pyramid Model of Strategy Adaptation, described in detail in Section 10.5.

You have now seen how your organisation can respond with resilience and agility. The next question is, respond to what? To answer this, you must be able to identify strategic risk.

10.3 Identifying strategic risk

As strategy progresses across its lifespan, there are many things that can knock it off course – these are *strategic risks*. An understanding of the nature of these risks and how to identify them serves as a foundation for a far more systematic approach to strategy adaptation than the default 'wait-until-it-happens-and-then-work-out-what-to-do' approach.

10.3.1 The nature of risk

At the heart of all risk lies uncertainty. Certainty gives rise to consequences; uncertainty gives rise to risks. This uncertainty, as far as strategy is concerned, raises the potential for harm, for opportunity or, often, for both.

To work well, strategy adaptation needs to recognise the risks standing in the way of strategy success, understand the nature of the underlying uncertainty, and decide how to mitigate any harm or exploit any opportunity arising from that uncertainty. For example, understanding your customer needs is nearly always strategically important. Customer needs changing is therefore a strategic risk. This will readily lead to harm if products your customers used to love are then loved less. It could, however, also lead to a huge opportunity. If customer needs have changed for you, they will also have changed for your competitors, and recognising these changing needs first is an opportunity that could give you significant strategic advantage.

Figure 205 shows these relationships as the Nature of Strategic Risk Model.

Figure 205 The Nature of Strategic Risk Model

If you are surprised to see risks connected to opportunities, you've been missing out. There is a whole world of possibilities waiting to be discovered for anyone open-minded enough to look for the positive implications of uncertainty, not just the harm it can cause.

Figure 206 shows a template for a 'Strategic Risk Register'. This is derived directly from the Nature of Strategic Risk Model and allows you to identify the underlying 'uncertainty' that a risk introduces, then explore and record both the potential harm and the exploitable opportunities available as a result of that uncertainty.

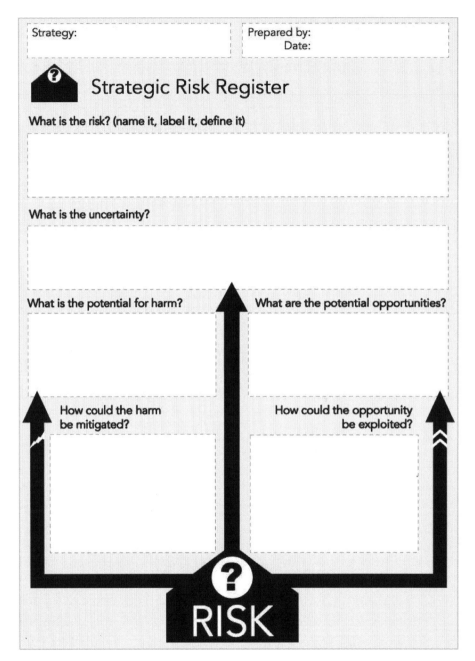

Figure 206 The Strategic Risk Register

10.3.2 Types of strategic risk

In order to identify the risks associated with strategy it is important to understand the different types of risk to look out for. There are four different types of risk to consider to begin with: marketplace risks, remote risks, knock-on risks and internal risks.

1. *Marketplace risks.* The most obvious risks are marketplace risks. Your customers don't end up buying what they said they wanted. You competitor launches the very same product you were about to spend a year developing. Advertising prices soar, making your perfectly crafted marketing campaign unaffordable.

2. *Remote risks.* Other risks in your operating environment may initially seem remote but could quickly turn into strategy-killers. A global pandemic, maybe. Or a trade war involving a country where some of your key suppliers are based.

3. *Knock-on risks.* Another type of risk from your operating environment is especially hard to handle because of its knock-on impact. These risks are triggered by events that have no direct impact on your strategy at all. But their knock-on consequences are what cause you the problems. A simple example might be a new company taking up tenancy in the building next to yours, which has no impact on your business until they start recruiting your key staff, who they've bumped into in local coffee shops and bars. Or a huge scandal breaks that has nothing to do with your organisation or your products… until your key social media brand ambassador is discovered to be deeply implicated and is tarnished badly enough to taint your brand as well.

4. *Internal risks.* It is important to recognise that strategic risks are not just things that happen to you from the outside world. You are a source of risks yourself, and these could have a big impact on your strategy. Your cash-flow is disrupted because bad debts weren't

pursued vigorously enough. Your website crashes in the middle of a peak trading period. Your newly-launched product needs to be recalled due to a safety issue.

Figure 207 shows these four different types of risk that can prompt strategy adaptation both from within the organisation and from its operating environment.

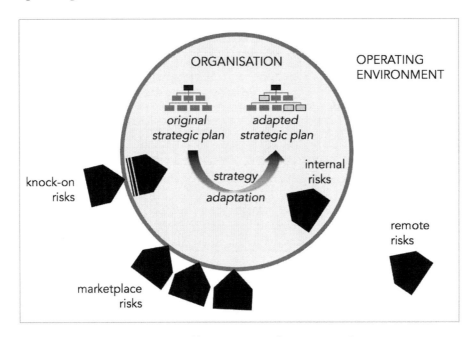

Figure 207 Different types of strategic risks

There is one final type of strategic risk that you need to consider which is harder than most to manage: emergent risks.

Emergent risks are ones you don't anticipate until they are upon you. A common reason for them is that they arise due to the changes brought about by strategy. Changing one aspect of your organisation will often put other aspects under strain. A new supplier, for example, might give you more customer value for less money, but may not be able to guarantee the 'just-in-time' deliveries your entire manufacturing process relies on. As Figure 208 illustrates, these types of risk can emerge from strategic change through two routes. The first is internal to your organisation. Marketing innovation disrupts sales. Sales innovation disrupts operations. Operational innovation disrupts finance. The second route to emergent strategic risk is from strategic change that has an impact on the operating environment, and the operating environment then responds. An example of this is how your competitors respond to the launch of your new products.

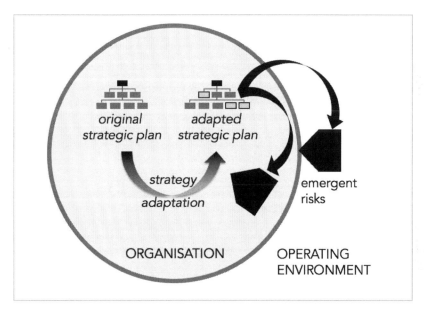

Figure 208 Strategic change can give rise to emergent risks

10.4 Prioritising strategic risk

How you prioritise risks is the next issue you need to consider. The inspiration behind the model you are going to use to prioritise strategic risk is Failure Modes and Effects Analysis (FMEA). This technique was devised by the US military in 1949,[15] adopted extensively by both automotive and aeronautic industries over the subsequent decades and is now used in everything from knitwear manufacturing[16] to semiconductor, food service, plastics, software and healthcare sectors.[17]

FMEA calculates the relative priority for different risks, given their *likelihood of occurrence*, their *severity* and how readily they are to be *detected* in order to be mitigated. Figure 209 shows an analysis of the risks involved in selling a sandwich, as might be undertaken by the owner of a small, independent, town-centre sandwich shop.

Failure Modes and Effects Analysis

Function: Sell sandwich

Likelihood	Severity	Ease of detection	Risk priority number (RPN)
Failure mode #1: sandwich is stale			
3	1	2	6
Failure mode #2: wrong label (wrong filling)			
4	2	2	16
Failure mode #3: wrong label (allergen not identified)			
2	5	3	30
Failure mode #4: bacterial contamination			
1	5	5	25
Key to effects:			
One in every ... 1. 1 million 2. 10,000 3. 1,000 4. 100 5. 10 ...sandwiches sold	Customer ... 1. Is disappointed 2. Complains 3. Never comes back 4. Warns friends 5. Is seriously ill	Detection is ... 1. Obvious 2. Easy 3. Difficult 4. Very difficult 5. Impossible	RPN = likelihood x severity x ease of detection

Figure 209 FMEA on the risks of selling a sandwich

The analysis starts by defining the domain in which you wish to compare risks, in this case the risks involved in selling a sandwich. The first task is to work out a scoring system that is meaningful for this domain. FMEA prioritises risks using three scores:

1. *Likelihood score* – The highest likelihood is taken to be the risk occurring one in every ten sandwiches sold. Given that they sell between 50 and 100 sandwiches per day, this highest likelihood would occur several times a day and is given a score of five. The lowest likelihood is one in a million; a likelihood that would occur once in every twenty to thirty years. In other words, a once in a business-lifetime event. This is given a score of one.

2. *Severity score* – The highest severity is making a customer seriously ill (score of five) and the lowest severity is a customer being disappointed (score of one).

3. *Ease of detection score* – The highest ease of detection score is 'impossible' to detect (score of five) and the lowest is 'obvious' (score of one).

A high risk is deemed to be something that is likely to happen, with severe consequences and is hard to detect. Thus, the risk priority number, by which risks are compared and prioritised, is *likelihood* multiplied by *severity* multiplied by *ease of detection*.

Four different risks are identified in selling a sandwich:

1. *The sandwich is stale.* This doesn't happen very often. Most sandwiches are made on the day. It is only those made late in the day and not sold that might be kept overnight and sold the next day. So, they are likely to be only slightly stale, if at all, and hence will only lead to customer disappointment. It is also pretty easy to spot, if you are looking for the signs. This ends up being the lowest risk priority (3x1x2=6).

2. *The sandwich is sold with a label indicating it has a different filling from the one it actually has.* This happens more frequently than selling stale sandwiches because of the huge range of different sandwiches made and sold. For some customers this will be merely disappointing but for others it will be a reason to complain. Again, it is not too hard to spot if you are looking for it. As a result of the slightly higher likelihood and slightly higher severity, it has a higher risk priority (4x2x2=16).

3. *The sandwich is sold with a label that fails to indicate it contains specific allergens.* This is far less common than 'wrong-filling' labelling mistakes, maybe one in ten thousand sandwiches, as tracking allergens from ingredient to label has always been a priority. The severity, however, could potentially be as high as it gets, making a highly allergic customer seriously ill. It is also difficult to detect. This scores the highest risk priority (2x5x3=30).

4. *The sandwich is sold with bacterial contamination.* This is the nightmare scenario for any food service business. It can cause serious illness in customers and is impossible to detect. Since it is extremely rare, however, it scores lower than the allergen mis-labelling (1x5x5=25).

The highest RPN values indicate the risks with the greatest priority: these are the ones that the business must tackle first. The conclusion from this analysis, for the sandwich shop owner, is that even more rigorous procedures need to be put in place to reduce the likelihood of allergens being missed from labels.

Now you have an understanding of FMEA, you can move on to discover the model, based on FMEA, that you can use to prioritise *strategic risk* – it is called PRiSM, the Prioritising Risk for Strategy Model.

10.4.1 The Prioritising Risk for Strategy Model (PRiSM)

The Prioritising Risk for Strategy Model (PRiSM) is shown as the 'prioritise' stage in Figure 210.

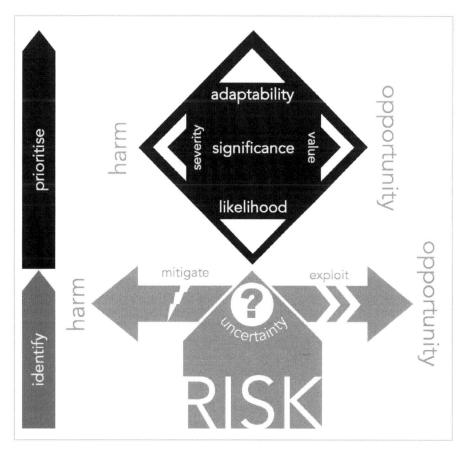

Figure 210 The Prioritising Risk for Strategy Model (PRiSM)

It has several similarities to FMEA and some key differences, a few of which are striking. Let's deal with them first:

1. FMEA only deals with failure modes likely to cause harm, and scores the severity of that harm. PRiSM deals with risks that may give rise to harm or may give rise to opportunity. In addition to measuring *severity of harm* it also measures *value of*

opportunity. This is called 'significance' in PRiSM and is the sum of the scores for severity of harm and value of opportunity.

2. FMEA uses *ease of detection* as one of the three determinants of risk priority. This acts as a 'risk moderator'; it amplifies or dampens other aspects of harm.[18] Risks with high likelihood and high severity are given a lower priority if they are easily detected. PRiSM uses a much richer risk moderator. It is 'adaptability', the capacity to adapt, which, as you will discover in a Section 10.5, includes sense-making, decision-making and change-making. It is, therefore, a lot broader than merely ease of detection. It is also more conducive to planning rather than just assessment and prioritisation.

FMEA and PRiSM are similar in these ways:

1. They both consider the factors contributing to the magnitude of risks and provide methods for comparing their priority;

2. FMEA looks at specific functions (e.g. selling a sandwich) and explores the different failure modes for that function. Similarly, PRiSM looks at strategic goals and explores the risks (of both harm and opportunity) that could result from pursuit of these goals.

3. They both have a scale for the likelihood of an 'event' happening (a failure mode for FMEA and an occurrence of risk for PRiSM);

4. Both models prioritise risks using a multi-factor scoring system. FMEA uses likelihood, severity and ease of detection. PRiSM uses likelihood, significance (in terms of severity of harm and value of opportunity) and adaptability.

Figure 211 shows a template that can be used for prioritising the risks affecting strategic goals using PRiSM. You can use risks identified in the Strategic Risk Register (see Figure 206) in this PRiSM template.

Strategy:			Prepared by: Date:	

◆ **PRiSM** (Prioritising Risk for Strategy Model)

Strategic goal affected by risks:

Define score for: Likelihood	Define score for: Significance		Define score for: Adaptability	Risk priority number (RPN)
	Severity of harm **+**	Value of opportunity		
Low = unlikely High = likely (over a time period)	Low = no harm High = extremely harmful	Low = no value High = extremely valuable	Low = easy High = extremely difficult	RPN = likelihood x significance x adaptability
1. 2. 3. 4. 5.	0. 1. 2. 3. 4. 5.	0. 1. 2. 3. 4. 5.	1. 2. 3. 4. 5.	Note: Significance = severity of harm + value of opportunity Adaptability = capacity to adapt to risk

Risk #1:

Likelihood score:	Harm score:	Value score:	Adaptability score:	RPN:

Risk #2:

Likelihood score:	Harm score:	Value score:	Adaptability score:	RPN:

Risk #3:

Likelihood score:	Harm score:	Value score:	Adaptability score:	RPN:

Figure 211 PRiSM template for prioritising risk for strategy

10.5 Adapting to risk

Having identified and prioritised strategic risks, it is now time to adapt your strategy to mitigate or exploit those risks. To do so, let's expand the *adaptability* factor in PRiSM (Figure 212).

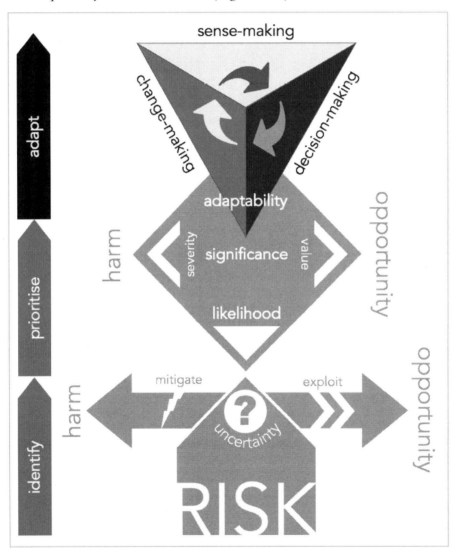

Figure 212 Expanding the adaptability factor in PRiSM

Adapting to risk requires three key activities (Fig. 213):

1. *Sense-making* - seeking out relevant information and giving it meaning;

2. *Decision-making* - recognising what's important; evaluating potential solutions; committing to action;

3. *Change-making* - accepting the need for change; planning change effectively; executing change efficiently.

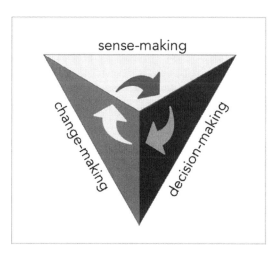

Figure 213 Activities at the heart of strategy adaptation

You make *sense* of what's happening (or likely to happen), you make *decisions* about what needs to be done (or not) and then you make the necessary *changes* happen. The arrows in Figure 213 indicate that these three activities are done in sequence and iteratively. Sense-making informs decision-making. Decision-making commits to change-making. Having made some changes, what you now need to make sense of may have changed, requiring you to revisit sense-making again. Iterating round the loop is the continuous process of strategy adaptation to risk.

These three adaptive activities can be depicted as the faces of a pyramid, each built on a robust base of capability, giving you the Pyramid Model of Strategy Adaptation (Fig. 214).

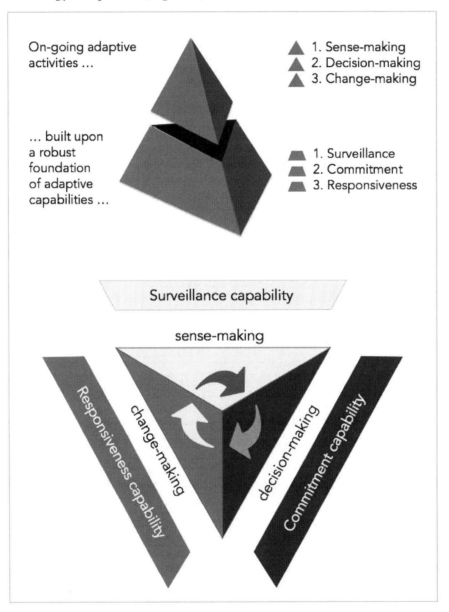

Figure 214 The Pyramid Model of Strategy Adaptation

You were introduced to these adaptive capabilities when you learned about strategic agility earlier in this chapter (Section 10.2.1). It is all very well saying you will make sense of lots of risks but what if you have no means of sensing those risks, their likelihood of occurring or their likely severity? Your sense-making will, in the words of Lord Kelvin at the start of Chapter 6, be of a 'meagre and unsatisfactory kind'.

1. Sense-making needs to be underpinned with a *surveillance capability* that enables effective sense to be made of the world. This includes:

    a. awareness of what needs to be sensed;

    b. the means of acquiring data of the key indicators and determinants of risk;

    c. operating systems and processes to monitor these data streams and recognise significant changes in risk status;

    d. having meaningful alert thresholds to trigger decision-making.

   A recent MIT Sloan Management Review article, suggested "sensemaking is key to effective leadership and yet doesn't figure into executives' mental models of great leaders … Not only do leaders fail to properly use sensemaking themselves, but it's a capability that is often ignored when hiring, evaluating, developing, and promoting leaders. As a result, leaders and organizations aren't nearly as effective as they could be." [19]

2. Decision-making needs to be underpinned by a *commitment capability*. This includes:

    a. a proficiency at assimilating information and insights;

    b. the information processing skill of being able to discern the best course of action from many options;

   c.   the social skill of securing commitment by key decision-makers to a preferred course of action.

3.   Change-making is underpinned by a *responsiveness capability*. This includes:

   a.   a readiness and willingness to take action quickly;

   b.   the flexibility to change priorities and commitments to make room for that action;

   c.   the skill to undertake action effectively and efficiently, so it has the desired impact.

Of course, all these capabilities need to work thoroughly, efficiently and at speed.

Figure 215 gives a template that can be used as a Strategic Risk Adaptation Plan, based on the Pyramid Model of Strategy Adaptation. You can use the high-priority risks recognised in the PRiSM analysis as the basis for your adaptation plan (see Figure 211).

Figure 216 explores these interconnected models using a real historical example: how, with the benefit of hindsight, should organisations have adapted their strategies to handle the threat, and then introduction in 2018, of the General Data Protection Regulation (GDPR) by the European Union.

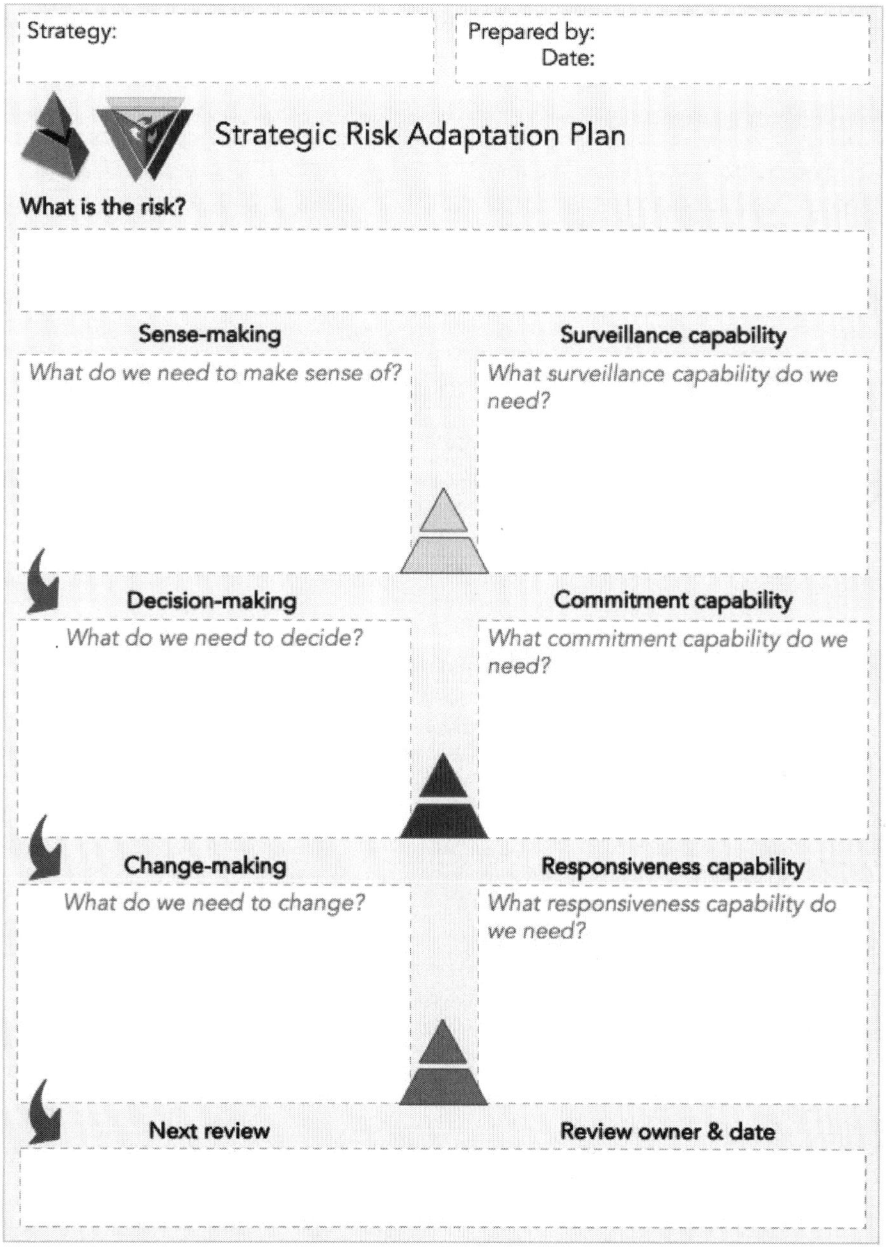

Strategic Risk Adaptation Plan

Strategy: Prepared by:
                                             Date:

What is the risk?

Sense-making

What do we need to make sense of?

Surveillance capability

What surveillance capability do we need?

Decision-making

What do we need to decide?

Commitment capability

What commitment capability do we need?

Change-making

What do we need to change?

Responsiveness capability

What responsiveness capability do we need?

Next review

Review owner & date

Figure 215 Strategic Risk Adaptation Plan

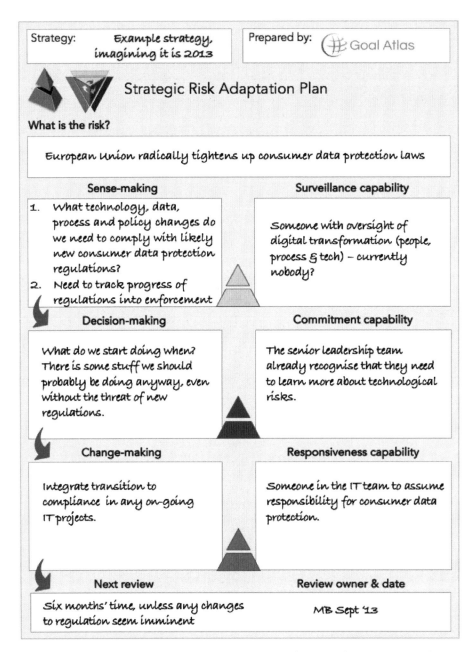

Strategy: **Example strategy, imagining it is 2013**

Prepared by: Goal Atlas

Strategic Risk Adaptation Plan

What is the risk?

European Union radically tightens up consumer data protection laws

Sense-making

1. What technology, data, process and policy changes do we need to comply with likely new consumer data protection regulations?
2. Need to track progress of regulations into enforcement

Surveillance capability

Someone with oversight of digital transformation (people, process & tech) – currently nobody?

Decision-making

What do we start doing when? There is some stuff we should probably be doing anyway, even without the threat of new regulations.

Commitment capability

The senior leadership team already recognise that they need to learn more about technological risks.

Change-making

Integrate transition to compliance in any on-going IT projects.

Responsiveness capability

Someone in the IT team to assume responsibility for consumer data protection.

Next review

Six months' time, unless any changes to regulation seem imminent

Review owner & date

MB Sept '13

Figure 216 Strategic Risk Adaptation Plan – historical GDPR example

10.6 Anticipating the future

A critical issue in building any type of strategic adaptability is understanding and anticipating the future. There are two tools of particular value that can be used in combination here. The first is called the Futures Cone and the second is called VACU analysis.

10.6.1 The Futures Cone

As you gaze into the future, there are a great many things that could potentially happen emanating from the current moment in time. The further into the future your gaze extends, the broader the range of potential futures that come into view. The Futures Cone, originally devised by Charles Taylor of the Strategic Studies Institute,[20] visualises this expanding range of potential futures as a set of nested cones, with each cone representing a different degree of future likelihood (Fig. 217).

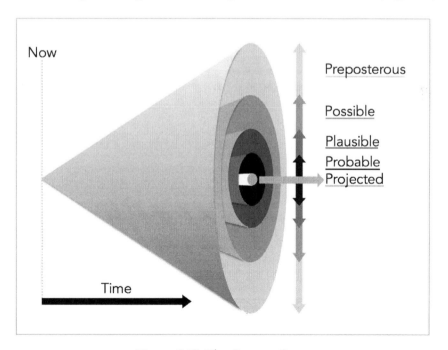

Figure 217 The Futures Cone

The horizontal centre-line of the cone is the *projected* future. This is the default option. This is what will happen if nothing changes. This is the business-as-usual line.

Around the projected future lies a range of *probable* futures. They are likely to happen, given present circumstances. The level of planning you undertake to accommodate these futures should be proportional to:

1. their probability – the higher the probability of them happening, the firmer your plans should be;

2. the extent to which you feel circumstances today are going to continue to shape the future as they are currently shaping the present. In other words, do you see disruption on the horizon?

Next you have *plausible* futures. Since they are outside the cone of probable futures, you are saying they are improbable, yet they could still come about. The means by which they could come about are known and are credible. Here, you possibly don't need elaborate plans yet, but you do need vigilance to spot when a plausible future becomes more probable.

Possible futures are both improbable and implausible, yet substantial changes in circumstances could still see them occur. The only planning needed here is to look for possible futures that would hugely impact you and which could be planned for relatively easily and inexpensively.

Preposterous futures are the ones that you scoff at and dismiss, yet still occasionally come about. These can often be useful provocations in futures-planning sessions. Identify a handful of preposterous futures that are improbable, implausible and impossible. Now try to work out why they are so preposterous and what would need to change to make them possible? Now, do you still think they are as preposterous as you did originally?

Part of the value of the Futures Cone is the recognition that things frequently move from preposterous to actually happening, and hence need to be planned for. President Kennedy's plan to land a man on the moon before the end of the decade was considered preposterous by many commentators in 1961.[21] Within a matter of months landing a man on the moon was realised to be possible and within a few years, it became plausible. It was only in the last year or two before the actual landing that it started to be considered probable.

A very different preposterous future was the United Kingdom crashing out of the European Union with no deal governing any aspect of our future relationship with our former European partners. For the first 18 months after the original Brexit referendum most people (politicians and public alike) were focused on the withdrawal negotiations.[22] What kind of deal would we get? A no-deal Brexit was considered by most to be preposterous. By January 2019, when the Government had secured a negotiated withdrawal agreement but that agreement was rejected by Parliament, a no-deal Brexit turned into a possibility. When Boris Johnson became the UK Prime Minister in June 2019, a no-deal Brexit became plausible[23] and after his prorogation of Parliament it looked probable.[24]

Envisioning the future is hard. Structured and systematic processes like the Futures Cone make it just that little bit less hard. Figure 218 gives a template for exploring the range of futures for any given issue.

Once you have identified potential futures you think are worthy of consideration, the question is what to do next. 'VACU analysis' provides an answer.

| Strategy: | Prepared by: |
| | Date: |

Futures Cone Analysis

Note: *Risk includes harm to be mitigated and opportunity to be exploited*

What is the issue?

Projected risks

Business-as-usual; what will happen if nothing changes.

Probable risks

Likely to happen, given present circumstances.

Plausible risks

Improbable, yet could still come about.

Possible risks

Improbable and implausible, yet substantial changes in circumstances could still see them occur.

Preposterous risks

Improbable, implausible and impossible, yet still occasionally come about.

Figure 218 Template for Futures Cone Analysis

10.6.2 VACU Analysis

The VACU model is a minor but significant adaptation of the VUCA framework (Volatility, Uncertainty, Complexity and Ambiguity), which is cited frequently by online sources and originally attributed to General Maxwell Thurman in 1991.[25]

Volatility, ambiguity, complexity and uncertainty, as ordered in the VACU model, represent a continuum of decreasing understanding and increasing unpredictability about the future (Fig. 219). More crucially, and much more usefully, they represent different types of unknowns and different ways of turning ignorance into insight.

	Volatility	**A**mbiguity	**C**omplexity	**U**ncertainty
Decreasing understanding, increasing unpredictability →				
What does the future hold?	One probability, sometime	A few possibilities	Lots of possibilities	Anything's possible
Challenges ☹	Know what will happen but not when	Dilemmas, dichotomies, alternatives	Too many moving parts, too many interactions	Confusion and complete unpredictability
Solutions ☺	Have better sensors & build in more slack	Do more tests / experiments	Get more / better knowledge expertise	Get more / better information

Figure 219 The VACU model of future challenges and solutions

When something is *volatile*, you know it is likely to happen, you just don't know when. In which case, you may be able improve your surveillance capabilities. The sooner you know things are about to happen, the better you will be able to respond. If that isn't possible, you may be able to build greater resilience to withstand the stress, even if it arrives undetected.

In *ambiguous* situations, there are only a few possibilities, but they all seem equally probable. In which case, the time may have come for small scale tests and experiments. Minimum viable products may need to be prototyped. You need to get out of the office and start asking customers key questions.

If the situation is *complex*, there are lots of moving parts and lots of interactions between them. Out of that comes too many possibilities and insufficient insight into which of the many possibilities are plausible, which are probable and hence which you should plan for. The solution is likely to come from greater knowledge and expertise: does experience of similar situations in the past lead to a set of more (or less) likely outcomes?

Under circumstances of *uncertainty*, anything's possible. It is typified by high levels of confusion and complete unpredictability. In which case, what is needed is more information or better information. The more that a confusing situation can have its causes and effects identified and named, the more likely it is that these causes and effects can be connected.

Figure 220 shows a template for analysing any issue using the VACU framework.

Strategy: | Prepared by:
                                   | Date:

VACU VACU Analysis

What is the issue?

Where does the issue lie on the VACU continuum ?

V [ ]   A [ ]   C [ ]   U [ ]

   Volatile   Ambiguous   Complex   Uncertain

Decreasing understanding, increasing unpredictability

	Volatile	Ambiguous	Complex	Uncertain
What does the future hold?	One probability, sometime	A few possibilities	Lots of possibilities	Anything's possible
Challenges ☹	Know what will happen but not when	Dilemmas, dichotomies, alternatives	Too many moving parts, too many interactions	Confusion and complete unpredictability
Solutions ☺	Have better sensors & build in more slack	Do more tests / experiments	Get more / better knowledge expertise	Get more / better information

So, what do we do about it?

Figure 220 VACU Analysis template

10.7 The practicalities of strategy adaptation

You've seen strategy adaptation represented as a stage in the strategy lifecycle that commences after the strategic plan is produced. This is useful because it focuses attention on the fact that this strategic plan is dynamic, evolving and adapting to changing circumstances. Preparation for strategy adaptation, however, begins earlier in the strategy lifecycle. You saw in Chapter 5 on Strategy Governance that a key goal for the executive governance of strategy was the management of strategic risk.

The roots of strategic risk management lie in strategy development, where the risks associated with different aspects of the emerging strategic plan need to be defined. Risk assessment then continues during strategy adoption. As the strategic goals get elaborated and stretch across the organisation, the risks associated with those goals also need to be elaborated. Using our Artigence case study, you can explore some of the ways this can be done.

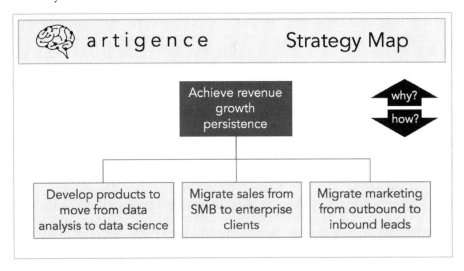

Figure 221 Strategy map for the Artigence strategy

Figure 221 shows the top-level goals in the strategy map for the Artigence case study. A strategy map is a great place to start risk assessment. Every goal in the strategy map can be reviewed to explore the uncertainties associated with it, and how these can lead to the risk of harm, or to potential opportunities (as described in the Nature of Risk model). These risks, if credible and significant, can be added to your Strategic Risk Register, outlining plans to mitigate harm or exploit opportunities.

One of the core methods in Artigence's strategy map is to *migrate marketing from outbound to inbound leads*. A well-recognised challenge is converting inbound leads to sales. Figure 222 shows Artigence's Strategic Risk Register for poor conversion of inbound leads. This allowed them to recognise both the potential for harm, and the opportunities to be exploited from this risk.

They then reviewed what would be required to accommodate this risk using the Strategic Risk Adaptation Plan, based on the Pyramid Model of Strategy Adaptation (Fig. 223). Adapting to risk requires resilience and agility in terms of sense-making, decision-making and change-making. In reviewing this risk, the Artigence team considered what capabilities they might need in place to make themselves more resilient and agile. They quickly realised that, as a whole team, they lacked experience in inbound marketing. They knew the theory, they had read lots about how others had made it work, but none of them had actually done it. Since this was a key method of achieving their entire strategy, they concluded that they needed to recruit a senior, experienced, inbound marketer.

This analysis gave them confidence that this element of the strategy had now been sufficiently risk assessed. They knew what they needed to do. All the actions they'd identified were feasible and affordable. That job was done, for now, and would be reviewed at the next board meeting.

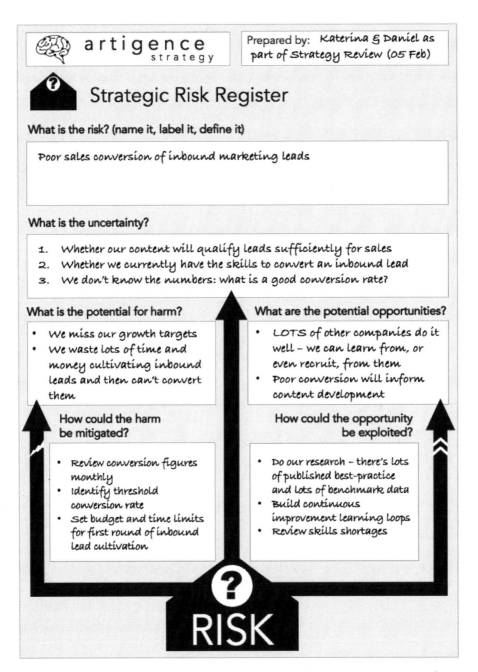

Figure 222 Artigence's Strategic Risk Register on poor conversion of inbound leads

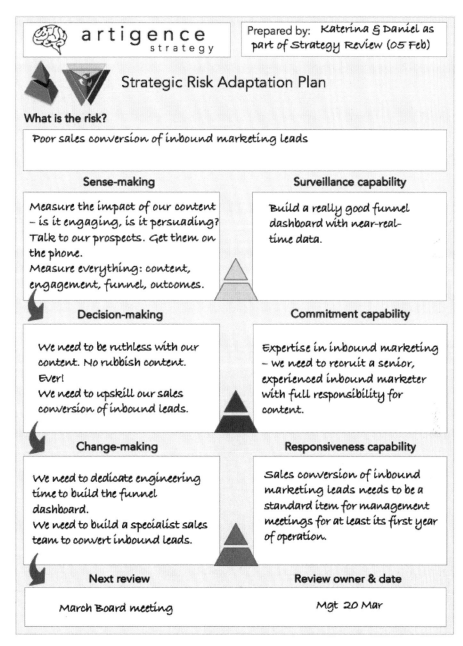

Figure 223 Artigence's Strategic Risk Adaptation Plan for poor sales conversion of inbound marketing leads

Working through the strategy map was a great way for Artigence to build an initial strategy risk register. They were aware, however, that this only covered certain types of risks, the ones they brought on themselves by setting a goal and then not being able to achieve it. There were many more that would come at them from the outside world and no amount of analysis of their own strategy would identify them. They needed different models and frameworks for that.

Artigence decided to apply two techniques, Futures Cone Analysis and VACU Analysis, to explore the future strategic risks involved in a subject that co-founder, Daniel, had been troubled by for a few months: quantum computing. Quantum computing is one of those fast-moving, highly complex areas of technology that are as hard to keep track of as they are to understand. Essentially, quantum computing can accomplish tasks that would not be feasible using traditional digital computers. Google, for example, recently reported completing a task in 200 seconds on their latest quantum computer.[26] They estimated that the same task would have taken 10,000 years in a state-of-the-art classical supercomputer. Clearly this will open up huge advantages for machine-learning and artificial intelligence and would enable Artigence to offer undreamt-of power in their data science solutions. Quantum computing, however, comes with the risk of serious harm, such as all the data Artigence stores for their clients suddenly becoming vulnerable to theft because a hacker with access to a quantum computer could crack their data encryption.

Figure 224 shows the Futures Cone Analysis that Artigence did on quantum computing. Figure 225 shows how they applied VACU Analysis to explore the same issue.

Prepared by: *Katerina & Daniel as part of Strategy Review (15 June)*

Futures Cone Analysis

Note: *Risk includes harm to be mitigated and opportunity to be exploited*

What is the issue?

Quantum computing enables hugely faster computation than classical computing

Projected risks

No current risk

Probable risks

Not yet, but maybe soon?

Plausible risks

In 2020, both IBM and Google demonstrated quantum computers working on a small scale. They just need to be made scalable.

Harm: our data security can be breached

Opportunity: new more powerful Artigence products

Possible risks

Shor's algorithm (1994) proved how quantum computation could crack common encryption methods. It just needed the quantum computer to work on.

Preposterous risks

The original notion that if you make encryption algorithms big and complex enough it takes conventional computers too long (i.e. 1,000 years) to crack them. NO LONGER THE CASE WITH QUANTUM COMPUTING

Figure 224 Artigence's Futures Cone analysis of the risks from quantum computing

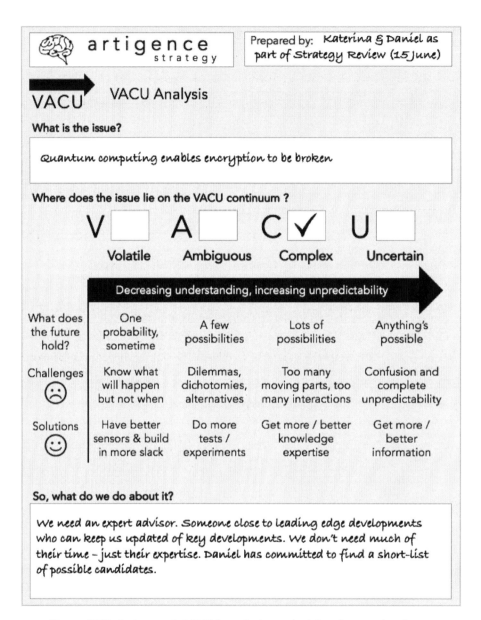

Figure 225 Artigence's VACU analysis to decide what to do about Quantum Computing

10.8 Summary and key takeaways from Chapter 10

1. **Strategy adaptation occupies most of the lifespan of a strategy** – more than strategy production and strategy adaptation combined. What you are adapting is actually the strategic plan, not the strategy itself. The strategy continues to provide clarity of direction throughout. As soon as the strategic plan has been adapted so much that it no longer reflects the strategy, that's the time for a new strategy.

2. Strategy adaptation comes about by building **resilience** (the ability to withstand challenges or recover rapidly and fully from them) and **agility** (the ability to adapt swiftly by means of innovation).

3. **Strategic risks arise out of uncertainty.** Strategy adaptation needs to **identify risks**, understand the underlying uncertainty, and decide how to **mitigate any harm** or **exploit any opportunity** arising from that uncertainty.

4. **There are different types of strategic risk:**

    a. **marketplace risks,** such as risks from your competitors or the changing needs of your customers;

    b. **remote risks,** that may seem distant threats in your operating environment but can have significant effects on your strategy;

    c. **knock-on risks,** that are triggered by events in your operating environment that have no direct impact on your strategy at all;

    d. **internal risks,** from inside your organisation;

    e. **emergent risks,** that arise from the changes brought about by strategy.

5. **Prioritising strategic risk** can be achieved by analysing the features of risk: **likelihood** of occurrence, **significance** (defined as **severity of harm** and **value of opportunity**) and the **adaptability** of your organisation in response to the risk.

6. The **Prioritising Risk for Strategy Model (PRiSM)** scores the features of risk to give a **Risk Priority Number (RPN).**

7. **Adapting to risk** requires three key activities: **sense-making, decision-making** and **change-making.** These activities are built upon a foundation of three adaptive capabilities: **surveillance capability, commitment capability** and **responsiveness capability.**

8. A critical issue in building any type of strategic adaptability is **understanding and anticipating the future.** Two techniques that can be used to do this are:

    a. **The Futures Cone,** which looks at the likelihood of events happening in terms of whether they are projected, probable, plausible, possible or preposterous.

    b. **VACU Analysis,** which represents the Volatility, Ambiguity, Complexity and Uncertainty of an issue as a continuum of decreasing understanding and increasing unpredictability about the future.

10.9 Let's talk about ... strategy adaptation

Use these questions to prompt deeper conversations on strategy adaptation across your organisation:

   1. How well is your organisation able to adapt your strategy? Is this good enough? Would it be better if you had more or less adaptability?

2. *Are the concepts of resilience and agility well understood across your organisation? How good would you say you are at building strategic resilience? And how good at being strategically agile?*

3. *Do you have processes in place to think about, and plan for, future opportunities and obstacles? How effective do you believe them to be? How could they become more robust?*

Notes on Chapter 10

(all web content accessed between April and September 2020)

[1] American Psychological Association, 2012. *Building your resilience.*
https://www.apa.org/topics/resilience

[2] Department for International Development, 2016. *What is Resilience?*
https://assets.publishing.service.gov.uk/media/57a08955ed915d3cfd0001c8/
EoD_Topic_Guide_What_is_Resilience_May_2016.pdf

[3] Wikipedia. *Resilience (materials science).*
https://en.wikipedia.org/wiki/Resilience_(materials_science)

[4] Oxford English Dictionary. *Agile.*
https://www.lexico.com/definition/agile

[5] Word Hippo. *What is another word for agile.*
https://www.wordhippo.com/what-is/another-word-for/agile.html

[6] Cambridge Dictionary. *Agile.*
https://dictionary.cambridge.org/dictionary/english/agile

[7] Perkin N and Abraham P, 2017. *Building the Agile Business Through Digital Transformation.* Kogan Page, London. p83.

[8] Cancialosi C, 2020. *Organizational Agility And Resilience - Two Critical Sides Of The Same Coin.* Forbes Magazine.

https://www.forbes.com/sites/chriscancialosi/2020/03/10/organizational-agility-and-resiliencetwo-critical-sides-of-the-same-coin/#23616198614a

[9] X Directions. *Resilience & Agility: The New Leadership Currency.* https://xdirections.com/resilience-agility-the-new-leadership-currency/

[10] Wikipedia. *Yin and Yang.* https://en.wikipedia.org/wiki/Yin_and_yang

[11] Hansell S, 2001. *After the Attacks: The Backup Sites; One Contingency Plan in Action: Amex Bank Keeps Money Moving.* The New York Times, 15 Sept 2001.

[12] Lengnick-Hall CA, Beck TE and Lengnick-Hall ML, 2011. *Developing a capacity for organizational resilience through strategic human resource management.* Human Resource Management Review 21: 243–255.

[13] Perkin N, 2020. *Agile Transformation.* Kogan Page, London.

[14] Perkin N, 2020. *Agile Transformation.* Kogan Page, London. p66.

[15] United States Department of Defense, 1949. *Procedures for performing a failure mode effect and critical analysis.* United States Department of Defense. MIL-P-1629.

[16] Ozyazgan V and Engin FZ, 2013. *FMEA Analysis and Applications in Knitting Industry.* Tekstil ve Konfeksiyon 23(3): 228-232.

[17] Fadlovich E, 2007. *Performing Failure Mode and Effect Analysis.* Embedded Technology. https://web.archive.org/web/20120320122624/http://www.embeddedtech mag.com/component/content/article/6134

[18] Kraemer CH, Stice E, Kazdin A, Offord D and Kupfer D, 2001. *How Do Risk Factors Work Together? Mediators, Moderators, and Independent, Overlapping, and Proxy Risk Factors.* American Journal of Psychiatry, 158 (6): 848-856.

[19] Ancona D, Williams M and Gerlach G, 2020. *The Overlooked Key to Leading Through Chaos.* MIT Sloan Management Review, 8 Sept 2020. https://sloanreview.mit.edu/article/the-overlooked-key-to-leading-through-chaos/

[20] The Futures Cone idea originated in a 1990 study by Charles Taylor for the Strategic Studies Institute of the US Army War College, entitled *Creating Strategic Visions* (https://apps.dtic.mil/dtic/tr/fulltext/u2/a231618.pdf). In it, he sketched a Cone of Plausibility (p 12-15). It was Joseph Voros who popularised the idea

in his 2015 blog article *On examining Preposterous! Futures.*
https://thevoroscope.com/2015/12/28/on-examining-preposterous-futures/

[21] Wikipedia. *Apollo 11: Background.*
https://en.wikipedia.org/wiki/Apollo_11#Background

[22] See background, timescale and key votes at Wikipedia. *Parliamentary votes on Brexit.*
https://en.wikipedia.org/wiki/Parliamentary_votes_on_Brexit

[23] Wikipedia. *Premiership of Boris Johnson.*
https://en.wikipedia.org/wiki/Premiership_of_Boris_Johnson

[24] Wikipedia. *British prorogation controversy.*
https://en.wikipedia.org/wiki/2019_British_prorogation_controversy

[25] Goal Atlas's VACU framework is a minor but significant adaptation of the VUCA framework (Volatility, Uncertainty, Complexity and Ambiguity), which is cited frequently by online sources. This VUCA framework is originally attributed to General Maxwell Thurman in 1991 (https://usawc.libanswers.com/faq/84869) although most sources cite Bennett N and Lemoine GJ, 2014. *What VUCA Really Means for You.* Harvard Business Review. January–February 2014. The issue we have had with the original VUCA framework is making sense of the order in which the 4 issues are presented. The acronym present them in order of volatility, uncertainty, complexity then ambiguity. Alternatively, the Harvard Business School article presents them in a two-by-two matrix, with complexity and volatility being presented as more predictable than ambiguity and uncertainty and volatility and uncertainty being better known than complexity and ambiguity. Having tried and failed to make either of these arrangements work in a number of different strategy projects, I realised they all fell beautifully into a continuum of decreasing understanding and increasing unpredictability about the future, when rearranged as VACU – volatility, ambiguity, complexity and then uncertainty. Hence the change for the VUCA model to our VACU model.

[26] Arute F, et al, 2019. *Quantum supremacy using a programmable superconducting processor.* Nature 574: 505–510.

Chapter 11

Strategy review

---

*Progress, far from consisting in change,
depends on retentiveness...*

*Those who cannot remember the past are
condemned to repeat it.*[1]

Figure 226 Strategy review as part of the strategy lifecycle

Through resilience and agility your strategic plan has adapted as much as it can without parting company from its overarching strategy. The time has come to put this current strategy to bed and produce a brand-new strategy. If the transformational change that has been brought about by your current strategy is to retain momentum, your new strategy must be informed by what has gone before it and build on the lessons learned, whilst simultaneously setting a new direction for the next era of transformational change. As such, the last step in your current strategy lifecycle, and, at the same time, the first step in the production of a new one, is the strategy review (Fig. 226).

11.1 The summative strategy review

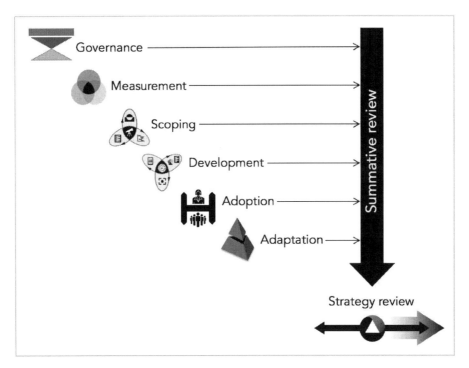

Figure 227 The summative strategy review

Reviewing strategy ought to be a habit that happens throughout strategy, not just at the end of the strategy lifecycle. The strategy documentation, logs and records you have produced during the scoping, development, adoption and adaptation of strategy can form the basis of a strategy review at any time. The idea of a 'summative strategy review' is that you now produce a summation of your review insights and embed the lessons learned so your strategy works even better next time (Fig. 227).

Whether you have maintained a strategy review habit throughout the strategy lifecycle or are starting from scratch now, the way strategy review works is the same.

11.2 Strategy review – how it works

The strategy review looks both backwards and forwards. Looking back, you evaluate the extent to which your strategic goals were met and what lessons can be learned to feed into the next strategy lifecycle. Applying these lessons looking forward embeds them into your new strategy and maintains the momentum of the transformational changes you have just brought about. Figure 228 shows these two key components which form the Strategy Review Model.

Figure 228 The Strategy Review Model has a look-ahead and look-back component

11.2.1 The look-back component of strategy review

The look-back component follows the well-established principles of an after–action review[2] or a post-implementation review[3]: it looks for answers to the questions '*what* happened, *why* did it happen, and *how* can it be done better?' from those that were both involved in and responsible for the actions taken. The strategy review seeks to evaluate the extent to which the strategic goals set out in the original strategy were met and what lessons need to be learned from the entire strategy lifecycle.

Such reviews are not always easy to manage and don't always end up with productive outcomes. They can all too readily descend into accusations and recriminations. Here, however, are some good-practice tips, inspired by the excellent NOBL Academy's article on *Agile Retrospectives.*[4]

1. *Agree the scope and structure of the review.* Which elements of strategy are you setting out to review in this session (it may take several sessions to review an entire strategy)? What milestones or deliverables best mark out the process undertaken?

2. For each milestone / deliverable, *set out the facts.* No opinions and no evaluation is permitted at this stage. Stick to the facts. What activities were undertaken? What information / data was acquired and used? What outputs were produced?

3. *Objective evaluation.* What evidence is there to indicate how well / badly each milestone worked? What evidence is there that the entire process you are reviewing here today worked well or badly?

4. *Lessons learned.* What ought you do differently next time? Why do you think this would be better? What evidence do you have that this would produce better outcomes?

5. *Commitment to action.* These can happen in two forms: processes and projects.

    a. *Processes* (NOBL actually labelled this 'policies', which suggested a degree of formality that many organisations may not be comfortable with): ways of working that should be done differently in the future. Ideally, these should be decided by consensus, especially if a team is deciding how this same team ought to work differently next time. For larger organisations, this may not be possible. The learnings from a small team may be useful for many teams across the organisation. Where this is the case, the conclusions from a strategy review may need to be referred to a decision-making group with broader authority.

b. *Projects*: a discrete initiative to be undertaken to make strategy work better next time. It could be research, training or method of measurement. Here, a key principle is that projects go ahead if someone can be found to lead it and be held accountable for its outcome. Again, in larger organisations, undertaking this type of project may not be possible for the team undertaking the strategy review. In which case, a project recommendation may need to be referred elsewhere for approval.

It is vital that, if time and effort is committed to a look-back strategy review, evidence must be presented back to the team involved to demonstrate that their commitments to action were impactful. If they are going to enter into any subsequent reviews in good faith and with commitment, they need to feel that their work had value.

11.2.2 The look-ahead component of strategy review

The look-ahead component seeks to apply the lessons from this strategy to make the next strategy better... or at least try to avoid repeating the same mistakes again. Inevitably, this look forward component of strategy review will blend into the strategy scoping for the new strategy (Fig. 229). From a strategy governance point of view, clarification is needed on whether the review of this strategy and the scoping of the next strategy are actually going to be a single activity. This ought to be the default, unless there are compelling reasons for keeping them separate.

Figure 229 The look-ahead component of strategy review will blend into strategy scoping

The look-back and look-ahead components inevitably lead to a degree of symmetry in strategy review. So, for example:

1. *Looking back*, you seek to evaluate whether the current strategy succeeded. Did it meet its 'success-defining' KPIs?
   Looking forward, could the same kind of success-defining KPIs be used for the new strategy?

2. *Looking back*, did vision, mission, values and strategy work well together? In the twilight of the current strategy, are you closer to achieving your vision than when the strategy began? Are you still 'on-mission' and did you remain on-mission throughout the entire strategy lifecycle? Are your values still valid? Did they tangibly shape your actions during this strategy?
   Looking forward, should vision, mission and values continue as they are or do they need to be re-worked alongside the new strategy?

3. *Looking back*, did the strategy destination in your current strategy serve you well? Did it continue to provide a North Star to guide decisions and actions across the organisation in a purposeful and aligned way?

Looking forward, do you have any pointers on what would make a good destination for the next strategy? Or conversely, do you have any pointers on what to avoid in choosing your next destination?

4. *Looking back,* did the core methods enable you to reach your strategy destination, as anticipated?

   Looking forward, can the core methods be carried forward into the next strategy? Are there lessons to be learned about how to find better core methods for the next strategy?

11.3 Six aspects of strategy to be reviewed

There are six aspects of strategy to be included in a strategy review. Here is a summary of them:

1. **Strategy governance.** Did the relationship between the board and senior leadership work well on strategy? Did senior leadership secure the engagement and commitment of strategic change-makers across the organisation?

2. **Strategy measurement.** Was the strategy measured effectively? Did the strategy have its intended impact? Was it possible to track the progress of strategy across the organisation throughout its lifecycle? Was that tracking good enough to highlight where the plan needed to change to improve outcomes?

3. **Strategy scoping.** Did strategy scoping get the development process off to a good start? Did everyone have a clear understanding of what needed to be done to produce this new strategy and who was doing what?

4. **Strategy development.** How well did the development process work? Was it creative enough? Was it systematic enough? Did it

have the right inputs, robust analysis, clear insights? Did it, in retrospect, come up with the right strategy?

5. **Strategy adoption.** How well did the strategy 'land', across the organisation? Did senior leaders engage with front-line change-makers? How well did that work? Was there clarity across the organisation about who was committed to which changes? Did everyone feel there was a coherent strategic plan?

6. **Strategy adaptation**. Did you manage to strike the right balance between the strategy remaining unchanged, whilst the strategic plan adapted to circumstances? How strategically resilient were you? How strategically agile were you?

You can now work through the following six frameworks to undertake each aspect of the strategy review (Fig. 230 to Fig. 235).

Strategy:	Prepared by:
	Date:

 Look-back review of Strategy Governance

Executive governance

- *How was the relationship between the board and senior leadership defined regarding strategy? Formally? Informally?*
- *In what ways did this relationship work well? In what ways did it work badly?*
- *How effective was the relationship? Did it end up with good decisions and commitments?*
- *How efficient was the it? Was it wasteful of time and resources?*
- *Any relevant documents to attach?*

Working governance

- *What process did senior leadership use to secure the engagement and commitment of strategic change-makers across the organisation?*
- *In what ways did this process work well?*
- *In what ways did it work badly?*
- *Was the outcome good?*
- *Did everyone, who needed to, engage with and commit to the strategy?*

 Look-forward review of Strategy Governance

What should we do differently?

Process	Process owner
How should we change the way we do strategy governance next time? For a process to change, a process-owner, with the authority to make those changes, needs to be identified. They also need to commit to the changes.	

Project	Project sponsor
A project is a discrete piece of work intended to make a process work better. Projects go ahead if they have a sponsor with the time and resources to complete them, and willingness to be held accountable for their outcome.	

Figure 230 Review of Strategy Governance

Strategy:	Prepared by: Date:

← ● Look-back review of Strategy Measurement

Strategy measurement, in general

- *Was strategy measured well?*
- *Were key performance indicators (KPIs) defined, widely discussed and used to inform strategic decisions?*
- *Were they actionable, meaningful and purposeful?*

Success-defining KPIs	**Critical-to-success KPIs**
Were success-defining KPIs: - *Produced at all?* - *Good for defining success? How could they have been better?* - *The 'beacon' guiding strategic efforts that they should have been?* - *Tracked frequently enough and by the right decision-makers?* - *Achieved? Did this equate to genuine strategic success?*	*Were the critical-to-success KPIs:* - *Broad enough in their coverage of the whole strategy?* - *Specific enough to relate to front-line change?* - *Well enough connected to aggregate up to strategic success?* - *Too numerous, too confusing?* - *Not precise enough in measuring important change?*

● → Look-forward review of Strategy Measurement

What should we do differently?

Process	**Process owner**
How should we change the way we do strategy measurement next time? For a process to change, a process-owner, with the authority to make those changes, needs to be identified. They also need to commit to the changes.	

Project	**Project sponsor**
A project is a discrete piece of work intended to make a process work better. Projects go ahead if they have a sponsor with the time and resources to complete them, and willingness to be held accountable for their outcome.	

Figure 231 Review of Strategy Measurement

Strategy:	Prepared by: Date:

Look-back review of Strategy Scoping

Strategy scoping, in general

- *Did strategy scoping get the development process off to a good start by clarifying beforehand what was known, assumed or needed to be decided?*
- *Did it do that effectively? Were sufficient records kept?*
- *Was there a 'strategy announcement'? If so, how did that work?*
- *Looking back, was strategy scoping useful? Were its conclusions and proposals as good as they could have been?*

Horizon scoping	**Development scoping**	**Success scoping**
• *Did you get clear strategic insight from your current situation, aspirations and drivers?* • *Did you set a strategy time-horizon?*	• *Were key decisions identified, along with the evidence needed to make them?* • *Were 'jobs to be done' identified?* • *Were responsibilities and timescales set?*	• *Did strategy scoping do a good job of setting criteria for the acceptance of the new strategy towards the end of its development?*

Look-forward review of Strategy Scoping

What should we do differently?

Process	**Process owner**
How should we change the way we do strategy scoping next time? For a process to change, a process-owner with the authority to make those changes, needs to be identified. They also need to commit to the changes.	

Project	**Project sponsor**
A project is a discrete piece of work intended to make a process work better. Projects go ahead if they have a sponsor with the time and resources to complete them, and willingness to be held accountable for their outcome.	

Figure 232 Review of Strategy Scoping

| Strategy: | Prepared by: |
| | Date: |

 Look-back review of Strategy Development

Strategy development, in general

- *Did strategy development proceed as intended?*
- *Were there major surprises?*
- *If so, should these have been anticipated?*
- *Looking back, was the strategy as good as it could have been?*
- *Was the strategy destination a good one?*
- *Were the core methods the right ones?*

Create	Inform	Validate
- *Was development both creative and bounded?* - *Were enough strategy ideas generated?* - *Was enough time set aside for creativity?* - *Did people work together enough on new strategic ideas?*	- *Was strategy development as evidence-based as it should have been?* - *Were any data or insights missed?*	- *Was strategy development validated thoroughly enough?* - *Were aspects of strategy accepted that ought to have been challenged?* - *Were aspects of strategy rejected that ought to have been accepted?*

Look-forward review of Strategy Development

What should we do differently?

Process	Process owner
How should we change the way we do strategy development next time? For a process to change, a process-owner with the authority to make those changes, needs to be identified. They also need to commit to the changes.	

Project	Project sponsor
A project is a discrete piece of work intended to make a process work better. Projects go ahead if they have a sponsor with the time and resources to complete them, and willingness to be held accountable for their outcome.	

Figure 233 Review of Strategy Development

| Strategy: | Prepared by: |
| | Date: |

 **← Look-back review of Strategy Adoption**

Strategy adoption, in general

- *Was strategy adoption successful?*
- *Did the necessary change-makers across the organisation all engage with and commit to the strategy? Did they find their work purposeful?*
- *Did adopting the strategy contribute to a positive culture?*
- *Was the strategic plan seen as the driver of transformational change across the organisation?*

Did the strategic plan produced during adoption:
- *Effectively organise the change-makers and the changes they needed to bring about in an orderly, structured and aligned way?*
- *Give all the change-makers a clear understanding of their goals and how their goals connected to the goals of others and to the strategy 'destination'?*
- *Prioritise strategic work effectively, meaningfully and impactfully?*
- *Provide clear targets for key strategic goals and timescales for those targets? Were these targets taken seriously? Did the goal owners feel they mattered? Did meeting or not meeting targets have consequences?*

Look-forward review of Strategy Adoption →

What should we do differently?

Process	Process owner
How should we change the way we do strategy adoption next time? For a process to change, a process-owner with the authority to make those changes, needs to be identified. They also need to commit to the changes.	

Project	Project sponsor
A project is a discrete piece of work intended to make a process work better. Projects go ahead if they have a sponsor with the time and resources to complete them, and willingness to be held accountable for their outcome.	

Figure 234 Review of Strategy Adoption

Strategy:	Prepared by: Date:

 Look-back review of Strategy Adaptation

Strategy adoption, in general

- *Did you have a clear process for reviewing whether the strategic plan needed adapting? Did it work?*
- *Did you have a clear understanding of the risks arising from the strategy?*
- *Were these risks prioritised meaningfully?*
- *Did the identification of risks enabled you to mitigate their impact?*
- *Were any risks identified but still dealt with badly?*
- *Did the identification of risks give rise to new opportunities?*

Resilience

- *What steps did you take to make the strategic plan more resilient?*
- *Were you able to withstand challenges? Were you able to recover rapidly and fully from them?*
- *What additional resilience measures do you wish you had taken?*

Agility

- *What steps did you take to ensure you were prepared to be strategically agile, if necessary?*
- *How well did they work?*
- *Where was strategic agility needed?*
- *Were there times when you should have been more agile?*

Look-forward review of Strategy Adaptation

What should we do differently?

Process	Process owner
How should we change the way we do strategy adaptation next time? For a process to change, a process-owner with the authority to make those changes, needs to be identified. They also need to commit to the changes.	

Project	Project sponsor
A project is a discrete piece of work intended to make a process work better. Projects go ahead if they have a sponsor with the time and resources to complete them, and willingness to be held accountable for their outcome.	

Figure 235 Review of Strategy Adaptation

11.4 Summary and key takeaways from Chapter 11

1. Strategy review happens **at the end of the strategy lifecycle**, but it should also **be a habit** that is undertaken throughout the strategy.

2. **Strategy review has two components**: look-back and look-forward.

3. The **look-back** component seeks to find the lessons that can be learned throughout the lifecycle of the strategy.

4. The **look-forward** component looks to see how these lessons can be applied to the next strategy as part of strategy scoping.

5. **Good-practice tips for the review process** include:

    a. Agree the scope and structure of the review;

    b. Set out the facts of what actually happened in the last strategy;

    c. Evaluate the facts objectively, using evidence;

    d. Extract the lessons learned to apply to the next strategy;

    e. Commit to action, in the form of processes to adopt and projects to undertake that will ensure strategy works even better next time.

6. **Six aspects of strategy should be reviewed**:

    a. Strategy governance;

    b. Strategy measurement;

    c. Strategy scoping;

    d. Strategy development;

    e. Strategy adoption;

    f. Strategy adaptation.

11.5 Let's talk about... strategy review

1. *How continuously are you reviewing your strategy? Are you doing it enough?*

2. *When you DO review are you really learning lessons and changing how you work as a result? Or are you just going through the motions?*

3. *Is the success or failure of your review processes a reflection of something deeper about your organisational culture? If so, should you celebrate it or repair it?*

Notes on Chapter 11

(all web content accessed between April and September 2020)

[1] Santayana G, 1905. *Vol. I, Reason in Common Sense, The Life of Reason: The Phases of Human Progress.* C. Scribner's Sons, 1905. p 284.

[2] Wikipedia. *After Action Review.* https://en.wikipedia.org/wiki/After-action_review

[3] Westland J, 2018. *What is Post-Implementation Review in Project Management?* https://www.projectmanager.com/blog/post-implementation-review

[4] NOBL Academy 2016. *The Definitive Guide to Agile Retrospectives and Post-Mortem Meetings.* https://academy.nobl.io/definitive-guide-to-agile-retrospectives-and-post-mortem-meetings/

Glossary - the language of strategy

With something as complex as strategy, it is vital that you have a collection of key words and phrases that you use in the same way to mean the same thing when you discuss strategy. Here are the main definitions of key terms and models used in this book. Entries marked with a star (★) indicate models or frameworks devised by Goal Atlas.

Adoption conversations: a key enabler of strategy adoption. These are conversations which spread out across the organisation as the core goals defined in the strategy are elaborated to fill out the strategic plan. They involve an exchange of knowledge and expertise to ensure that front-line teams understand the intentions and aspirations of the new strategy and senior leaders understand the front-line context in which strategic change must take place.

Agility: the ability to think or move quickly, easily or nimbly in order to respond at pace to either the need or opportunity to change. Being agile in relation to strategy means being ready and able to make innovative changes to the strategic plan in response to new circumstances.

★ AMP Model of Good KPIs: model proposing that a good Key Performance Indicator (KPI) is one that is Actionable, Measurable and Purposeful.

Annual Recurring Revenue (ARR): a performance measure, often used by SaaS companies with subscription-based customer accounts, of how much money they expect to make cumulatively from the customers who signed up this year plus those they retained from previous years. This is relevant for understanding the Artigence case study.

Average Revenue Per Account (ARPA): a performance measure, often-used by SaaS companies with subscription-based customer accounts, of how much revenue they make from each customer per year. This is relevant for understanding the Artigence case study.

★ **Binary Star Model of KPIs:** In astronomy a binary star system is a pair of stars locked in orbit around each other. This concept is used to explain the interdependence of the two main types of strategic Key Performance Indicators (KPIs): Success-Defining KPIs and Critical-to-Success KPIs.

★ **Boundary Model of Strategy:** This model assumes that strategy is about the management of transformational change over a long period of time (typically years). It proposes that an important early decision about any new strategy is what proportion of the organisation's resources are to be allocated to strategic initiatives, as opposed to the maintenance of business-as-usual. The 'boundary' is the dividing line between the resources allocated to strategy and business-as-usual, respectively.

Bounded creativity: a best-practice approach to creative thinking, informed by research. Creativity is most effective and most valuable when constrained to the right extent; too tightly constrained and creativity is stifled, too few constraints and creativity is too unfocused and, usually, not relevant enough to the challenge that the creativity is trying to address.

Candidate strategy: a set of ideas contending to become the new strategy. If the *mediated assessment protocol* is to be used to decide on the new strategy, it requires more than one candidate strategy to be compared.

★ **Cascade Model of Goal Prioritisation:** starts with a simple priority allocation system (typically one, two or three stars) for individual goals in a strategy map and then cascades a calculated priority score across the map, taking into account the inheritance of priority from parent to child goals. This model is adapted from Thomas L Saaty's well-established and well-respected Analytic Hierarchy Process (AHP)

★ **Cascade Model of KPIs:** proposes that wherever you have a strategy map, you can cascade Key Performance Indicators (KPIs) over that map, thereby revealing the logical connection between the individual KPIs. A well-constructed KPI cascade will ensure that achieving all of the KPIs for a given set of sub-goals leads to the achievement of the KPI for their parent goal.

Change-makers: the people, across your organisation who make the changes happen that are necessary for strategic success.

Convergent thinking: often thought of as simply selecting the best or the correct idea produced during *divergent thinking*. This, however, is an over-simplification. Part of convergent thinking, as the name suggests, is the bringing together, the combining, the hybridisation or the synthesis of multiple individual ideas – this is creative convergence and is much more than simply idea-selection.

Critical-to-success KPIs: one of two types of strategic Key Performance Indicator (KPI) (the other being *success-defining KPIs*). Critical-to-success KPIs define the target performance thresholds for all goals in a strategy map that are critical to the success of the entire strategy. They are, therefore, a lot more numerous than success-defining KPIs.

Culture: the ideas, customs, attitudes and social behaviour of particular people or society (see also *Organisational culture*).

Divergent thinking: from the word diverge, meaning to move apart, divergent thinking is the ability to think of lots of ideas. It is one of the two stages in creative thinking, the other being *convergent thinking*.

Effectiveness: what you do to deliver value to your beneficiaries; how, and how well, you deliver value. Effectiveness can be defined as 'doing the right thing'.

Efficiency: how you make good use of resources. Efficiency can be defined as 'doing the thing right'.

Enforcement principle of governance: one of two principles shaping the *working governance of strategy*, the other being the *engagement principle of governance*. The enforcement principle recognises that rules and formalities need to be imposed, complied with and enforced, as part of the management of strategy. Mechanisms of enforcement include organisation design, the line management relations inherent in that design, policies and standards and managerial decisions about the allocation of budget.

Engagement and commitment: active interest in, and a willingness to commit to strategy, brought about by high levels of consultation, influence and autonomy being afforded to individuals and teams across your organisation. *(See also Working governance of strategy).*

Engagement principle of governance: one of two principles shaping the *working governance of strategy*, the other being the *enforcement principle of governance*. The engagement principle recognises that for strategy to succeed, individuals and teams across the organisation need to co-create, engage with and commit to strategic goals, and a set of norms and conventions for pursuing them.

Executive governance of strategy: ensures the board and senior leadership are working effectively together towards strategy success. This requires the board and senior leadership to work together to serve the best interests of the organisation. *(See also Governance).*

FAST diagram: diagram showing an interconnected cascade of functions, derived using Function Analysis System Technique, developed by Charles Bytheway for analysing cause and effect relationships.

First principles thinking: also called 'reasoning from first principles', it breaks down a complicated issue into basic elements and builds back up a more rational, assumption-free, unbiased understanding of the issue than would be possible by analogy.

Formalisation of authority: a systematic approach to working governance employing organisation design, RACIs (definitions of who is Responsible, Accountable, Consulted or Informed about a decision-making process), policies and standards, budget distribution and performance measurement against defined targets. The formalisation of authority is how the *enforcement principle of strategy governance* is applied. *(See also Working governance of strategy).*

Frame-setting: a convergent thinking process designed to select, refine and combine the creative ideas generated for a new strategy (typically by *frame-stretching*). (See also *Framing).*

Frame-stretching: a divergent thinking process designed to come up with new ideas about what could potentially be included in the new strategy. The creative thinking about new strategy ideas is prompted by a variety of models (e.g. SWOT analysis or Value Proposition Design) that are placed at the centre of the frame to stretch the imagination into new ways of thinking about strategy. Typically followed by *frame-setting.* (see also *Framing).*

★ **Framing:** a technique used in the creative loop of the strategy development process. It stimulates the divergent thinking component of creativity by frame-stretching (see *frame-stretching)* and then the convergent thinking component of creativity by frame-setting (see *Frame-setting).*

Futures Cone: The Futures Cone visualises an expanding range of potential futures, emanating from the current moment in time as a set of nested cones, with each cone representing a different degree of future likelihood.

Goal: an action with a purpose.

Goal owner: an individual to whom a goal (in the context of this book, typically a strategic goal) has been delegated.

Governance: the means by which your organisation: i) structures and delineates authority, and thereby defines strategic roles; ii) sets goals (e.g. strategy) and the rules by which these goals can be pursued (e.g. policies, compliance) and iii) establishes reporting and enforcement mechanisms. *(See also Strategy governance; Executive governance of strategy; Working governance of strategy).*

★ **Hallmarks of Good Strategy Model:** proposes there are five hallmarks of good strategy: strategy is about change; strategy is about choice; strategy is about coherence; strategy is about challenge; strategy is about cascade. These hallmarks provide a way of checking whether your draft strategy is a 'good' strategy prior to launch.

★ **'H' Model of Strategy Adoption:** proposes that, if strategy is to be adopted effectively across an organisation, senior leadership needs to secure the engagement and commitment of individuals all the way through to front-line teams. The 'H' Model illustrates how this is enabled by *adoption conversations,* that ensure front-line teams understand the intentions and aspirations of the new strategy and senior leaders understand the front-line context in which strategic change must take place.

★ **Hourglass Model of Strategy Governance:** illustrates the relationship between *executive governance of strategy* and *working governance of strategy* and how *formalisation of authority* needs to work together with *engagement and commitment* within the working governance of strategy.

★ **House of Strategy Model:** provides the foundation, walls and roof within which your new strategy is going to live. It shows graphically how vision, mission, values and strategy come together for your organisation. It can be used to audit an existing, or create new, vision, mission, values and strategy.

★ **Iceberg principle of strategy scoping:** uses the metaphor of an iceberg, most of which is invisible under the surface of the sea, to explain that strategy scoping needs to acknowledge that most of the forthcoming strategy cannot possibly be visible during strategy scoping. The part that is visible, however, can, and indeed should, be described as meaningfully as possible.

Identity marks: signals showing what type of organisation you are, what you stand for and what you aspire to, such as your vision, mission, values, strategy and brand.

Impact: how much value you are actually able to deliver, by means of the work you do.

★ **Innovation Pyramid:** a visual representation of the rule of thumb for innovation management first proposed by Sergey Brin of Google, suggesting 70% of resources are spent on maintaining business as usual, 20% on refining the way you do business as usual and 10% re-inventing how you will do business-as-usual in months or years to come.

Investment Pyramid: illustrates how good investment decisions set out to balance the different risk and return profiles of different types of investments. The pyramid shape reflects typical investment advice to keep the majority of your investment assets in low risk, low potential return investments, and a minority in high risk, high potential return investments

Key Performance Indicator (KPI): a critical measure of progress towards an intended outcome *(see also Strategic Key Performance Indicator).*

KPI trajectory: a depiction of how a Key Performance Indicator (KPI) is expected to change over time and hence how interim targets over the course of the strategy need to be set.

Lagging and leading indicators: two different types of Key Performance Indicator (KPI). A lagging indicator is a measure of output or impact; usually the impact you seek to bring about (e.g. did your strategy result in the increased revenue you sought?). Such measures of impact commonly take some time to take effect and be measurable – hence 'lagging'. A leading indicator is a measure of input (e.g. marketing expenditure) that often causes the impact we seek to bring about and is available quickly – hence 'leading'.

Mediated Assessment Protocol (MAP): a structured process for committing to a new strategy late in the strategy development process. It involves having more than one candidate strategy to decide between, defining how they will be assessed in advance, having the assessment done independently by multiple people and making the final evaluation after all the mediating assessments are complete.

Mission: one of the identity marks for your organisation (vision, mission, values and strategy). Mission is a statement of the core purpose and focus of your organisation. It provides a sense of identity for employees, customers, suppliers etc. It is about NOW! Why do you exist, right now?

★ **Nature of Strategic Risk Model:** illustrates how to recognise the risks standing in the way of strategy success, understand the nature of the underlying uncertainty, and decide how to mitigate any harm or exploit any opportunity arising from that uncertainty.

Organisational culture: the ideas, customs, attitudes and social behaviours typical of an organisation. Organisational culture is often characterised as being positive (good communication, a clear sense of purpose, opportunities for growth and development, reward and recognition for good work, feelings of trust and adherence to clear values) or negative / toxic (hyper-competitive, giving rise to lots of conflict, distrust, fear of authority and pressure to over-work).

Organisation design: is the creation of roles, processes and structures to enable an organisation to achieve its objectives. An important output is organisational structure, which defines the line management relationships between individuals across the organisation.

Performance indicator: a measure of progress towards an intended outcome.

Price-Value map: a graphical representation of your products and your competitor's products showing how they compare on two axes of a scatter-graph: price and some measure of the value delivered to customers.

★ **Prioritising Risk for Strategy Model (PRiSM):** a systematic and structured way for scoring risks and then calculating a relative risk priority number so that different risks can be compared and decisions taken on which to take action on. PRiSM is adapted from the well-established risk prioritisation tool in engineering called Failure Modes and Effects Analysis (FMEA).

★ **Pyramid Model of Strategy Adaptation:** a graphical depiction of the three activities needed for strategy adaptation (sense-making, decision-making and change-making) as well as the three underlying capabilities needed to make these activities effective (surveillance capability, commitment capability and responsiveness capability).

RACI: a means of defining working relationships in terms of who is Responsible, Accountable, Consulted and Informed.

Recursion: is a repeating pattern-within-a-pattern. It occurs in biology (e.g. trees branching repeatedly with ever-smaller and smaller branches) in mathematics and computer science. Russian dolls that nest inside one another are a physical example of recursion. The concept of recursion applies to *strategy mapping* where the method of one goal is the purpose of the goal below it.

Residual value: the value you receive, after costs, in exchange for the value you deliver.

Resilience: the ability to withstand or accommodate changes both inside your organisation and outside in its operating environment.

SaaS: acronym for Software as a Service, describing a business model where software applications are developed and hosted by the business and licensed to customers on a subscription basis. This is relevant for understanding the Artigence case study.

★ **SaNity Check Model:** checks both the sufficiency and necessity of goals in a strategy map. Once the entire strategy map has been checked for the sufficiency and necessity of all of its goals, the strategy map is considered to be validated.

★ **Separation Model of Strategy:** proposes that strategy and strategic planning need to be forced apart so they can serve their different purposes within the organisation. Whilst strategy provides a compelling vision of the future, strategic planning devises the transformational change programme to get there. Whilst strategy is all about destination and path, strategic planning is all about people, priorities, resources and deadlines. Perhaps most critically, strategy doesn't change, but strategic plans can, and usually do, change.

Situation analysis: is part of strategy scoping and reviews the current situation of your organisation in preparation for strategy development. The *House of Strategy Model* can be useful for situation analysis.

★ **Six Elements of Strategy:** six different things strategy is claimed to be: analysis, choice, positioning, design, storytelling and commitment.

These elements are used to synthesise a coherent view of what strategy is.

Small/medium-sized business (SMB): defined here as a business with less than 1,000 employees and less than £10M turnover.

Socratic questioning: a set of questions suggested by Plato (a student of Socrates) for getting to the root of knowledge and ideas (see also *First principles thinking*).

Strategic Key Performance Indicator: a critical measure of progress towards the change specified in a strategy.

Strategic plan: a transformational change program, initially designed to achieve *strategic success* and then adapted to cope with changing circumstances for the rest of the *strategy lifespan*.

Strategic planning: a process that translates high-level, organisation-wide strategic goals into the actionable goals that front-line individuals and teams can achieve, and identifies priorities, timescales and targets for strategic success. The outcome from strategic planning is a completed *strategic plan*.

Strategic risks: The five key types of strategic risks are: 1. Marketplace risks, typically involving actions of your customers or competitors; 2. Remote risks that initially seem remote but could turn into strategy killers, such as a global pandemic or a trade war; 3. Knock-on risks are triggered by events that have no direct impact on your strategy at all, but their knock-on consequences are what cause you the problems; 4. Internal risks are caused by changes within your organisation; 5. Emergent risks are the risks you don't anticipate until they are upon you, commonly because they arise due to the changes brought about by strategy.

★ **Strategic Risk Register:** a way of analysing and describing strategic risks, to identify the underlying 'uncertainty' that a risk introduces and then explore the potential harm and exploitable opportunities available as a result of that uncertainty. The strategic risk register is derived from the *nature of risk model*.

★ **Strategic Risk Adaptation Plan:** a way of analysing and describing how you could adapt to the uncertainties posed by strategic risks. The strategic risk adaptation plan is derived from the *pyramid model of strategy adaptation*.

Strategic success: a state (identified by *success-defining KPIs*) aspired to and moved towards throughout the *strategy lifespan*.

Strategy: can be defined in quite different ways depending on whether you are focused on the process of creating it or the purpose it is intended to serve. The process-focused definition: strategy requires choices to be made, based on analysis and clarification of strategic positioning. It is, however, more than merely choosing between options; strategy designs a future you then strive to bring about. Doing so requires the commitment of change-makers and hence strategy must be conducive to engaging and inspiring them. The purpose-focused definition: strategy defines the future state you seek to bring about, the value of achieving that state and the core methods by which you intend to get there.

Strategy acceptance criteria (a term used during strategy production): one or more factors used to evaluate whether the strategy under development is good enough to be signed-off and launched.

Strategy adaptation: one of the three stages in the strategy lifecycle (Produce, Adopt, Adapt), during which a strategic plan is adapted to cope with changing circumstances. Strategy adaptation focuses on both strategic resilience and strategic agility.

Strategy adoption: one of the three stages in the strategy lifecycle (Produce, Adopt, Adapt), during which a new strategy is adopted across the organisation and, at the end of which the new strategic plan is produced. Strategy adoption gets everyone across the organisation to engage with the strategy and commit to its success.

Strategy adoption gap: the challenge of turning the intentions of strategy, originally owned by senior leadership, into actions driven by front-line teams that lead to strategic success.

Strategy announcement: the moment when the commitment to produce a new strategy becomes official, at the end of strategy scoping and prior to the start of strategy development. The strategy announcement is usually marked by some sort of announcement event.

Strategy aspirations: part of the strategy scoping process to identify what you, as an organisation or as leaders of that organisation aspire to in the forthcoming new strategy.

Strategy cascade: the process of elaboration and aggregation by which strategic choices at the top of the cascade set the context for the choices below, and choices at the bottom influence and refine the strategic choices above.

★ **Strategy Design Model:** a model comprising eight interlinked elements that good strategies should be designed to feature: destination, methods, alignment, innovation, priority, performance, adaptability and adoption.

Strategy destination: the desired future state for your organisation, identified in your completed strategy and defined by your *success-defining Key Performance Indicators* (KPIs).

Strategy development: how you analyse, synthesise, imagine and commit to a new strategy, and how you write it and prepare it for dissemination throughout the organisation, following *strategy launch*.

Strategy development log: documentation that logs each key step in your thinking and decision-making throughout *strategy development*.

Strategy drivers: part of the strategy scoping process to identify what you feel compelled to include in the forthcoming new strategy.

Strategy governance: the means by which your organisation exercises authority to make a concentrated and coordinated effort to achieve strategic success. (*See also Governance*).

Strategy governance charter: a document defining how governance works and specifying how the roles and responsibilities of the board and senior leadership align.

Strategy horizon (a term used during strategy production): a characterisation of the likely ambitions for the strategy under development, as far as can be seen at the present moment in time.

Strategy launch: The moment when the strategy officially begins, usually heralded by some launch event to publicise the new strategy and its aspirations. The strategy launch is also a key moment marking the start of strategy adoption.

Strategy lifecycle: the functionally-different stages through which strategy progresses.

★ **Strategy Lifecycle Model:** the model used in this book depicting the strategy lifecycle as having three stages: produce, adopt and adapt.

Strategy lifespan: the planned duration of a strategy from the time of strategy launch to the intended time when strategy success will be achieved.

★ **Strategy mapping:** a process of connecting goals together using why-how logic to link methods and purposes in a validated map. It can be used to systematically connect the strategic aspirations of senior leadership to the tactical actions of front-line teams, and can facilitate strategic innovation, strategy adoption and strategic planning.

Strategy production: one of the three stages in the strategy lifecycle (Produce, Adopt, Adapt), during which a new strategy is produced, and, at the end of which, the new strategy is launched. This stage is comprised of two processes: strategy scoping and strategy development.

Strategy review: a process of gathering insights and embedding the lessons learned so your strategy works even better next time. Ideally a habit that happens throughout the lifespan of your strategy, with a summative review at the end of its lifecycle.

★ **Strategy Review Model:** a representation of the summative review process that happens at the end of the strategy lifespan (or earlier, if it is decided to terminate the strategy early and develop a new one). This review should include look-back (what happened? why did it happen? how could it have worked better?) and look-ahead components (what lessons from this strategy could make the next one better?).

Strategy scoping: one of the processes within the 'Strategy production' stage of the strategy lifecycle. Strategy scoping defines what you can see of the new strategy from where you are standing right now.

Strategy scoping log: documentation that logs each key step in your thinking and decision-making throughout *strategy scoping.*

Strategy success: a situation in which all strategy success criteria have been met, on time and to a satisfactory quality.

Strategy success criteria: one or more factors that will be used to judge the ultimate success of a strategy.

Strategy timeline: a (usually graphical) depiction of key events, processes and outcomes across the lifespan of a strategy.

Strategy validation: one loop of the *triple-loop model of strategy development,* which sets out to check if the strategy is fit-for-purpose by evaluating it against 1. the *strategy acceptance criteria* devised during *strategy scoping* and 2. the *hallmarks of good strategy*. Strategy validation also refers to the process of checking the final *strategy map* that underpins the *strategic plan*, using the *SaNity check model*.

Success-defining KPI: sets the threshold at which your strategy will ultimately be judged to have succeeded or failed.

Timeline of strategy: a graphical illustration of the strategy lifespan, showing key events and processes and their timings.

★ **Triple-Loop Model of Strategy Development:** a visual representation of the three activities that occur iteratively during strategy development: create, inform and validate.

★ **Triple-Loop Model of Strategy Scoping:** a visual representation of the three activities that occur iteratively during strategy scoping: horizon scoping, development scoping and acceptance scoping.

★ **VACU Model:** represents four stages in a continuum of decreasing understanding and increasing unpredictability about the future (developed from the previously published VUCA model). Volatility is where you know what will happen but not when, nor for how long. Ambiguity is where there are a few possibilities. Complexity is where there are lots of possibilities. Uncertainty is where anything is possible. Representing unpredictability in this way prescribes what to do in response; e.g. in volatile situations, have better sensors, whereas in complex situations, get more or better knowledge and expertise.

Value: who benefits and how. In the Value Model of Strategy, value refers to a value exchange between you and the world.

★ **Value Model of Strategy:** a model representing strategy in terms of the three key defining features of strategic action: value, effectiveness and efficiency.

Values: important and lasting beliefs or ethical ideals shared by the members of your organisation. Used to guide what is acceptable and unacceptable, what is desirable and undesirable. Good values are significant and impactful.

Vision: a picture of the potential of your organisation. An audacious dream of your future. Intended to inform, inspire and energise everyone to realise that shared vision. Vision is the counterpoint to mission – it is not where you are now, but where you want to be.

Wicked problem: problems are difficult or impossible to solve because of incomplete, contradictory, and changing requirements that are often difficult to recognise. They have better or worse solutions, not right or wrong ones – wicked problems are said to be 'tamed' rather than solved.

Working governance of strategy: ensures that strategy is effectively adopted across the organisation. This requires senior leadership to ensure that people and teams across the entire organisation know about the strategy, are committed to it and empowered to contribute to its success. Working governance encompasses the formalisation of authority and engagement and commitment. (*See also Governance*).

Index

Printed in Great Britain
by Amazon

53809312R00251